Petrarch's Guide to the Holy Land

Francisci .P. Laureati itinerarii ad sepleñi dñi nri
yhu xpi ad Iohem de Mavello icipit feliciter .p. pheuiz.

ARS admodum spei nre rerum
eventus respondet. Sepe premeditata
destituunt. insperata contingunt.
ρ neqz id mirum cuiqz esse debet. Mirum potius
siqd aliter accidat. Siquide ratio principia
rerum regit. euentu fortuna moderat. nichil
autem magis aduisum rationi qp fortuna.
Itaqz sepe telam quam ingeniose illa quidez
ordita erat, hec impetuose ante tps abrumpit.
Quod probatione utina egeret. neqz his que
relis adeo uita hominum plena esset. ut ia
fere nil aliud ingemiscat. Sed ut ad rē nraz
ueniam. Decreueras quidem me uolentez
fateor optantemqz me comitem bre. nam
que usqp optabilior aut sanctior uia est q
iustior peregrinatio qp ad sepulcrum ubi ille
iacuit cuius tpralis mors imortalem nobis
et eternam uitam peperit. Sepulcrum ubi si
dici fas est et uicta mors simul et uictrix
uita sepulta est. O beatum iter et inuidio
sum xpiano animo spectaculu. hinc ego
nunc nescio quibus peccator uectibus arceor

PETRARCH'S GUIDE TO THE HOLY LAND

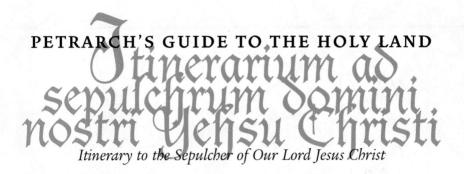

Itinerarium ad sepulchrum domini nostri Yehsu Christi

Itinerary to the Sepulcher of Our Lord Jesus Christ

*Facsimile edition of Cremona, Biblioteca Statale,
Deposito Libreria Civica, manuscript BB.1.2.5*

With an Introductory Essay, Translation, and Notes by
THEODORE J. CACHEY, JR.

University of Notre Dame Press
Notre Dame, Indiana

Copyright © 2002 by University of Notre Dame
Published by the University of Notre Dame Press
Notre Dame, Indiana 46556
www.ndpress.nd.edu

The facsimile edition of Cremona, Biblioteca Statale, Deposito Libreria Civica,
manuscript BB.1.2.5, reproduced on pages 84–160 is reproduced by permission of the
Italian Ministero per i Beni e le Attività Culturali,
Biblioteca Statale di Cremona,
Deposito Libreria Civica.

FRONTISPIECE
First page of Petrarch's *Itinerarium.*
Cremona, Biblioteca Statale, Deposito Libreria Civica, manuscript BB.1.2.5, f. 1r.
(*By permission of the Ministero per i Beni e le Attività Culturali, Biblioteca Statale di Cremona, Deposito Libreria Civica.*)

Book design by Nancy Berliner
Jacket design by Hafiz Huda
Set in type by Berliner, Inc., New York, New York
Printed and manufactured in the United States of America by Edwards Brothers

Library of Congress Cataloging-in-Publication Data
A record of the Library of Congress Cataloging-in-Publication Data is
available upon request from the Library of Congress.

This book was printed on acid-free paper.

For my mother and father

INTRODUCTION

What is not *a journey?*
Tzvetan Todorov

Every narrative is a travel narrative.
Michel de Certeau

The mental and material aspects of travel have been in tension from the beginning of history across a wide variety of cultural contexts. Dominant intellectual traditions have tended to disparage the physical journey and movement in space in favor of the Stoic and Christian, as well as Eastern, preference for interior travel and explorations leading to the discovery of an immensity within. Lieh Tzu, a Taoist author of the fourth century, observed: "Those who take great pains for exterior journeys do not know how to organize visits that one can make inside oneself." And Francis Petrarch, standing at the summit of Mt. Ventoux, read aloud from his copy of St. Augustine's *Confessions* (book 10): "And they go to admire the summits of mountains and the vast billows of the sea and the broadest rivers and the expanses of the ocean and the revolution of the stars and they overlook themselves" (*Fam.* 4.1). The desire and aspiration for freedom from the limitations of space and time has informed an irreducible resistance to physical and material travel, favoring instead journeys of the mind and spirit—the motionless quest.

The ongoing interaction between mental and material travel constitutes a complex relation of mutual reinforcement, particularly in the West, where the relative geographical stasis of the Middle Ages was followed by the mobility of the modern period, whose political and scientific appropriations of space on a global scale have characterized the last half millennium. Coming at the "end of the journey," after five centuries of material geohistorical exploration, discovery, and conquest, and during a period of renewed space-time compression owing to the twin forces of globalization and technology, we have grown increasingly sensitive to the interrelation between mental and material travel. Consequently, anthropologists, historians of travel, and students of travel literature are exploring the possibility of new perspectives on the role of travel in history and are considering the complex interaction of spatial and textual topographies in both their material and mental aspects.[1] These emerging critical perspectives enable a new appreciation for the role of Petrarch in the history of travel.

Petrarch's relation to travel has been generally neglected by Petrarchan criticism, in spite of the fact that Petrarch defined himself as a "peregrinus ubique" (a pilgrim everywhere), and one distinguished critic has characterized him as an "irrequieto turista" (an anxious tourist).[2] Both the reality and metaphor of travel are found everywhere in Petrarch's life and works. An Augustinian notion of life as a pilgrimage is pervasive in Petrarch's writings, and the poet's incessant travels are recorded and memorialized throughout his texts. Nevertheless, Petrarchan travel has, with rare exceptions, been treated only in passing in the critical literature.[3]

Symptomatic of this neglect, Petrarch studies have suffered from the marginalization of Petrarch's contribution to the medieval genre of the pilgrimage itinerary, the *Itinerarium ad sepulcrum domini nostri Yehsu Christi* (*Itinerary to the Sepulcher of Our Lord Jesus Christ*). Composed over three days between March and April 1358, the work takes the characteristic Petrarchan form of an epistle, addressed in this instance to a friend, Giovanni Mandelli. A distinguished military and administrative figure at the Visconti court in Milan, Mandelli planned to undertake a pilgrimage to the Holy Land and invited Petrarch to join him.[4] Petrarch wrote this "brief itinerary" (as he describes it in the proem to the work) to accompany Mandelli on his journey and to stand in for the poet, who would not join the pilgrimage, as he explicitly states in the work's proem, because he feared storms at sea. One might expect this contribution to one of the most important genres of medieval travel writing, by one of the most inveterate travelers and travel writers of the late Middle Ages, to have attracted greater scholarly attention. In exploring why it has not, we gain insight into the relation between material and literary travel and their contribution to the development of an Italian cultural identity, as well as a critical context from which to undertake a fresh consideration of the work.

Italian Literary History of Travel

If the inadequate state of studies on the *Itinerarium*—for a long time in fact considered somewhat the Cinderella of Petrarch's writings—may displease the literary critic and philologist, those concerned with historical matters must lament this lack of interest because it constitutes an eloquent symptom of the deafness of Italian scholarship faced with the testimonies relative to the pilgrimages in the Holy Land.

Franco Cardini[5]

Historians have made significant progress since Franco Cardini lamented the scholarly neglect of the tradition of travel to the Holy Land, thanks to Cardini's own work and to that of his circle of Italian medieval historians.[6] Nevertheless, the "Cinderella" status of Petrarch's *Itinerarium* endures. A critical edition of the work is still not available, and even the title of the work is a topic of some unresolved controversy (see About the Text and Translation). Cardini's call to action points to a neglect of Italian medieval travel that is broader than that of the Petrarchists. As G. R. Cardona wrote in a seminal essay on Italian travel literature, "Italian literature does not willingly include in its canon the journeys with which it is nevertheless rich. . . . In the literary histories there is lacking therefore a chapter on travel."[7] Indeed, Petrarch's *Itinerarium,* like other pilgrimage texts of the Italian Middle Ages, belongs to a type of writing that has long been devalued by canons of Italian literary historiography, which have traditionally excluded travel literature from their jealously classicizing precincts.

This historiographical resistance to travel has everything to do with the peculiar nature and history of Italy's cultural construction as a national identity. If Italy had had another history—a national political history dating from the Renaissance instead of from the nineteenth century—and had that history been informed by the profound economic and political impacts of early modern colonial travel as were the histories of France, Spain, and England, a work like Petrarch's *Itinerarium* might have enjoyed a different critical fortune. Instead, emerging from the Renaissance with a legacy of literary monuments rather than foreign conquests and colonies, Italy existed as a quintessentially literary territory, and without a national political identity. This conglomerate of cities and regions came to form a spiritual destination for literary travelers from all the diverse regions of Italy and beyond. As Carlo Dionisotti wrote, Italy's

> was . . . a humanistic tradition, nourished by linguistic and literary
> successes, founded upon the persuasion that if the Italians suffered indeed
> the violence of historical events, only they were nevertheless capable, by
> election and by education, to oppose to that ephemeral and blind violence
> the perennial lucid validity of discourse, of writing.[8]

Italy's national cultural identity privileged writing and literary culture as the means by which an "imagined" national literary community might be formed and by which geographical and cultural diversities, as well as the violence of Italian history, might be transcended.[9] All travel not directed to Italy in the sublimated linguistic and literary sense fell outside the necessarily centripetal and aulic rhetorical trends of post-Renaissance Italian literary and cultural identity. Material travel represented a competing trajectory with respect to the journey toward Italy as an ideal territory of the imagination because its regional points of departure inevitably called attention to the lack of an Italian home. Writing and literature meanwhile came to represent characteristic Italian forms of resistance to the alienations of material space, and to the journey of temporality itself.

At the origin of this Italian cultural paradigm, Francis Petrarch, the son of a Florentine exile, overcame the challenge and alienation of his *apolide* (stateless) status by means of an exquisite literary operation that was to become a model for the subsequent Italian tradition.[10] Marco Santagata's account of Petrarch's lyric poetic position vis-à-vis his vernacular precursors effectively portrays his biographical, intellectual, and institutional situation in relation to the disarticulated polity of fourteenth-century Italy. Santagata describes how Petrarch's exilic status enabled him to transcend the geographical connotations and articulations that characterized the Italian lyric tradition: "Petrarch was enabled to look from above and with detachment upon the entire course of vernacular literature."[11] Unlike the exiled Dante, who aspired to return to Florence but never did, Petrarch refused the opportunity to return when it was offered to him and instead maintained his "Italian" and "cosmopolitan" status, traveling abroad and throughout Italy without ever making a permanent home.

Petrarch's travels were part of a larger project of constructing Italy as a literary territory that transcended any municipal or regional space. Despite G. R. Cardona's quick dismissal of the *Itinerarium* (he characterized it as simply "an occasion for the erudite display of an ample series of readings"),[12] an Italian literary history of travel might well take Petrarch's "brief itinerary" as an appropriate point of departure. The *Itinerarium* contributed to Petrarch's status as the authoritative center and point of reference for an alternative Italian territory. The work allowed Petrarch to establish literary mobility, particularly literary mobility to Italy, as the Italian tradition's privileged form of travel, designed to transcend the historical reality of Italy's oppressed and disarticulated concatenation of disparate political entities. For this reason, the critical problem of Petrarchan travel, and the significance of a work like the *Itinerarium,* far from being marginal concerns, actually come close to the heart of a Petrarchan constitution of Italian cultural identity. In fact, as we shall see, Petrarch's *Itinerarium* is more an itinerary to Italy than a guide to the Holy Land. The little book is more about figuring Petrarchan heroic literary travel and consolidating an Italian home than it is about a pilgrim's pious journey to the religious center of the Christian world.

Petrarch's writing of a travel guide to the Holy Land when he had never been there might seem to disqualify him from the annals of travel literature rigorously limited to the narratives of "real" journeys. Yet it is precisely the too rigid distinction between real and virtual travel that needs to be reconsidered, since this distinction has led to a severing of Italy's splendid legacies of travel writing from the traditional canon and has blinded historiography to the importance of both the reality and metaphor of travel in Italy's cultural construction. From the perspective of both the mental and material aspects of the journey, Petrarch's *Itinerarium* offers a point of departure for investigating the relationship between the beginnings of both modern literature and modern travel.

Petrarch and Travel

Widely recognized as the first modern poet and traditionally considered the father of humanism, Petrarch is not normally thought of in relation to the history of travel. He was, however, among the most well traveled of his age, and he occupied, in terms of intellectual history, a position at the forefront of geographical and cartographic knowledge of his time. The poet's oeuvre cumulatively constitutes a *representation of space*, in Lefebvrian terms,[13] that can be considered canonical for the crucial period in spatial history that witnessed, on the horizon of the classical Mediterranean world, the dawning of the new Atlantic age of discovery, exploration, conquest, and colonization (marked by the mid-fourteenth-century rediscovery of the Canary-Fortunate islands).[14]

Travel has usually been taken as a sentimental or romantic theme in Petrarch's life and works. Only very rarely, or in isolated cases, as when analyzing his famous letter describing the ascent of Mt. Ventoux (*Fam.* 4.1), has travel been utilized as a critical perspective or a key to interpretation. A more holistic approach to the function of travel in Petrarch's career in the light of recent anthropological studies of travel and travelers reveals the ideological and political significance of Petrarch's self-conscious mastery of geographical distance and space, in both metaphorical and material terms. That geographical knowledge should play a vital role in Petrarch's construction of a culturally authoritative position in his society should come as no surprise. According to anthropologists, in fact, those few members of traditional societies who were able to become familiar with geographically distant phenomena and with geographical knowledge in general were often accorded an aura of prestige and "awe" that approached "the same order if not always the same magnitude as that accorded political-religious specialists or elites in general."[15] A significant measure of Petrarch's cultural authority derived from his prestige as a heroic traveler and as the possessor of distant knowledge in precisely these anthropological terms.

For example, Petrarch self-consciously cultivated his reputation as heroic wayfarer by repeatedly comparing himself to famous explorers and military travelers throughout his writings, including crucial texts like *Familiares* 1.1: "Compare my wanderings to those of Ulysses. If the reputation of our name and of our achievements were the same, he indeed traveled neither more nor farther than I."[16] Petrarch typically describes his desire for travel as the expression of a noble aspect of his character, even when his restless mobility appears to serve as a rhetorical cover for more strategic calculations of political advantage and expediency, as in *Familiares* 15.4 "to Andrea Dandolo, Doge of Venice, a justification for his frequent moves,"[17] or in the "Letter to Posterity" (*Sen.* 18.1).[18] In fact, in terms of his metaphorical and material negotiations of contemporary political space, Petrarch was a master of what anthropologists call *establishing spatial zones*, that is, recognizing and exploiting territorial dichotomies[19]—as, for example, in his famous dilemma about whether to accept the laurel crown in Paris or in Rome (cf. *Fam.* 4.4), or in the fundamental spatial differentiation he repeatedly reconstituted along the length of his career between town and country retreat (Avignon / Vaucluse; Parma / Selvapiana; Padua / Arquà). Especially important was the contrast between France and Italy, around which Petrarch's career turned like a hinge.

Petrarch's social and cultural authority derived from his reputation as someone highly informed about matters not generally known, which included esoteric and recondite geographical information deriving from both his firsthand reconnaissance of places and his investigations into the poetic and historical literature of the past. Petrarch's unsurpassed geographical knowledge of the poetic and historical literary sources was achieved by means of groundbreaking philological studies, and this particular genre of long-distance knowledge represented a primary feature of his reputation. For example, in a letter to Boccaccio (*Sen.* 5.1), Petrarch memorably expressed his disappointment at receiving a portion of Leontius Pilatus's translation of Homer concerned with the underworld: "For I had no wish to know what went on in the Greeks' hell; it is enough to know what goes on in the Latin hell." Instead, what Petrarch really wanted to know was how Homer "described the remote places of Italy, such as Aeolia, Lake Avernus, or the Mount of Circe."[20] Together with his disciple Boccaccio, Petrarch is generally credited with launching humanist historical geography, which, by way of new encyclopedic geographical works like Boccaccio's *De Montibus,* prepared the way for the Renaissance Age of Discovery and Exploration.

It is perhaps not by chance that Petrarch's self-fashioning as a master of geographical space appears to intensify in the period leading up to his definitive relocation to Italy between 1347 and 1353 (focused in part by his acquisition of a copy of Pliny's *Natural History* in 1350). During this period he conceived the epistolary collection of the *Familiares* and composed and backdated many of the travel letters in first several books (including *Fam.* 4.1, the "ascent of Mt. Ventoux"). These letters were clearly intended to promote Petrarch's reputation as a traveler and as a possessor of long-distance knowledge, even to the very edges of the earth, as in *Familiares* 3.1, in which he reports from the very shores of the Ocean on "various opinions regarding the location of the island Thule."[21] Also during this period Petrarch wrote the early version of the "Letter to Posterity," which emphasized the heroic restless mobility that characterized his life, as well as the famous "travel page" of the *Secretum,* in which he put into the mouth of Augustine the recommendation that he travel to Italy. In support of this recommendation, Augustine recalls a metrical epistle of Petrarch's in praise of Italy, in which the poet had assumed, as he had in the travel letters of the *Familiares,* the role of experienced world traveler and investigator of distant knowledge who nevertheless preferred Italy to every other country.[22]

Petrarch's detailed knowledge and mastery of specifically Italian geographical space was an essential aspect of his reputation among his contemporaries and found expression along the entire length of his career, often in polemical counterpoint to the putative cultural hegemony of France.[23] The poet's detailed knowledge of Italian topography, evident in both his prose and poetry, apparently contributed to the tradition that he co-authored, with the Angevin King Robert of Naples, the first modern map of

Italy, a tradition that is authoritatively credited during the fifteenth century by Biondo Flavio, who claims to have used this map in his *Italia illustrata*.[24] Clearly, by the time Petrarch composed the *Itinerarium ad sepulchrum domini nostri Yehsu Christi* in Milan in the late 1350s, he had established himself as one of the leading "long-distance specialists" of his age. Petrarch achieved this distinction through his manipulations of the metaphor and the reality of travel, and this status constituted one of the most important and influential aspects of his cultural authority and aura from the perspectives both of his contemporaries and of the humanists who followed him. An anthropological perspective on the theme of travel in Petrarch, particularly sensitive to the political and ideological contexts within which the poet's long-distance interests and activities were conducted, might eventually offer a general interpretative key to his life and works. Meanwhile, this perspective reveals why Petrarch's *Itinerarium* is not as marginal a work as it has sometimes been made out to be within the canon of Petrarch's writings and helps to explain why Giovanni Mandelli requested, and Francis Petrarch composed, a pilgrimage guidebook to the Holy Land in the first place.

Early Reception of the *Itinerarium*

Petrarch's *Itinerarium* penetrated a wide variety of Tre-Quattrocento (fourteenth- and fifteenth-century) social and geographical contexts, including libraries of the Florentine humanists (both in Tuscany and in the eastern Mediterranean), as well as the courtly environs of Niccolò III d'Este in Ferrara, Lorenzo il Magnifico in Florence, and the Kingdom of Naples. The full history of the work's early reception—over forty manuscripts survive—would no doubt constitute an important chapter in an Italian literary history of travel. An early translation into the Tuscan vernacular of the *Itinerarium,* attributable to Petrarch's intimate friend Donato Albanzani and dated to the beginning of the fifteenth century, illustrates the precocious vernacular fortune of Petrarch's guide, and the dissemination of Neapolitan vernacular versions derived from this translation points to the work's currency before 1500.

The end of the fifteenth century, when journeys of exploration and discovery increasingly displaced pilgrimage as a privileged and prestigious mode of travel, appears to mark an end to the *Itinerarium*'s late-medieval, early-Renaissance fortunes. The dawning Atlantic world was the harbinger of the progressive displacement of the Italian peninsula from its traditional position at the geographical heart of Western economic and cultural space, a shift that would contribute to a concomitant transformation and consolidation of the Italian literary system along the classicizing and travel-resistant lines described earlier in the essay. Thus, the Tre-Quattrocento reception of the *Itinerarium,* more than merely a material bibliographical record of the work's dissemination, reveals something about Petrarch's role in the incipient establishment of an Italian home and point of departure for travel, a process that was eventually interrupted by historical events. The new early modern history of travel had as its protagonists the emerging nation-states that followed in the wake of an Italian-based avant-garde who had led the way in both the literary and geographical realms.

In general, the network of early reception of the *Itinerarium* (see Appendix 1) constitutes in literary terms what, to adopt an anthropological concept of Victor Turner's, can be called a *catchment area* of Italian pilgrimage.[25] Turner found that in medieval Europe, "any region possessing a certain cultural, linguistic, or ethnic unity, often corresponding also to an area of economic interdependence, tended to become at once a political unit and a pilgrimage catchment area."[26] While Italy did not achieve political unity during the Renaissance, both the reception of Petrarch's *Itinerarium* and, as we shall see in the final section of this essay, the text itself figure virtually, in literary terms, an Italian home or point of departure for travel.

The Neapolitans utilized the text as a prestigious guide to local natural, classical, archeological, and literary sights, especially those associated with Virgil. Petrarch's incisive and memorable descriptions of these places were immediately received into the local Neapolitan tradition as a form of validation of Neapolitan identity. Meanwhile, the Florentine tradition received and celebrated the work as an authoritative exemplar of humanistic travel, a model for contemporary wandering scholars traveling about with pen in hand, as well as for those engaged in virtual journeys undertaken from their desks at home. The Ferrarese no less than the Florentines and the Neapolitans found a model of travel in Petrarch's *Itinerarium*. The work was part of the cultural background that informed Niccolò III d'Este's 1413 pilgrimage to the Holy Land, which was designed to consolidate the power of the *signoria* at home.[27]

The literary territory called *Italy* as figured in the *Itinerarium* functions as a point of departure for Italian travel. Petrarch's contribution to the genre of medieval pilgrimage is distinguished by its *italianità*[28]—how it transcends the diversity of Italian homes by virtue of its representation of Italy from Petrarch's unifying point of view. Moreover, the work's combination of material and metaphorical modes of travel enabled it to succeed subsequently in a wide variety of contexts as a model for Italian travel, beginning with landlocked Ferrara, which, in spite of the city's geographical marginality to the Atlantic discoveries and its political vulnerability within the context of ongoing struggles between the peninsula's major regional powers, eventually emerged as a central point of reference in the Italian Renaissance history of travel. The world of travel beyond the city's walls, both real and virtual, continued to offer Ferrara an important means of affirming its place in the world and shoring up its identity as a home during the Age of Discovery. For example, the city's preoccupation with geographical exploration and travel finds expression in the Cantino *Carta da navigar* (1502), a large-scale world map that was among the earliest to record the Columbian discoveries; the map was commissioned for Ercole d' Este by Albert Cantino, who was in Portugal gathering information on behalf of the Ferrarese court.[29] The presence of the so-called Zorzi anthology in Ferrara, dating from the same period, similarly attests to Ferrarese virtual participation in the earliest period of New World discoveries. The Zorzi codex was among the first to gather together the New World discovery narratives and is considered a more or less direct precursor of

Giambattista Ramusio's *Navigazioni e viaggi* (Venice, 1563–1606).[30] Ultimately, the geographical scenographies traversed by the imagination of Ludovico Ariosto in his *Orlando Furioso* (1516, 1521, 1532) can be taken to represent both Ferrara's and Italy's most mature response, in terms of literary mobility and virtual travel, to the contemporaneous material journeys of the Renaissance Age of Discovery and Exploration.[31]

Modern Reception of the *Itinerarium*

Eighteenth-century scholar Girolamo Tiraboschi offered an alternative to the narrowly classicizing and rhetorically focused system of Italian literary history in his monumental *Storia della letteratura italiana*.[32] At a time when the preeminence and classical status of the Italian literary canon was under severe pressure from the competing modern national literatures of France, England, and Spain, Tiraboschi sought to bolster Italian cultural identity by means of a prodigious recovery of the cultural and historical context surrounding the Italian canon, including an appeal to Italy's traditions of travel.[33] Accordingly, he offered an innovative critical perspective on Petrarch the traveler and on the *Itinerarium*. Preoccupations with national identity and travel current in late-eighteenth-century society no doubt sharpened Tiraboschi's sensitivity to the connection between Petrarch's travels and the question of Italian cultural identity. Representing a significant and instructive exception to Cardona's view that histories of Italian literature have ignored the literature of travel, the *Storia* is the first and the last Italian literary history to give Petrarch's *Itinerarium* any kind of prominence. The chapter dedicated to Italian travel during the Trecento reveals an Enlightenment sensitivity to Petrarch's role as a prototypical or model traveler and departs from the canonical Italian rhetorical view of Petrarch, which largely derived from the status of the *Canzoniere* as a vernacular classic. Tiraboschi grants special status to Petrarch's travels and his travel writings, treating him alongside some of the most prominent names of Trecento Italian travel literature, including Odorico da Pordenone and the Zeno brothers.[34]

Petrarch could not be admitted among the travelers if that category were limited to those who travel to less well-known countries, Tiraboschi recognized; nevertheless he asserted that Petrarch ought to be considered a perfect model for the "enlightened" Grand Tour traveler of the eighteenth century, "since in the descriptions that he has left us of the countries that he saw, he shows what ought to be the aims, method, and the kinds of observations that distinguish an erudite traveler."[35] Tiraboschi's presentation of Petrarch as "erudite traveler" subtly promotes an appreciation of Italy's leading role in the history of travel: Petrarch provides a model for Grand Tour travelers three hundred years before modern, "enlightened" Europeans began to go abroad.

Tiraboschi's treatment of Petrarch and travel shows a sure grasp of the poet's self-fashioning as a traveler and brings together Petrarchan texts that are the point of departure for any discussion of the metaphor and reality of travel in the poet's work. The historian begins by recalling the letters from the first book of the *Familiares* (1.3, 1.4, 1.5), which recount young Petrarch's journeys through France and Germany during the 1330s. The significance of these travels and an account of Petrarch's shifting attitude toward them remain open questions for Petrarchan criticism.[36] Tiraboschi goes on to recall Petrarch's account of the ascent of Mt. Ventoux (*Fam.* 4.1), perhaps the most famous and commented upon of Petrarch's travel narratives: "Elsewhere he recounts the climb that he made one day to the top of Mount Ventoux in the County of Venassin, and the things that he encountered there most worthy of observation."[37] Tiraboschi also discusses Petrarch's journey to the Kingdom of Naples, narrated in several letters from book 5 of the *Familiares:* "The report that he has left us of his journey through the Kingdom of Naples is also beautiful."[38]

Tiraboschi identifies journeys referred to only obscurely in Petrarch's writings: "He alludes also, albeit vaguely, to having coasted the shores of Spain, to having sailed upon the Ocean, and also, as it seems, to having reached England, but concerning this he has not left us more exact information."[39] These hyperbolic extensions of Petrarch's range contributed to his fame and prestige as world traveler and represent another critical problem for the assessment of Petrarch's self-fashioning as a heroic wayfarer.

Tiraboschi concludes with a discussion of Petrarch's *Itinerarium*—and in this way grants prominence to the work:

> He had the intention of journeying also to the Holy Lands of Palestine, as one gathers from the preface of a small work, of which we will now speak; but terrified of the long navigation and of the dangers that on other occasions he had encountered upon the sea, he did not make the trip. Instead, however, he wrote a small book entitled the *Itinerarium Syriacum* and addressed it to his friend who was undertaking that journey and who had asked him to accompany him. In this work, beginning from Genoa, Petrarch describes minutely all the places that his friend should see in the course of the journey and those things that he should most attentively observe; it is a book that casts not a little light on the historical and the geographical knowledge of those times, and I marvel that the Abbot de Sade in his three tomes of memories of the life of Petrarch never made mention of it.[40]

Not content simply to offer a paraphrastic synthesis, Tiraboschi goes on to speak of the dedicatee, who is not named in the text or the printed editions but whose name, "Johannem de Mandello," appeared in the manuscript of the work consulted by Tiraboschi in the Estense Library; Mandelli is further identified as being "of an ancient and noble family of Milan, and he is probably the same who was podestà of Piacenza in the year 1347."[41]

The attention to the problem of Petrarch the traveler that characterizes Tiraboschi's literary history is an exception to the general trend of Petrarchan scholarship. As Tiraboschi pointed out, Jacques François de Sade (*Memoires pour la vie de F. Pétrarque,* 1764–67) made no mention of the *Itinerarium.* Ugo Foscolo, writing in the 1820s from a documentary and critical perspective, reported that most of Petrarch's travel letters "are still unpublished";[42] while Foscolo translated the description of the tempest at Naples (*Fam.* 5.5) as a sample of the poet's travel writing, the historian does not otherwise comment on the travel writings or the *Itinerarium*. Alfred Jean François Mézières attempted in 1867 to take into greater consideration Petrarch's Latin prose, especially the epistolary, and made some advance in the treatment of Petrarch the traveler; nevertheless Mézières's paragraph on the topic, while it gives some prominence to the *Itinerarium,* is unfocused and represents only the barest of premises for what will be the discovery of Petrarch the geographer-traveler by erudite philological and positivist Petrarchan scholarship in the late nineteenth century.[43] The learned and more recent investigations of Pierre de Nolhac and Giuseppe Billanovich brought the *Itinerarium* to the surface again in scholarship dedicated to Petrarch's humanism, especially in connection with his knowledge of classical geography.[44] Because the poet's travel writings and the history of his travels have been relegated for the most part to discussions of Petrarch the erudite humanist geographer and philologist, discussion of the *Itinerarium* and of Petrarchan travel in general has tended to be divorced from broader questions of Petrarchan poetics. This tendency to treat travel and geography in Petrarch purely as topics of intellectual history has impeded an appreciation of the original unity of travel as metaphor and reality in Petrarch's life and works.

Signs of a new attitude toward Petrarch the traveler and the *Itinerarium* have appeared more recently, however, since Cardona's essay and the Columbian Quincentenary, which contributed to a renewed interest in the literary dimensions of Italian Renaissance travel and in the literature of travel generally in Italy.[45] In particular, new light has been cast upon this previously neglected corner of the Petrarchan canon by Francesco Lo Monaco's edition ("vulgata *editorum in usum*") and translation of the *Itinerarium* (1990)[46] and by Alfonso Paolella's critical edition of the Neapolitan vernacular tradition of the text (1992).[47] Perhaps, as in Tiraboschi's time, the current moment allows renewed critical interest in the "Cinderella" of Petrarchan studies. "Postnational" perspectives on cultural change and globalization have brought the history of travel and of space to the forefront of contemporary debates. The challenge will be to reconsider the *Itinerarium* within the context of Petrarch's real and metaphorical travels and to reconnect that system to a general history of travel.

Earliest Reception: Mandelli and Boccaccio

Tiraboschi's identification of Giovanni Mandelli as the work's dedicatee was the first step in recovering the immediate context that inspired the *Itinerarium.* Mandelli was probably the first to read the work; in any event the man to whom it was addressed was at least ideally the first to receive it. According to Billanovich's reconstruction of the work's initial publication beyond Mandelli, Giovanni Boccaccio was apparently among the first to read and copy the *Itinerarium,* around the time when he was completing his geographical encyclopedia, the *De Montibus.* Subsequent reception of the work can be understood as a negotiation between the claims of its earliest readers—the courtly military pilgrim Mandelli and Boccaccio the humanist scholar.[48]

Petrarch himself provided a striking portrait of Mandelli the pilgrim in a letter of commendation addressed to Francesco Nelli,[49] written from Milan on Christmas Day 1355 (*Fam.* 19.6).[50] Mandelli was passing through Florence on a pilgrimage to Rome, and Petrarch recommended his friend to the protection of Nelli, prior of the Tuscan city's Church of the Holy Apostles. Petrarch may as well have been presenting Mandelli to posterity and particularly to future readers of the *Itinerarium,* which the poet had yet to write but for which he had already found an ideal dedicatee:

> This man whom you see is a humble little man devoted to Christ, a true despiser of the world and transitory things and zealous for eternal things, and what is more—a tiny addition to so much praise but your love for me will make you consider it very large—he is also very dear to me, and he is on his way to Rome. And so, look upon him as you would me; he possesses a good soul. I know the man; we have served in the same army and have not yet been discharged, although our common commander has been killed. If he needs advice or any favor in order to complete his pious pilgrimage, I believe that you would comply without being asked; nevertheless I do ask you. For what could be more acceptable to Christ whom you serve, or to His apostles who are your guests, than for you gladly to give assistance and advice to this devout man who has left behind the court's deafening roar to make his way to their silent dwellings. If you wish to learn anything about me (surely there will be much that you wish to know), although our different interests may mean that he does not know everything about me, he will still be able to tell you something about my private life, and nearly all of my public life. This letter I have written in haste from a remote corner of Milan, from a secluded section in the convent of St. Ambrose on the day and at the hour when a living light from earth shone upon a world immersed in shadows and upon blind mortals. Farewell, and remember me.[51]

Petrarch's description of Mandelli's pilgrimage to Rome, in flight from "the court's deafening roar to make his way to their [the apostles'] silent dwellings," parallels Petrarch's own isolation from the Visconti court as he writes in "a remote corner of Milan, from a secluded section in the convent of St. Ambrose." Mandelli and Petrarch clearly share the same public sphere—proximity to and dependence upon the Visconti political world. Their deeper bond, however, is their shared desire to put distance between themselves and that world: Mandelli by undertaking a pilgrimage and Petrarch by isolating himself in the seclusion of his study. This mirrors precisely the respective situations of the two friends three years later on the occasion of the *Itinerarium,* when Mandelli is planning a journey to the Holy Land while Petrarch will stay behind in Milan, writing and reading. Their shared desire to distance themselves from the political world offers a key to understanding the deeper inspiration of the *Itinerarium.* In fact, the letter of recommendation to Nelli states that the nature of the relation between Petrarch and Mandelli is based upon their having "served in the same army" from which they have not been discharged although their "common commander has been killed." This reference to Archbishop Giovanni Visconti, who had died 5 October 1354, locates Petrarch and Mandelli squarely in the Visconti political and courtly world.

In *Familiares* 19.6, the *Itinerarium*, and *Dispersa* 69 (the last surviving letter Petrarch addressed to Mandelli, written ten years after the *Itinerarium* and discovered by Novati only at the beginning of this century), Petrarch consistently portrays his friendship with Mandelli as transcending the political context of their association. Both the pilgrimage to Rome in 1355 and the putative one to the Holy Land were counterpoints to periods of intense political upheaval and activity for the Visconti and thus for Mandelli, who served them as one of their most important political operatives. Moreover, Petrarch addresses *Dispersa* 69 to Mandelli, who was by that time a political exile, estranged from the Visconti and described by Petrarch as an "eminent and undeserved exile." As we shall see, this last letter to Mandelli expresses Petrarch's solidarity with his friend and reaffirms the alternative character of their relationship, a fraternal *communitas* forged through shared experience of exile and pilgrimage.[52]

The *Itinerarium* can be considered in this light to express a peculiarly Petrarchan literary strategy. Petrarch sought to transcend the political situation in Milan and northern Italy during the Italian crisis of the late 1350s by placing himself and his friend Mandelli above and beyond that crisis at the same time as they were engaged by it in their "public life." In terms of both social practice and literary genre, pilgrimage, especially pilgrimage to the Holy Land, was an ideal way to evade the divisions and conflicts of Italian political reality and to establish an alternative *communitas* involving both Petrarch's friend and posterity (see Appendix 2).[53]

Further documentary evidence, especially of Mandelli's presence at the Visconti occupation of Novara in June 1358, suggests that Mandelli never undertook the proposed pilgrimage to the Holy Land that occasioned Petrarch's composition of the *Itinerarium*. For if the text had been delivered to Mandelli on 4 April, as the Cremona manuscript subscription attests, his reappearance in Italy barely two months later would have required the most rapid pilgrimage to the Holy Land recorded during the period (in fact, according to Billanovich, Mandelli was in Pisa on 4 June, a week before the occupation of Novara).[54] G. Nori considered Niccolò III's 84-day pilgrimage extremely short when compared to other fifteenth-century journeys, including the 92-day pilgrimage of Mariana da Siena, the 141 days required by Santo Brasca, and the 225-day journey of Roberto da Sanseverino.[55] More than likely, Mandelli never made the trip, although one of the *Itinerarium*'s recent editors is agnostic on the point.[56]

Given the chronological restrictions, the *Itinerarium* likely represented a virtual and purely literary pilgrimage for the dedicatee as well as for the author. The project of the pilgrimage, conceived during a break in political tensions, quite possibly came up against altered political circumstances that continued to require Mandelli's presence. In addition, Mandelli's putative point of departure from Genoa and the Tyrrhenian itinerary described are highly unusual (practically unique in the literature) and may correspond to a Petrarchan literary program rather than to a genuine plan for a journey. Petrarch had plenty to write about the Ligurian, Tuscan, and Neapolitan areas that he knew well and had visited numerous times in his life and writings, while the Adriatic, besides being comparatively, and notoriously, unpoetic,[57] receives only glancing mention in his works. In this light, a quixotic, if not utopian, aspect of Petrarch's contribution to pilgrimage literature comes into view.

Mandelli belonged to a class of itinerant courtly military figures with whom Petrarch shared evident affinities. This class constituted a literary public for Petrarch's writings that was contiguous to, but distinguishable from, his readership in chanceries and monasteries on the one hand and princes, popes, and emperors on the other. Petrarch shares with this military administrative class an analogous political space and mobility, a heroic and highly vulnerable mobility tantamount to exile and pilgrimage.

The *Itinerarium* might usefully be considered within the context of this particular social network and sector of Petrarch's readership. Petrarchan pilgrimage as figured by the *Itinerarium*, dressed in appropriate military metaphorical garb, could effectively serve as a model of travel, mental or material as the case might be, for otherwise politically alienated and itinerant "Italian" political subjects like the Mandellis, the de' Pepolis, the Malatestas, and the Luchino del Vermes who dot the map of Petrarch's epistolary. The type corresponds roughly to that of the "pilgrim functionaries" whose vital role Benedict Anderson has studied in his work on the creation of virtual communities that led to the early modern nation.[58]

Indeed, Petrarch's faithfulness to these relationships in the face of the vicissitudes of their political fortunes goes beyond the model of spiritual guide or simple cultural hero and points to a deeper structural or anthropological affinity. For example, saddened by the death of Galeazzo Visconti's chief minister and counselor Giovanni de' Pepoli, Petrarch wrote to another friend, Pietro da Moglio, minister to Francesco da Carrara (*Dispersa* 68 [*Var.* 27]) that he would not under any circumstances take Giovanni de' Pepoli's place as chief counselor of Galeazzo: "No economic advantage could induce me to do so, I'd rather go begging. It's not that if I knew how I'd refuse my counsel to such a lord but I'm no good at such things."[59] Foresti observed how in a delicate political moment Petrarch wants to clarify that he does not wish to be too closely associated with the Visconti.[60] The very fact, however, that Petrarch felt it necessary to make clear that he would not be taking over Giovanni de' Pepoli's role indicates how compromised the poet was by his associations with the Visconti. Petrarch's own position was not as different from de' Pepoli's as it might seem. At moments like this, Petrarch's position at the authoritative center of a courtly network of readership emerges as an alternative space—above the fray, so to speak—to the conflict-ridden and divisive system of political alliances and relations that made up "Italian" political reality.

Petrarch's network of "pilgrim functionaries" constituted a virtual community organized around Petrarch's authority, which depended in large measure upon his authorship of an Italy that existed as an alternative to the reality of contemporary politics above and beyond the borders of Italian regional and political divisions and conflicts. The trajectory of Petrarch's pilgrimage to the Holy Land is accordingly primarily concerned with figuring "Petrarch's Italy" as a point of departure and an object of contemplation for this virtual community. The organization of Italian travel in the form of a pilgrimage to the Holy Land offers an alternative to the checkerboard of Italian political boundaries.[61]

Giovanni Mandelli's relation to the Visconti court ended in exile. Petrarch's letter to his friend on 6 July 1368 is a poignant conclusion to their relationship as recorded in the poet's epistolary. *Dispersa* 69 documents the continuation of the bond of friendship that linked Petrarch and Mandelli and evidently transcended changing political fortunes—Mandelli's exile and Petrarch's departure from Milan after 1361 following eight years of residence there.[62] The same preoccupation with the reality and metaphor of travel that had characterized both *Familiares* 19.6 and the *Itinerarium* continues in this letter, which in some senses represents an epilogue to the pilgrimage text. The theme of pilgrimage that had characterized the friends' relationship is displaced, however, by the topic of exile, political exile from Visconti Milan for Mandelli, spiritual exile of the Christian soul for Petrarch. The poet consoles his friend by reaffirming their common status as pilgrim-exiles, a state that the friends share in an Augustinian sense despite superficial contrasts between Mandelli's exile and Petrarch's prestige.

Dispersa 69 begins with a description of the *vulnus ciceronianum,* a wound on Petrarch's left leg, which since 1359 had been repeatedly injured by collisions with a massive codex of Cicero's letters *ad Atticum.*[63] On this occasion the wound causes pain and indignation, but, says Petrarch, "I believe this trouble and as many others as afflict me are a gift of heaven intended to make me realize my condition and to put a brake on a vagabond soul."[64] Just as in *Itinerarium* Pr. 5, where fear of sea travel, shipwreck, and nausea "has put this bridle on a vagabond soul and on an eye insatiable for new things," the wound caused by the Ciceronian codex curbs or limits the poet's mobility. It recalls to him the futility of a ceaseless motion driven by a desire for a peace that cannot be achieved in this life. This Augustinian theme of human life as exile / pilgrimage is evoked explicitly in connection with the tribulation caused by the *vulnus ciceronianum* taken as a figure for the human condition: "And there is no doubt that man is born for tribulations, for forcing himself to walk in the opposite direction and aspiring in vain to achieve peace down here where there is no possibility of reaching it, he nevertheless travels with ardor always seeking it."[65]

Dispersa 69 also brings together other Petrarchan motifs linked to the thematics of travel, including the pleasures and pain of travel by horseback and Petrarch's partiality for river travel. Petrarch looks forward to his travel on the Po and the Ticino and gives thanks to God for these two "obsequious" rivers that will transport him "without both the help and the bother of travel by horseback" to Venice. The rivers in fact will shortly transport Petrarch on his triumphal trip back to the Veneto, as more famously recounted in *Seniles* 11.2.[66] *Dispersa* 69 reprises many of Petrarch's favorite travel themes and thus establishes continuities with the *Itinerarium* as well as with other travel texts from Petrarch's ouevre.

The letter also suggests something about the political dimension of Petrarch's mobility in both natural and metaphorical senses. In particular, Petrarch's river travel placed him above the contending parties in the war that was taking place in the valley of the Po. This political meaning of Petrarch's free passage between the warring parties will be especially emphasized in *Seniles* 11.2. Meanwhile, in *Dispersa* 69, addressed to the exiled

Mandelli, Petrarch explicitly refers to the protection that he enjoys at the hands of both the Visconti and the emperor: "I came with his permission and by his command I return, not without, both coming and going, the consent of these Lombard lords." In the same sentence that Petrarch suggests the political implications of his unimpeded passage under the protection of the emperor and the lords of Lombardy, he also evokes a no less important theme that he had already touched upon earlier in the letter when he had described himself as a "most humble and abject particle of his [God's] creative work, anxious and toilsome animal" and referred to the insignificance and insubstantiality of his physical being: "I tell you this because I don't want you to be in any doubt about the state of your friend which is never still, but is carried away faster than the wind."[67] The poet emphasizes his smallness among God's creatures at the same time as he makes a point of calling attention to his protection by the highest authorities of both sides in the current war. Petrarch's description of his state as being so insubstantial as to be "carried away faster than the wind" calls to mind another topos of Petrarchan mobility, that of fog or dust blown by the wind:

> A mist or dust caught in the wind, I flee
> to be no more a pilgrim in this life,
> and let it happen if it be my fate.[68]

In passages like the one from *Dispersa* 69, one can observe and admire the structural ambiguities, or rather adaptability, of Petrarch's troping of travel. On the one hand, his mobility is a sign of cultural authority and power, while on the other hand, travel evokes the Augustinian notion of earthly life as an exile or pilgrimage. *Dispersa* 69 tellingly expresses multiple meanings and ambivalences of Petrarchan travel—as an alienating state of exile, as Christian pilgrimage, and as political privilege—at the same time that it constructs an authoritative self-portrait on the basis mobility.

Not unexpectedly, Petrarch's river travel and the image of being blown by the wind lead directly to reflections on earthly life as a state of exile with respect to heavenly life after death. Petrarch compliments Mandelli on the freedom of his soul, judging his political exile "not miserable but happy," as well as "joyous, even worthy of envy." He concludes by expressing the wish "after this exile, not yours alone, but shared by all of us, that in this death, which is called life, where we find ourselves held back by the straps and the prison of the body, we will see ourselves in the end free in the country and the land of the living. Be happy, oh illustrious and unmerited exile." Leaving behind Mandelli in his material political state of exile, Petrarch returns to the warm and honorable reception by Francesco da Carrara at Padua, as described in *Seniles* 11.2.[69]

But Giovanni Mandelli and the pilgrim-functionaries of Petrarch's circle were not the only readers of the *Itinerarium* and Petrarch's other travel writing. Giuseppe Billanovich imagined in his reconstruction of events that Mandelli recounted—to no less a figure than Boccaccio, Petrarch's "greatest disciple"—descriptions of his pilgrimage to the Holy Land while Boccaccio was visiting Petrarch in Milan between the middle of March and the beginning of April 1359, less than a year after Mandelli's putative pilgrimage.

In addition, Billanovich reports that at that time Boccaccio "certainly was permitted to copy the 'opuscolo' [booklet] offered to Mandelli," which Boccaccio "loved with an attraction to pages which were devout in their aim, ordered and ingeniously balanced by the usual profound doctrine, rich with the geographical and exotic curiosities which we know by many indications—from the *Filocolo* to the *De Montibus*—to have stimulated Boccaccio."[70]

The association of Boccaccio's *De Montibus* with Petrarch's *Itinerarium* is natural enough given the friendship, the history of contact between the two authors, and their shared interest in geographical questions. Petrarch and Boccaccio together played a vital role in launching the humanist renewal of geographical studies that came to inform the Renaissance Age of Discovery and Exploration. Billanovich emphasized the influence of these geographical studies for the subsequent tradition, noting that they were originally inspired by a literary motivation: "Petrarch and his friends began gathering flowers in the garden of rhetoric: they were seeking useful assistance for reading classical authors." From these beginnings there emerged "a transformation of the geographical discipline, an altered vision of landscape, that opened the way to the great geographical discoveries."[71] This line of modern commentary, particularly concerning early humanist geography, has remained largely undeveloped.[72] As a result, the *Itinerarium* tends to be reduced to an expression of Petrarch's literary-geographical curiosity and erudition, a perspective that—especially in associating the *Itinerarium* with an encyclopedic work like Boccaccio's *De Montibus*—underestimated the distinctive and innovative aspects of Petrarch's pilgrimage guide. The *Itinerarium* is less important for its historical or geographical erudition than as an exhilarating manifestation of Petrarchan literary self-fashioning. The *Itinerarium* points the way toward modern travel and modern travel writing in which the self that writes "I" becomes as much the subject of that writing as the landscape being traversed.

Petrarch's pilgrimage guide also opens the way to the great geographical discoveries in what one might term the imperial (albeit virtual) geographical ambition that it expresses. Petrarch never wanted to relinquish the idea that he was the center of the world. As a poet, a primary means of expressing this conviction of his own centrality was through his manipulations of geographical space, which he sought to control and to rearrange by placing the Petrarchan self at its center. Petrarch's transformation of the study of geography and the "invention of landscape" were mutually reinforcing and ultimately turned on the same hinge, which was a Petrarchan subject that everywhere sought to leave its mark, to write its signature. In his "colonially" inflected orientations of space around the self, Petrarch is a direct precursor of Columbus in Haiti, who described trees "flourishing and adorned as they usually are in Spain in the month of May. . . . The nightingale chattered, and other sparrows . . . in the month of November where I myself went strolling among them."[73]

Petrach's study and annotation of passages in minor Roman geographers like Pomponius Mela and Vibius Sequester, authors whom Petrarch put back into circulation in learned circles, was not simply a philological operation and gathering of information in support of his reading of literary texts.[74] Those same texts provided the materials for the poet's construction of a kind of "cosmic menagerie" in *RVF* 135, "Qual più diversa et nova" (the strangest rarest thing).[75] There, a diversity of marvels, including fabulous fountains Petrarch had recently "discovered" in Mela, are gathered together within the unifying perspective of the poet's gaze and ordered in relation to the "closed vale where Sorgue springs" (verse 93).

Petrarch's geographical studies supported his heroic quest to leave some record of his passage and to project some shadow of fame. He sought to situate the Petrarchan self in relation to a network of topographical coordinates that bridged the frontier between the literary and geographical dimensions of space. By enabling the frontier between text and territory to be crossed, geographical knowledge represented a privileged means of authorizing and authenticating the Petrarchan self for posterity.

Thus, even within the genre of geographical annotations to his manuscripts, Petrarch frequently memorialized his physical journeys to literary sites, including several of those visited in the *Itinerarium*.[76] Petrarch recorded his passage in these places and his participation in their aura with his *vidimus*—"We have seen"—in the annotation in his Ambrosian Virgil to the Servius commentary (*Aeneid*, 3.386) at the mention of the "inferni . . . Lacus," where Servius had located the entrance to the underworld ("There is a cave in the side of the mountain, . . . where I visited not too many years ago"),[77] and in the *Rerum Memorandarum Libri* 4.30.8, where Petrarch mentions the Sibyl ("whose place near Cuma in Campania I recently saw").[78] He also records his visit to the site of the Acheron by adding a postil to the discussion of the place in Servius's commentary (*Aeneid*, 6.107): "description of a place that I diligently contemplated with my own eyes a few years ago." Elsewhere he records his desire to visit Literno, the site of his hero Scipio's noble exile (see Notes to the Text and Translation, note 73).

The imperialistic dimension of Petrarch's aspiration to dominate space perhaps finds its counterpoint in the humility and vulnerability of these fragmentary, discontinuous annotations. Petrarch's heroic desire to overcome the bounds of time and space through his writing was always and everywhere haunted by a no less compelling recognition of the inevitability of death and of the ultimate futility of imperial ambition. In this perspective, the intimate gesture of these annotations corresponds to snapshots of modern sightseers next to historical monuments and famous places, from which the tourist hopes to bring home testimony of having "been there" and to affirm at some deeper level, against the background of authoritative coordinates of time and space, the reality of his or her "being."

Petrarch's *Itinerarium*

Petrarch immediately puts the reader on notice that his contribution to a genre of medieval travel usually characterized by lack of originality and individuality will be anything but anonymous or short of personality. The proem turns the impersonal generic characteristics of the *itineraria* upside down by displaying prominently the temperament and forceful presence of the work's celebrity author, and might even be taken to question the very institution of pilgrimage that the author purports to promote. From the outset, Petrarch's trademark ambivalence threatens to overshadow pilgrimage as an institution of medieval piety. While affirming that there exists "no more desirable and holy route," the point of the introduction is to advise Giovanni Mandelli of Petrarch's decision *not* to go along with his friend on a pilgrimage to the Holy Land.

The justification for not going on the pilgrimage takes the typically Petrarchan form of confession and self-revelation.[80] "Speechless shame," he says, quoting Horace, keeps Petrarch from stating his reasons but "imperious truth" commands that he speak and excuse himself (*Itin.* Pr. 3). One's suspicions that the disclosure will be less an act of contrition and more an expression of authorial exhibitionism are confirmed when we learn that an old Petrarchan standby is what holds the poet back from undertaking the journey: fear of the sea and shipwreck, or, more precisely, of "slow death and nausea worse than death itself" (Pr. 5). In addition, Petrarch attributes the blame to "fortuna" (Pr. 6: "Fortune begrudges that I should be a member of your group"). While incongruous as a motivation or justification for his refusal to accompany Mandelli, "fortuna" does correspond to another Petrarchan thematic preoccupation around 1358, exactly the period when work on the *De Remediis Utriusque Fortune* was drawing to a close. In the *Itinerarium* the theme thus serves as a kind of Maileresque "advertisement for the self" and its literary investments (as we shall see, the *Itinerarium* is rife with these self-promotions). Finally, instead of his companionship on the journey, Petrarch offers his correspondent or "fan" Mandelli a "brief itinerary" and pilgrimage guide, a literary artifact that can stand as "the more stable effigy of my soul and intellect" (Pr. 7). The implementation here of yet another Petrarchan topos—the literary work as the "effigies animi ingeniique"— has the paradoxical effect of making Petrarch's *Itinerary* both a "description of places," as he explicitly terms it at one point (2.2), and a portrait of the poet's soul.[81] The result is a geographical work, an itinerary or pilgrim's guide, that is at the same time a Petrarchan self-portrait, and this peculiarity sets the work outside the traditional genre of *itineraria*. The subject who writes is no less prominent a subject and object of the writing than the external geographical world that the text undertakes to describe. The tension between these two aspects of the work—the projection of Petrarch's personality and the description of an environment "external" to the author—is central to an appreciation of how the text explores the relationship between poet and world, between writing and space.

Petrarch's resistance to the idea of travel to the Holy Land is unique and needs to be distinguished from more traditional oppositions to travel presented both by some of the church fathers and by medieval ecclesiastical authorities on pilgrimage. While these arguments included a series of practical criticisms, opposition ultimately derived from a rejection of the notion that salvation could be connected with any one place in a greater measure than with any other.[82] Giles Constable, in an authoritative essay on the subject, even included Petrarch among his anti-pilgrimage authorities, noting, for example, that Petrarch in the *Secretum* "put into the mouth of Augustine the view that a change of location only adds to the labor of someone who is already burdened with evil, citing the Socratic maxim that 'You peregrinate with yourself.'"[83] Petrarch often expressed this philosophical commonplace against travel. In the *Itinerarium*, however, Petrarch does not invoke any of these traditional strictures against pilgrimage.

Instead, the argument that no place is any holier than another emerges incongruously in Petrarch's statement that he does not know where it is better to die, since "that which makes men happy or miserable is not to be found in any place but in the soul" (*Itin.* Pr.3). The commonplace on the irrelevancy of physical location to happiness appears in the middle of a nervous discussion in which Petrarch confesses his fear of shipwreck as the motivation for his refusal to undertake the journey (Pr. 3). Perhaps lurking behind the entire passage's shiftiness is the author's deeper, even subconscious, preoccupation with final resting places, especially his own, a typically Petrarchan theme expressed repeatedly throughout the works (as, for example, in the last chapter of the contemporary *De Remediis*, "On dying without burial"). At the outset of the *Itinerarium* the reader detects the implicit tension between Petrarch's eventual sepulcher and the Holy Sepulcher itself. Despite his protestations to the contrary in his "Testament," Petrarch was as concerned with his eventual resting place as he was with avoiding storms at sea.[84] Indeed, his desire to control the place of his burial was no doubt directly related to his horror at the thought of losing his place in the world somewhere on a trackless sea. To state that he is not afraid of death and that it is madness to concern oneself with the place and time of one's death, only to admit finally that he is afraid "of slow death and nausea worse than death itself," displays the Petrarchan self in all of its heroic vulnerability. Petrarch appears to court censure by saying that his aversion to seasickness causes him to decline undertaking the most holy of medieval journeys. The theme of shipwreck holds as strong an attraction for Petrarch as that of pilgrimage, to say nothing of a real journey to the Holy Land.

The shipwreck motif pervades Petrarch's works and represents a signature theme. In general terms, the poet's obsessive reiteration of the topic enacts a literary strategy for neutralizing and mastering anxieties about shipwreck in both material and more metaphorical terms. Petrarch's preoccupation with the theme derived from real experiences at sea[85] and from no less compelling literary anxieties about the integrity of his poetic self and identity. In a sonnet like *RVF* 189, "Passa la nave mia colma d'oblio" (My ship full of forgetful cargo sails), for instance, the poet achieves the composure to which he is exhorted by Augustine in the *Secretum,* that is, to stand upon the shore, compassionately observing the shipwreck of history as well as his own.[86] At the beginning of 1358, with the storm clouds between the Visconti and the imperial league beginning to clear and a few months before writing the *Itinerarium*, Petrarch uses the shipwreck theme to characterize his own tranquility (*Fam.* 20.10, to Giovanni Aghinolfi):

> As for me, however, know that I am safe in the midst of perils (O thick head of mine!) and so tranquil amidst the tempests that if I did not see others strewn about in the stormy sea and were not struck by the seafarer's

clamoring, I would not realize that I was at sea. I sit at the helmsman's feet and stand on the heaving prow, not motionless but certainly unshaken, awaiting the end with a mind that considers nearly every wind as favorable and every port as acceptable.[87]

Here Petrarchan detachment elaborates a variation on the Lucretian shipwreck-with-spectator: as spectator on the deck of a ship tossed by the storm, the poet describes himself as "safe," "tranquil," "not motionless but certainly unshaken."

Petrarch was enjoying the relative isolation of his literary *otium* and one of the most productive periods of his Milanese years at the same time as Giovanni Mandelli was planning a pilgrimage to establish some distance between himself and the political storm that had caught him in its tempest.[88] Petrarch chooses not to compromise the stability he had recently achieved in the literary realm of his study; instead he invokes his fear of the sea and of shipwreck as justification for refusing to go on the pilgrimage with Mandelli. While explicitly praising pilgrimage, and Mandelli for undertaking it, the poet chooses forthrightly and freely not to go.

For the anthropologist Victor Turner, pilgrimages represent "an amplified symbol of the dilemma of choice versus obligation in the midst of a social order where status prevails."[89] Thus, Petrarch's choice not to go on the pilgrimage expresses an extremely high degree of freedom vis-à-vis the structures of social constraint and duty that the institution of late-medieval pilgrimage was designed both to mitigate and to reinforce.[90] The pilgrimage to the Holy Land offered to Mandelli a means of exercising a measure of freedom, choice, and volition outside the everyday political framework of his duties on behalf of the Visconti. The pilgrimage could not have had the same appeal for the poet, who already enjoyed an even higher level of autonomy and status than what undertaking a pilgrimage to the Holy Land would have offered him. Petrarch's nonchalant refusal to accompany Mandelli eloquently indicates the eccentric and simultaneously central position of the poet with respect to the institution of pilgrimage and, by extension, to "local and international relations within a system of shared religious values."[91]

The *Itinerarium* not only expresses the freedom of the poet in terms of social status but, from a literary perspective, the work also asserts and celebrates the poet's capacity for overcoming the alienation of the journey and of space through writing. Petrarch constantly explores and exploits the power of writing as a higher form of travel throughout his works. The dedicatory letter to the *Familiares,* for instance, is carefully constructed around tropes of travel and presents Petrarch's epistolary as a kind of travel writing that will recover, after the apocalypse of the Black Death, what the rich trading voyages of the "Indian or Caspian or Carpathian Sea" could never recompense. In *Familiares* 1.1, writing emerges as a higher form of travel, as a means for overcoming the alienation of the material journey in space and time: "In the meantime I shall continue along the path I have been following, and shall avoid any exits so long as there is light. And the sweet labor will serve for me almost as a place of rest."[92] Writing also serves Petrarch in a material fashion by overcoming the alienation of space and time insofar as the genres of Petrarchan writing, from letters to treatises to lyric fragments, bring together minds and bodies that are otherwise separated in space and time. The virtual pilgrimage of the *Itinerarium* presents an ideal means for Petrarch to exhibit the power of his literary authority over space and to demonstrate his unrivaled capacity for long-distance travel while staying at home.

The advantages of Petrarchan virtual travel are celebrated in a memorable passage from *Seniles* 9.2, which perfectly captures the conception of travel informing the *Itinerarium*:

> I decided not to travel just once on a very long journey by ship or on horse or on foot to those lands, but many times on a tiny map, with books and the imagination, so that in the course of an hour I could go to those shores and return as many times as I liked to those distant shores, not only unscathed, but unwearied too, not only with sound body, but with no wear and tear to my shoes, untouched by briars, stones, mud, and dust.[93]

The benefits of literary mobility are repeatedly emphasized in the *Itinerarium*: "I will complete a very long journey in a concise style" (*Itin.* 1.0); "From here I hope that you will reach the ends of Italy as easily brought by favorable winds and smooth sailing, as I am by a simple and swift style" (12.0); "Your journey of three months I have completed in three days" (21.0). The ease and brevity of the virtual journey and the text's qualities of "lightness" and "quickness" are vital both to the work's meaning and to its success as a literary artifact.

Thus, when Petrarch compared himself to Ulysses in the dedicatory letter of the *Familiares*—"Ulysses indeed traveled neither more nor farther than I"— he referred not only to material travel but to literary mobility as well. The fear of shipwreck evoked in the proem of the *Itinerarium* accordingly needs to be considered in relation to the figure of Ulysses, who as model for Petrarchan travel makes one of his most striking appearances in the Petrarchan canon toward the end of the *Itinerarium*. The passage, in spite of its apparently marginal location in the context of Petrarch's works, represents a focal point gathering together various strands of the motif's significance. Petrarch encourages Mandelli, after having visited Jerusalem and having viewed the sacred sights, to continue his journey and visit Egypt, Alexandria, and the Nile. In doing so, the poet recalls the example of Ulysses:

> But what are you thinking now? Hasn't the desire to see us again taken you yet; hasn't the desire to return to your home, your fatherland, and friends entered your soul yet? I believe so and am sure it could not be any other way. But there is no greater stimulus than virtue. Virtue inspires the generous soul to overcome every difficulty; it does not suffer one to remain in one place, nor that one should look back; it forces one to forget not only pleasures but also more just duties and affections; it does not allow one to choose anything but the ideal of virtue and it does not allow one to desire or think of anything else. This is the stimulus that made Ulysses forget Laertes, Penelope, and Telemachus, and now keeps you far from us, I am afraid, longer than we should like. (*Itin.* 17.0)

Ulysses offered Petrarch a metaphorical way to create for himself a profile within the traditions of heroic travel and travelers. Beyond this, foremost among the relationships Petrarch is negotiating in this particular passage is the vexed one with his vernacular predecessor, Dante, who had so heavily mortgaged Ulysses by bringing the Greek hero and his journey to a divinely ordained *naufragio*. Tellingly, Petrarch's exhortation to Mandelli to emulate a Ulysses forgetful of Laertes, Penelope, and Telemachus, echoes Dante's own condemnation of Ulysses' neglect of his son, father, and wife: "Neither fondness for my son, nor reverence for my aged father, nor the due love that would have made Penelope glad, could conquer in me the longing that I had to gain experience of the world."[94] Petrarch reverses Dante's judgment and urges Mandelli in terms that Dante had used to condemn Ulysses. Petrarch's positive assessment of Dante's character in a famous letter to Boccaccio (*Fam.* 21.15) also praised Dante in these same terms: "In this I can scarcely admire and praise him too highly when nothing—not the injustice suffered at the hands of his fellow citizens, not exile, poverty, or the stings of envy, not his wife's love or his devotion to his children—diverted him from his course once he had embarked upon it."

The passage from the *Itinerarium* should thus be read within the context of Petrarch's renewed encounter with Dante under the stimulus of Boccaccio during the 1350s. The public discussion of Dante between Petrarch and Boccaccio, documented by *Familiares* 21.15, takes place only a year after the composition of the *Itinerarium*. Given that Petrarch praises Dante in *Familiares* 21.15 for Ulyssean qualities that led—according to Dante's fiction—to the hero's demise, it will come as no surprise that Petrarch's treatment of Ulysses generally avoids the inconvenient detail of the hero's shipwreck. Petrarch no less adroitly evades the *scoglio* or reef represented by Dante, whose words concerning Ulysses Petrarch so deftly (albeit passive-aggressively) and radically revises. Ultimately, however, Petrarch's avoidance of Ulysses' shipwreck is a clear sign of the poet's acute awareness of its inevitability.[95]

In fact, the swerve around Ulysses' shipwreck, both in the letter to Boccaccio and in the *Itinerarium*, suggests that the threat of shipwreck at the beginning of the *Itinerarium* is connected to the problem of poetic identity vis-à-vis Dante as well, who was clearly on Petrarch's mind as early as the work's proem, where Petrarch uncharacteristically uses the expression "second death" in the patently Dantean sense of damnation (*Itin.* Pr. 4).[96] In both the *Itinerarium* and in the correspondence with Boccaccio, Petrarch combines an ostensibly detached, even dismissive, attitude with pointed rewriting. In this sense, Petrarch offers in his own pilgrimage text a partial response to Dante's and to Dante the pilgrim-poet. In a typically Petrarchan move, faced with the challenge of asserting poetic identity, the pilgrim-poet Petrarch exhibits and displays his marginality and vulnerability at the same time that he asserts his own centrality and independence vis-à-vis his predecessor.

Petrarch's adaptation of Ulysses as a model pilgrim also points to a historical tension between the trajectories of *travel* and *pilgrimage* that underlies the *Itinerarium*. The tension is expressed in the philological uncertainty that persists concerning the title of

Petrarch's pilgrimage guide: *Itinerarium ad Sepulcrum Domini Nostri Yehsu Christi* (*Itinerary to the Sepulcher of Our Lord Jesus Christ*), according to the Cremona manuscript; or *Itinerarium Domini Francisci Petrarche de Ianua Usque Ierusalem et Alexandriam* (*The Itinerary of Lord Francis Petrarch from Genoa to Jersualem and Alexandria*), according to Tedaldo Della Casa's copy of the text (see About the Text and Translation). The question must wait to be resolved until the appearance of a critical edition of the text, but the second option, with its supplemental "et Alexandriam" is suggestive (as is the possibility that it represents an authorial variant). The latter title expresses the same impetus or paradigm of travel as expressed in the Ulysses passage that urges the pilgrim to go on, to push farther. The title reflects a Petrarchan variation on pilgrimage understood as a return to the Center of the World. As soon as Petrarch gets there, he is anxious to move on.

Pilgrimage traditionally represented a movement toward the Center of the World, while travel came to be associated with movement in the opposite direction, "toward the Other, located beyond the boundaries of the cosmos, in the surrounding chaos."[97] According to anthropologists, "the Pilgrim's journey to the Center, though perilous, is in traditional cultures and societies ultimately legitimate; the Traveler's, in these societies, is ordinarily not."[98] For instance, the distinction Dante draws between the poet's sacralized pilgrimage and Ulyssean travel represents one of the fundamental structural motifs of the *Divine Comedy*. Dante also used the distinction between pilgrimage and travel to authorize his own potentially Ulyssean transgression of boundaries as a poet.[99] Historically, as the traveler's role gradually became more socially acceptable, the significance of Ulysses, which already caused a high level of interpretive tension in Dante (as is evident in centuries of debate among the commentators about Dante's attitude toward Ulysses), was progressively reinterpreted in a more positive light by the subsequent tradition. At the beginning of this process stands, conspicuously, Petrarch's version of Ulysses in the *Itinerarium*.

Petrarch's revision of the paradigm does not, however, consist in simply opting for Ulysses the traveler as opposed to Dante the pilgrim. Transforming Ulysses into a pilgrim to the Holy Land represents a characteristic Petrarchan gesture of self-fashioning. Petrarch's conflation of travel and pilgrimage legitimizes his own literary project, which might be described paradoxically as a *Ulyssean pilgrimage*—a pilgrimage to the Center of the World whose final destination is not the fixed Center of the Holy Land but the open-ended Center of the incessantly, heroically wandering Petrarchan self. In the *Itinerarium* the use of the framework of the sacred journey authorizes the emergence of the Petrarchan writing subject *ex itinere*.[100]

In terms of the history of travel the *Itinerarium* registers an important transition. The work marks a stage in the progressive "disenchantment of the world," during which a modern worldview with "neither a Center nor an Other of any great primeval, mystical significance" emerged.[101] Initially, new centers of political and cultural pilgrimage appeared alongside traditional centers of religious pilgrimage. Over time, "the range of new centers multiplied and gradually they were transformed into 'attractions' and their visitors, the one-time pilgrims, became 'tourists.'"[102] Certainly Petrarch's *Itinerarium* represents an early example of the delineation of Italy as a "tourist attraction" that not only competes with but surpasses the Holy Land in the importance attributed to it (even by virtue of the mere fact that the guide devotes more textual space to Italy than to the Holy Land). Petrarch offers the first recorded admiring tourist's gaze of the Ligurian coast and the Cinque Terre (*Itin.* 2.0–6.0), from what was at that time the unusual perspective of a boat coasting along those shores.[103] Elsewhere he casually distinguishes between the sites that should be visited if possible and those that cannot be missed. The poet recommends that the pilgrim visit a particular church in Naples, not to pray but to admire the frescoes by Giotto (10.2).

The *Itinerarium* thus marks a shift not only in terms of the directionality of travel but also and especially in terms of the priority given to the subject who experiences and writes about travel. The incessantly wandering, incessantly writing Petrarchan subject conflates the planes of textual and territorial space in order to extend the range of the Petrarchan self and to authenticate the reality of that self by fixing it against the backdrop of cartographical-geographical space. Petrarch's aspiration to construct an enduring literary portrait of the self vis-à-vis his contemporaries and posterity leads him to inscribe himself upon the new map of the world.

Petrarch and the *Itinerarium* stand at the beginning of an early modern literary form that has conveniently been termed *cartographic writing*.[104] His pilgrimage narrative marks the emergence of a modern literary subject and parallels the concurrent transition in cartography from cosmographical mapping to more empirical modes of representation, from the ideological mappamundi to empirically based portolan charts. (Compare the T-O maps of the world in Illustrations 10 and 11 with the empirical portolan map of Italy in Illustration 4.) In fact, Petrarch incorporates in his writing both of these traditions in a way similar to world maps like the one made in Parma in 1367 by the Pizzigani brothers, with whom Petrarch may well have had personal contacts.[105] Petrarch coordinates his literary project with geography in order to legitimize the self through its association with geographic truth. His cartographic writing projects upon the outline of a portolan-style map of Italy and the eastern Mediterranean a memory gallery of typical Petrarchan *loci* and a portrait of the Petrarchan self. In particular, he establishes himself as both the cause and effect, as "inventor" and "discoverer," of Italy as a pilgrimage site that he authors at the same time that he is authorized by it—and that is presented in implicit opposition to the Holy Land.

The artistic ambition and self-mythologizing scope of this cartographical aspect of the *Itinerarium* is one of its distinguishing features. The interrelation between textual and geographical topographies that one finds in Petrarch is, of course, not without precedent. An intimate connection between topography and literary composition goes as far back as the classical period, where it was explicitly treated in discussions of the *ars memoriae*. Quintilian, for example, suggested that specific locations within a memory system might be furnished by the experiences of travel. A student of the rhetoric of space in Republican and Augustan Rome, E. W. Leach, has observed how, "save for the greater freedom that it offers to personal invention, the organization of *loci* in a memory system is not unlike that of a periplus, or geographical catalog, reflected in certain passages of *Aeneid* 3."[106] While the *ars memoriae* was never a formula for literary description, the same deep connection between memory and place that informed the *ars* did provide the inspiration for topographical descriptions in classical texts like the *Georgics* and book 3 of the *Aeneid*, which profoundly influenced Petrarch's own rhetoric of space and his representations of Italy in prose and poetry.

In Petrarch, however, this model does not have as its referent any geopolitical imperial reality of the world as it did in Virgil; rather, the model provides a way to construct a memory system that takes the Petrarchan self as its central point of reference. Indeed, Leach's evocation of *Aeneid* 3 is significant in this context, inasmuch as the text is important for Petrarch's literary topography in general and in the *Itinerarium* in particular. For instance, the geographical passage recalled by Leach is pointedly cited and reversed by Petrarch in the *Itinerarium* at the point where he describes Scylla and Charybdis. Precisely as if to place his own signature upon that classically Virgilian "passage," Petrarch addresses the reader: "It should not surprise you that Virgil in the third book of the divine poem apparently placed them otherwise. He was describing in fact the voyage of one who was arriving while I the voyage of one who is departing" (*Itin.* 12.2).

Petrarch places his signature upon Italy, taking his cue from classical forms of cartographic writing, which derived largely from Virgil (but were common to late Roman republican and imperial literature and reflected the Roman predilection for cartographic drawing and map making).[107] Petrarch appropriated these, however, for his own literary purposes and, in the absence of Caesar Augustus and Rome, oriented them around the Petrarchan self. As in the Ciceronian art of memory, in which the rooms of a house or *loci* are arranged in space and associated with components of discourse,[108] the place names that make up Petrarch's *Itinerarium* constitute a verbal map of Italy as a surface of memorable things, people, and events, all of which bear and are certified by a Petrarchan signature.

In the construction of the Ligurian-Tuscan section of the text, for example (*Itin.* 2.0–7.4), Petrarch integrates toponyms that correspond precisely to those of fourteenth-century portolan charts as well as place names derived from his own biographical and poetic memory. The places that appear in the *Itinerarium* but not in the portolan charts (see, for example, Illustration 5)—such as Lerici, Luni, Sarzana, Avenza, Rio Freddo, Massa, and Pietrasanta—all correspond to Petrarch's perssonal travels in the area. Petrarch's description of the Ligurian-Tuscan seaboard is remarkably self-aware of the poet's role in the invention or discovery of that landscape. He asserts that these coasts are "surely second to no other place on earth" and marvels that they were "overlooked by classical authors and above all by the poets"; Petrarch attributes the cause of this silence to the fact that these places "had not yet been explored and were therefore unknown" (5.1).

The clear implication is that there are lands yet to be discovered that the classical authors and poets did not know. Far from expressions of anxiety about cultural belatedness or inferiority vis-à-vis the ancients, we are confronted here with the Renaissance trope of New World discovery, according to which the moderns surpass the ancients. This perspective inspires the poet "to describe these places in a passage of my *Africa*, where the ideal opportunity presented itself, in a kind of writing very different from any other" (*Itin.* 5.1). Petrarch concludes the passage by delineating a complex relationship between the literary topographical description of his never-to-be completed epic, the direct topographical experience of the coast, and the role that memory plays within the subjectivity of the traveler-addressee: "And if the brevity of life or slowness of intellect or the concurrent distraction of other books or obstacles of fortune without measure should not keep that work from coming under your gaze, it will recall to your memory these and other places that you are now about to see" (5.1). Meanwhile, the *Itinerarium* performs the function of a marker for future tourists to "Petrarch's Italy."[109]

While the section on the Ligurian coast in the *Itinerarium* refers us back to Petrarch's activity as a poet and poetic inventor of places, the Neapolitan section highlights his role as an antiquarian and classical philologist. Petrarch projects himself upon the map of Italy in this instance by memorializing his archeological and philological tourism around Naples (*Itin.* 10.0–10.3), which contributed to the work's fortune among Neapolitan readers. Petrarch repeatedly recorded the emotions of his Neapolitan tours of 1341 and 1343, most prominently in *Familiares* 5.4, to Giovanni Colonna, and in a metrical epistle (*Epyst.* 2.15) to Rinaldo Cavalchini. In particular, as Michele Feo has noted, *Familiares* 5.4 entered immediately into the museum of local Neapolitan glories and is cited in travel and geographical writing regarding the bay of Naples from Flavio Biondo's *Italia illustrata* to recent tourist guides. Petrarch started that tradition by citing himself and his travels in his own travel guide, the *Itinerarium*.

Petrarch visited Naples for the first time in 1341. He was examined by King Robert of Naples in preparation for his subsequent coronation as poet laureate in Rome. It was winter, and Petrarch had little opportunity for tourism; nevertheless, he wrote in the fall of 1343 a metrical epistle (*Epyst.* 2.7) to Barbato da Sulmona, in which he proposed an archeological tour and reevoked the memory of the dead king and the sights they had visited together during his first Neapolitan sojourn.[110] In the *Itinerarium* Petrarch also recorded the archeological and antiquarian aspects of his conversations with King Robert by means of a charming anecdote in which the king queries Petrarch about the legend that Virgil had excavated the *crypta neapolitana* (today known as the "grotta di Pozzuoli") with magic spells:

> And when King Robert, famous for his kingdom, but still more illustrious for his intelligence and his literary culture, in the presence of many other people, asked me what I thought about it, trusting myself to his regal humanity, in which he surpasses not only other kings but all other men, I answered playfully that I had nowhere read that Virgil was a marble worker. To which he assented with a nod of his serene brow, and confirmed that there were vestiges of iron and not magic. (*Itin.* 10.0)

This appealing autobiographical vignette reinforces an image of the poet's authority, which was such that King Robert would ask his opinion about the matter. The easy familiarity between the two, expressed by Petrarch's witty remark and the king's assent with a "serene brow," further consolidates Petrarch's personal prestige and authority against the background of the Neapolitan setting. As Petrarch had noted in the dedication of the *Africa* to King Robert, "Merely by inclining your brow, / you create glory where no glory was" (*Afr.* 1.30–31).[111] The passage also connects to other passages in Petrarch that reject the tradition of Virgil as a magician, which represented an indirect means of defending himself against (but at the same time flaunting) the same charge that was brought against him in the early 1350s by his enemies in Avignon, including most prominently Cardinal Etienne Aubert, who became Pope Innocent VI in 1352.

Petrarch further inscribed himself upon the Neapolitan coasts by documenting his evolving understanding of the philological questions surrounding the deaths of Misenus in the *Aeneid* and Elpenor in the *Odyssey*, that is, whether both occurred at cape Misenum and whether they were accidental or sacrificial (*Itin.* 9.3). Petrarch's opinion of the matter was influenced by his reading of the Latin version of Homer that Leontius Pilatus had completed by November 1362 at Boccaccio's request. Petrarch later learned, as late as 1365, from reading Pilatus's translation of the *Odyssey* book 11, that Elpenor's death was accidental and took place before Ulysses left Circe. A trace of Petrarch's new knowledge surfaces in *Itinerarium* 9.3, where the poet introduces the phrase (probably sometime during the late 1360s) "in any case the matter is very uncertain," thus distancing himself from the opinion he had earlier expressed that Aeneas had sacrificed Misenus in the same place as Ulysses had reportedly sacrificed Elpenor (an erroneous notion Petrarch took from Servius).

But Petrarch waited almost two and a half years before asking Boccaccio for this Latin version of Homer, in a *Seniles* dated 1 March 1365, a delay Feo characterizes as the expression of "a sort of constant self-defense, a periodic putting up of barriers against assaults from the outside, a jealousness of one's own identity. Even the always cordial openness to Homer (like that towards Dante) is dominated by the need to not allow himself to be invaded, to avoid destroying his own system."[112] In fact, Petrarch resists totally revising the passage to reflect his new knowledge. He simply avers that "the matter is very uncertain." The tentative nature of the revision reflects the extent to which Petrarch's identity was intimately involved in his philology. His research sought to establish a philological "truth" in relation to geographical and textual *loci,* but the enterprise, like Petrarch's travel writing in general, was as much about consolidating his own sense of self and inscribing himself in place and memory as it was about resolving a question of classical literary topography. Petrarch's topographical-philological investigations into the geography of the classics were tantamount to affirming the self in relation to a network of classical literary places by means of which traces of the Petrarchan self might endure.

When confronted with new philological knowledge, Petrarch made a point of carefully returning to all of the relevant *loci* in his works and intervening according to the new knowledge. Feo has opportunely drawn a parallel between this practice and Petrarch's compositional methodology of revising endlessly his vernacular lyrics and other writings: "The method of the poet and the philologist are superimposed: the principle that the work is ever perfectible, as long as it 'lives' together with the physical life of the author, dominates all of Petrarch. . . . Only death can interrupt forever the game or the drama, whichever way you prefer to see it."[113] Thus Petrarch's constant revisitations of philological sources no less than his revisions of the poetry express a deeper aspiration to avoid closure, to defer the end of the journey, as much as they reflect a desire for knowledge of an external reality or truth. This deeper motivation may in fact explain why Petrarch left open the question of Misenus's and Elpenor's deaths in his revision of the *Itinerarium* when he might well have resolved it.

The *Itinerarium* illustrates an important element of Petrarch's rhetoric of space that goes beyond the discovery of a characteristic landscape or the shaping and refinement of historical and archaeological memory: he develops what amounts to the literary "invention" of Italy—a *patria* that superseded any regional and municipal Italian home. Petrarch's fashioning of Italy corresponded to his need for an authorizing home of a higher order at a time when Italy did not exist as a national political home but simply as a geographical abstraction. Through Petrarch's pen, Italy is revived as a cultural ideal. A large measure of Petrarch's authority among his contemporaries and before posterity derives from his role as Italy's author in this literary sense, that is, by virtue of his role in the creation of an ideal Italian homeland that was shared both by the imagined community of contemporary readers and by posterity. The *Itinerarium* is an important example of Petrarch's authoring of Italy in the genre of cartographic writing, and no doubt contributed to the tradition that Petrarch, together with King Robert, had made an authoritative map of Italy.[114]

From its point of departure in Genoa to the "the end of Italy upon having touched at Otranto" (*Itin.* 14.0), Petrarch's *Itinerarium* figures cumulatively as a portolan-style outline of the peninsula that constitutes a unity of coast and culture, with repeated references to "Italy" reinforcing this unifying theme. To begin with, either possible derivation of the origin of the name *Genoa* suits Petrarch's Italocentric purposes—either from Janus, "the first King of Italy," or from *ianua*, door, as the city is "like a *ianua* (that is to say, 'door') to our territory" (2.1). The fact that the point of departure for the itinerary is really a point of arrival is also appropriate. Petrarch in fact dispenses with any account of travel between an empirical point of departure and the place of embarkation, as was typical; he leaves "aside the places in between, since they are continually before our eyes and to report them to the ears is superfluous" (1.1). The poet highlights Augustus Caesar's prudence in stationing a fleet at Misenum and another at Ravenna, "so that the sea above as well as the one below, which together surround the greater part of Italy almost like an island, would be protected by this double guard" (9.5). He notes (in point of fact, erroneously) that "the place where Italy grows most narrow is called Scalea" (12.1), that is, as seen from the point of view of one looking down upon a portolan chart at the point where there is the least distance between the Tyrrhenian and Ionian coasts.

Before leaving Italy, Petrarch stops at Crotone on the Ionian coast, which "was once un-surpassed among the peoples of Italy . . . is barely known even to the inhabitants of Italy" (13.0; the decadence of Crotone is another typical Petrarchan theme). Taranto is remembered as the birthplace of Ennius, where, perhaps, Virgil died; but finally, the city is remembered as a frontier or border of Italy—as the city that gave help to the invaders of Italy, King Pyrrhus and later Hannibal (13.1).

The *Itinerarium* cumulatively provides a vision of the whole that emphasizes the outline of Italy both as a cartographic and cultural unity. This kind of cartographic writ-ing was apparently an ideal vehicle for the poet, who sought to inspire a broader con-sciousness of place among his contemporaries. Whether the leglike shape of the Italian peninsula (which was already fairly clear from the time of the *Peutinger Table*) had been previously referred to as "the boot," as it is now, or by some similar expression, it is significant that Petrarch was the first to write it down in one of his metrical epistles (*Epyst.* 2. 11.26–29): "powerful on the sea and on land, by your very aspect you appear destined for empire, as if you would like to strike the world with your heel. Like a spur you stretch out your Otranto and oppose to the nordic waves two-headed Brindisi."[115] As in this metrical epistle, Petrarch constitutes in the *Itinerarium* a comprehensive vi-sion of Italy that has the easily recognizable shape, in words, of a modern map. The *Itinerarium* is just one of several instances in Petrarch's works in which the poet views Italy from the perspective of a portolan map. On the one hand, he constructs a periplus experienced from the perspective of the traveling subject, and on the other hand he pro-vides a simultaneous view of the whole from above.

But moving beyond the Italian portion of his writerly periplus, Petrarch's "de-scription of places" presents a portrait of the poet's soul, even in its more conventional account of the eastern Mediterranean, the Holy Land, and Egypt. Here, where the car-tographical model for the writing reverts to the perspective of the mappamundi,[116] Petrarch's *Itinerarium* continues to express an array of typically Petrarchan themes and attitudes. If, for example, as Thomas Greene has suggested, "the chartless, formless space of [Petrarchan] errancy finds a focus in the boundary or threshold whose cross-ing situates a drama," and if Petrarch is thus to be considered "a poet of thresholds,"[117] then we are not surprised to discover in the section on the Holy Land a fascination with thresholds and boundary crossings, whether it be the recollection of Christ's descent "to raid the realms of the enemy" (that is, the harrowing of hell following his death, *Itin.* 16.3), or the entrance of the divinely aided conquering Romans into Jerusalem (16.5), or Caesar entering into Alexandria, "almost as if to render religious devotion" (20.0).

Petrarch gives the visit to the Holy Sepulcher no particular prominence. He de-scribes the tomb (at *Itin.* 16.3) as almost secondary to the harrowing of hell, and the tomb simply appears in a list of Jesus' actions in particular places, to be recalled by the pilgrim. In terms of literary attention and prominence in the work, Christ's sepulcher pales in comparison to Alexander's tomb, visited very close to the end of the *Itinerarium* (*Itin.* 20.0–20.2). Indeed, the visit to Alexander's tomb is another Petrarchan com-monplace, and the poet introduces it by means of an anecdote (deriving from Suetonius) about Augustus Caesar's visit to the tomb, which Petrarch had previously utilized in the introduction to the *De Viris Illustribus*. According to the story, Augustus Caesar, when he visited the tomb of Alexander, was asked if he wanted also to see the tomb of King Ptolemy as well; but Caesar "elegantly answered that he wanted to see a king and not the dead" (20.1). Petrarch uses the anecdote here in the *Itinerarium* to urge Giovanni Mandelli to "admire this tomb" of Alexander "if it has not been overcome by time" (20.2). In the *De Viris* the story gave Petrarch a figure for the biographer's freedom to select his own subjects: the emperor Caesar reveals himself to be a true sovereign by his desire to see kings, not dead men. Petrarch the pilgrim-tourist similarly defines himself by the sites he seeks out and points to along his itinerary, and his unconventional and personal pilgrimage narrative culminates in a visit to Alexander's tomb rather than Christ's.

Recent scholarship on Renaissance literature has sought to trace the self's emergence in the context of "the correlation between mapping and the growth of a new medium—literature—in early modern print culture."[118] As we have seen, however, cartographic writing can be said to go all the way back to Virgil and Roman literature. The cartographic and literary institutions that emerged during the Renaissance are distinguished by their preoccupation with the self and can be traced genealogically through Petrarch. Just as Renaissance cartographic writing reflects the early modern subject's attempt to negotiate a space for itself in relation to emerging national spaces and identities, Petrarch, at the beginning of this history of "self-fashioning," attempts both to establish and to affirm his identity as a writer by his "invention" of Italy and by inscribing himself on the new map of the world.

Stephen Greenblatt, who first coined the term *self-fashioning*, described this cultural phenomenon as deriving from a modern need "to sustain the illusion that we are the principal makers of our identities."[119] Petrarch sustained that illusion by adapting classical imperial cartographic writing to the needs of an all-consuming subjectivity whose ethics, according to Giuseppe Mazzotta, were "the dream of an absolute viewpoint wherein the self appears as a fragment of a larger world, and the world itself comes into being through the poet's dream."[120] From an institutional point of view, Petrarch first responded to the pressures of modernity upon the identity and freedom of the poet by attempting to appropriate the new map of the world and to enlist it in the general effort to sustain the illusion that the poet was the principal maker not only of his own identity but also of the world. Petrarch's intense awareness of the fragility of that illusion and his profound sense of his own vulnerability perhaps account for—and certainly counterbalance—the heroic hyperbole of his cartographic writing in defense of the self.

Notes

1. For a dialectical account of historical space between the medieval and Renaissance periods, see Henri Lefebvre, *The Production of Space*, trans. Donald Nicholson-Smith (Oxford: Basil Blackwell, 1991; 1st French ed., 1974). For the concept of *renewed space-time compression*, see

David Harvey, "The Time and Space of the Enlightenment Project," in *The Condition of Postmodernity* (Oxford: Basil Blackwell, 1989), pp. 240–59. Among the other works that have informed this essay are E. J. Leed, *The Mind of the Traveler: From Gilgamesh to Global Tourism* (New York: Basic Books, 1988); Dean MacCannell, *The Tourist: A New Theory of the Leisure Class* (New York: Schocken Books, 1976); James Clifford, "Traveling Cultures," in *Routes: Travel and Translation in the Late Twentieth Century* (Cambridge: Harvard University Press, 1997); Mary Campbell, *The Witness and the Other World: Exotic European Travel Writing, 400–1600* (Ithaca: Cornell University Press, 1988); Stephen Greenblatt, "Marvelous Possessions," in *Marvelous Possessions: The Wonder of the New World* (Chicago: University of Chicago Press, 1991), pp. 52–85; James Romm, "Geography and Fiction," in *The Edges of the Earth in Ancient Thought* (Princeton: Princeton University Press, 1992), pp. 172–214; M. W. Helms, *Ulysses' Sail: An Ethnographic Odyssey of Power, Knowledge, and Geographical Distance* (Princeton: Princeton University Press, 1988); Georges Van Den Abbeele, *Travel as Metaphor from Montaigne to Rousseau* (Minneapolis: University of Minnesota Press, 1992); Tom Conley, *The Self-Made Map: Cartographic Writing in Early Modern France* (Minneapolis: University of Minnesota Press, 1996).

2. The tag "peregrinus ubique" is from Petrarch's metrical epistle (*Epyst.*) 3.19.16, to Barbato da Sulmona: "incola cev nusquam, sic sum peregrinus ubique" (I am nowhere a citizen and a foreigner everywhere). Ernst Hatch Wilkins entitled the first chapter of *The Making of the* Canzoniere *and Other Petrarchan Studies* (Roma: Edizioni di Storia e Letteratura, 1951) "Peregrinus ubique." Gianfranco Contini termed Petrarch "l'irrequieto turista," in "Preliminari sulla lingua del Petrarca," the introduction to his edition of the *Canzoniere* (Torino: Einaudi, 1964), p. xv.

3. With the exception of A. Levati's five-volume, novelistic reconstruction of Petrarch's life based on the letters, *Viaggi di Francesco Petrarca in Francia, in Germania ed in Italia* (Milano: Societá Tipografica de' Classici Italiani, 1820), Petrarchan criticism has treated Petrarch the traveler only intermittently. See, for example: Pierre de Nolhac, *Pétrarque et l'human-isme* (Paris: Champion, 1902), vol. 1, pp. 149–52, and vol. 2, pp. 77 and 87–100; G. Billanovich, *Petrarca letterato,* vol. 1, *Lo scrittoio del Petrarca* (Roma: Edizioni di Storia e Letteratura, 1947), pp. 219–25; Ernest Hatch Wilkins, "Peregrinus ubique," *Studies in Philology* 45 (1948), pp. 445–53, also in *Making of the* Canzoniere, pp. 1–8. Occasionally, criticism takes up the topic anecdotally, as in A. Sacchetto, *Il pellegrino viandante* (Firenze: Le Monnier, 1955); G. Frasso, *Itinerari con Francesco Petrarca*, preface by Giuseppe Billanovich (Padova: Antenore, 1974). The confluence of positivist literary scholarship and interest in travel as an expression of Italian cultural and colonial leadership appears to have inspired the still interesting if philologically unreliable contributions of F. Lo Parco: "Il Petrarca e gli antipodi etnografici in rapporto con la concezione patristica e dantesca," *Romania* 37 (1908), pp. 337–57; "L'ultima Thule nell'intuizione e nella di-vinizzazione di F. Petrarca," *Rivista geografica italiana* 17 (1911), pp. 459–74; "Il viaggio di Francesco Petrarca 'ad extrema terrarum,'" in *Studii dedicati a Francesco Torraca* (Napoli: F. Perrella, 1912), pp. 87–100. A distinguished exception to the general neglect of the theme by contemporary criticism is Thomas M. Greene, "Petrarch's *Viator:* The Displacements of Heroism," *Yearbook of English Studies* 12 (1982), pp. 25–57.

4. Ugo Dotti, *Vita di Petrarca* (Roma and Bari: Laterza, 1987), pp. 324–26. For more on Petrarch and Mandelli, see F. Novati, "Il Petrarca e i Visconti," in *Francesco Petrarca e la Lombardia* (Milano: Hoepli, 1904), pp. 42–45.

5. See Franco Cardini, "Viaggiatori medioevali in Terrasanta: A proposito di alcune recenti pubblicazioni italiane," *Rivista storica italiana,* vol. 80/2 (Napoli: Edizioni Scientifiche Italiane, 1968), pp. 332–39; quote is from p. 336.

6. See, for example, and for further bibliography, Franco Cardini, "I viaggi di religione, d'ambasceria e di mercatura," in *Storia della società italiana,* vol. 7, *La crisi del sistema comunale* (Torino: Einaudi, 1982); and *Toscana e Terrasanta nel medioevo,* ed. Franco Cardini (Firenze: Alinea, 1982). More recent titles include *Il pellegrinaggio nella formazione dell'Europa: Aspetti culturali e religiosi,* ed. Mary Maragno (Padova: Centro Studi Antoniani, 1990); Gabriella Bartolini, *Nel nome di Dio facemmo vela: Viaggio in Oriente di un pellegrino medievale* (Roma: Laterza, 1991); *Vie di pellegrinaggio medievale attraverso l'Alta Valle del Tevere, Atti del Convegno: Sansepolcro, 27–28 settembre 1996,* ed. Enzo Mattesini (Città di Castello [Perugia]: Petruzzi; Sansepolcro: Comune di Sansepolcro, 1998); *Il pellegrinaggio medievale per Roma e Santiago de Compostela: Itinerari di Val di Magra,* ed. Giulivo Ricci (Aulla: Assessorato all'Istruzione e Cultura del Comune di Aulla, Centro Aullese di Ricerche e di Studi Lunigianesi, 1992); *Santiago di Compostella: Il pellegrinaggio medievale,* ed. Giovanni Cherubini (Siena: Protagon, 1998); Franco Cardini, *La peregrinación: Una dimensión de la vida medieval* [= *Il pellegrinaggio: Una dimensione della vita medievale*] (Manziana [Roma]: Vecchiarelli, 1999); *Romei e Giubilei: Il pellegrinaggio medievale a San Pietro (350–1350),* ed. Mario D'Onofrio (Roma: Electa, 1999).

7. G. R. Cardona, "I viaggi e le scoperte," in *Letteratura italiana: Le questioni,* ed. A. Asor Rosa (Torino: Einaudi, 1986), vol. 5, pp. 687–716; quote is from p. 687.

8. Carlo Dionisotti, *Geografia e storia della letteratura italiana* (Torino: Einaudi, 1971), p. 27.

9. See Benedict Anderson, *Imagined Communities: Reflections on the Origin and Spread of Nationalism* (London: Verso, 1983).

10. For the political ambiguities of this "cosmopolitan" aspect of Petrarch's position, see Franco Gaeta, "Dal comune alla corte rinascimentale," *Letteratura italiana,* vol. 1, *Il letterato e le istituzioni* (Milano: Einaudi, 1982), pp. 149–255, especially part 3, "Petrarca: Un apolide disponibile e fortunato," pp. 197–212.

11. Marco Santagata, *Per moderne carte: La biblioteca volgare di Petrarca* (Bologna: Il Mulino, 1990), p. 19.

12. Cardona, "I viaggi e le scoperte," pp. 687–716; quote is from p. 689.

13. Lefebvre, *Production of Space,* pp. 39–44.

14. See Theodore J. Cachey, Jr., "Petrarch, Boccaccio, and the New World Encounter," *Stanford Italian Review: Perspectives on the Italian Renaissance* 10 (1991), pp. 45–59.

15. Helms, *Ulysses' Sail,* p. 5.

16. All translations of the *Familiares* are from Francis Petrarch, *Letters on Familiar Matters, Rerum Familiarium Libri,* trans. Aldo S. Bernardo, 3 vols.: vol. 1, *Fam.* 1–8 (Albany: State University of New York Press, 1975); vol. 2, *Fam.* 9–16 (Baltimore: Johns Hopkins

University Press, 1982); vol. 3, *Fam.* 17–24 (Baltimore: Johns Hopkins University Press, 1985). Quote is from vol. 1, p. 8. Concerning Ulysses, see below, note 95, and Notes to the Text and Translation, note 156.

17. *Fam.* 15.4: "I do not know whence its origin, but I do know that innate desire, especially in superior minds, to see new places and to change domiciles, something which I do not deny should be tempered and regulated by reason" (*Letters on Familiar Matters,* vol. 2, p. 260).

18. All translations from the *Seniles* are from Francis Petrarch, *Letters of Old Age, Rerum Senilium Libri,* trans. Aldo S. Bernardo, Saul Levin, and Reta A. Bernardo (Baltimore: Johns Hopkins University Press, 1992). *Sen.* 18.1: "At that time a youthful craving drove me to travel through France and Germany; and although I invented other reasons to have my elders approve my journey, the real reason was my ardor and curiosity to see many things" (vol. 2, p. 675).

19. Helms, *Ulysses' Sail,* pp. 22–23.

20. *Letters of Old Age,* vol. 1, p. 156.

21. The travel letters of the early books of the *Familiares* include those describing his travels through France and Germany (*Fam.*1.4, 1.5, 1.6) and his first journey to Rome (*Fam.* 2.12, 2.13, 2.14); about the island of Thule (*Fam.* 3.1) and the ascent of Mt. Ventoux (*Fam.* 4.1); on his second trip to Naples (including *Fam.* 5.3, 5.4, 5.5, 5.6); and "concerning the remarkable places in the city of Rome" (*Fam.* 6.2).

22. *Epyst.* 2.25, to Ildebrandino di Conte, bishop of Padua; the work was composed in 1349 in praise of Italy, as compared to other countries, especially France, Germany, England, and Flanders.

23. See in particular Francis Petrarch, *In difesa dell'Italia (Contra Eum Qui Maledixit Italie),* ed. Giuliana Crevatin (Padova: Marsilio, 1995). See also *Fam.* 9.13, "To Philippe de Vitry, musician, rebuking the ineptness of those so restricted to one corner of the world as to consider even a glorious absence undesireable"; and *Sen.* 7.1, "to Urban V, how the return of the Church to its own See, too long delayed, must be delayed no longer."

24. "La pittura d'Italia di Roberto re di Sicilia, e di Francesco Petrarca suo familiare, la qual noi in questa opera sequitiamo" (the map of Italy by King Robert of Sicily and by Francis Petrarch member of his court, which we follow in this work). See Biondo Flavio, *Roma ristaurata et Italia illustrata di Biondo da Forlì,* vernacular trans. by Lucio Fauno (Venezia: Tramezzino, 1542), f. 148r. There is no mention of this map attributed to Petrarch in his writing or in immediately contemporary sources. See G. A. Cesareo, "La 'Carta d'Italia' del Petrarca," in *Dai tempi antichi a tempi moderni* (Milano: Hoepli, 1904), pp. 221–25.

25. Victor Turner uses the term *catchment area* to refer to the geographical area from which the majority of pilgrims are drawn to a particular shrine. See "Pilgrimages as Social Processes," in *Dramas, Fields, and Metaphors: Symbolic Action in Human Society* (Ithaca: Cornell University Press, 1974), p. 179.

26. Ibid.

27. See G. Nori, "La corte itinerante: Il pellegrinaggio di Nicolò III in Terrasanta," in *La Corte e lo spazio, Ferrara estense,* ed. Giuseppe Papagno and Amedeo Quondam (Roma: Bulzoni, 1982), pp. 233–46.

28. For the Italian nationalism or *italianità* that found its champions in Dante and Petrarch, see Philip Jones, *The Italian City-State: From Commune to Signoria* (Oxford: Clarendon Press, 1977), pp. 52–53, where Jones speaks of an Italian nationalism that "turning geography into history . . . reinterpreted the past itself as a history of *romanitas*, lost and recovered, from a Barbarian Middle Age by an Italian Renaissance. . . . The Italian Renaissance was Italian as much as Renaissance, even among the élite; and there was more to *italianità*, as Petrarch confessed, than 'sangue latino.' Italian national sentiment itself, for all its conscious Latinity, was not antique but, like all Western nationalism, a new formation (and not simply Latin) of the post Carolingian and later centuries."

29. See Claudio Greppi, "Una carta per la corte: Il viaggiatore immobile," in *The Renaissance in Ferrara and Its European Horizons*, ed. J. Salmons and W. Moretti (Cardiff: University of Wales Press; Ravenna: Ed. del Girasole, 1984), pp. 199–222.

30. Alessandro Zorzi was a Venetian erudite who assembled a series of annotated anthologies of the earliest narratives of exploration and discovery. See R. Almagià, "Intorno a quattro codici fiorentini e ad uno ferrarese dell'erudito veneziano Alessandro Zorzi," in *La bibliofilia* 38 (1936), pp. 313–47.

31. Regarding Ariosto's virtual travels, see *Espaces réals et espaces imaginaires dans* Le Roland furieux, ed. A. Doroszlai, J. Guidi, M. F. Piéjus, and A. Rochon (Paris: Université de la Sorbonne Nouvelle, 1991).

32. Girolamo Tiraboschi, *Storia della letteratura italiana* (Modena: Pressa la Società Tipografico, 1771–82); 2d rev. ed., 15 vols. (1787–94).

33. Carlo Dionisotti has observed that, whatever Tiraboschi's intention might have been, his historiographical enterprise undermined the integrity of the classical Italian canon by dissolving its narrowly rhetorical statute into a historical perspective of unprecedented articulation and breadth: "The rhetorical frame of Italian literature dissolved, and its motionless, timeless mirage with it, revealing an immeasurable historical panorama of civil exertions produced over centuries amidst shifting vicissitudes and profound fragmentation, by generations of different peoples, who had lived and died on one and the same territory" (*Geografia e storia*, p. 29).

34. Tiraboschi's patriotism is understated but nevertheless present and needs to be taken into account. As he explicitly stated in his preface, the purpose of his *Storia della letteratura italiana* was to "increase new praise of Italy, and to defend her as well, as necessary, against the envy of some of those among the foreigners." In fact, the single substantial citation that Tiraboschi provides from Petrarch's travel writings eloquently reflects a proud and patriotic Italian subject's perspective in response to the realities of late eighteenth-century travel, when Italy, "Europe's internal Other," had become the object of a kind of colonial appropriation by European travelers from France, Germany, and England. In this light, Tiraboschi's evocation of Petrarch the traveler and the translation of a key passage from *Familiares* 1.4 represents a poignant gesture of resitance to that appropriation, tactfully provided without critical commentary or amplification: "Recently I traveled through France for no particular purpose, as you know, except for the youthful desire of seeing as much as possible. At one point I reached Germany and the shores of the Rhine River, carefully viewing the customs of the people and delighting in the sites of

an unknown country, comparing each thing to ours. And though I saw many magnificent things on both shores, I nevertheless did not repent being an Italian. Indeed to tell the truth the further I travel the greater is my appreciation of my native soil" (see *Storia*, vol. 5, pp. 130–33).

35. Tiraboschi, *Storia*, vol. 5, p. 130.

36. These journeys were repeatedly memorialized by Petrarch himself. He attributes them to his desire for knowledge in the *Posteritati*: "vera tamen causa [of his travels] erat multa videndi ardor ac studium"(the real reason was my ardor and curiosity to see many things). He blames them on his destiny in *RVF* 331.2: "non mio voler, ma mia stella seguendo"(following not my will but my star). He describes these same travels as being motivated by his desire to free himself of the thought of love for Laura in *RVF* 360.46–60, *Epyst.* 1.6.64–99, and *Secr.* 3: "et licet varias simulaverim causas, unus tamen hic semper peregrinationum rusticationumque mearum omnium finis erat libertas"(and although I simulated different reasons, the only end of all my travels and of my retreats to the country was always and solely liberty). All translations of the *Secretum* are from *Petrarch's Secret, or the Soul's Conflict with Passion,* trans. William H. Draper (London: Chatto and Windus, 1951); the quote here is from p. 164.

37. Tiraboschi, *Storia*, vol. 5, p. 131.

38. Ibid.

39. Ibid.

40. Ibid., p. 132.

41. Ibid.

42. Ugo Foscolo, *Saggi e discorsi critici, Saggi sul Petrarca, Discorso sul testo del Decameron, Scritti minori su poeti italiani e stranieri, (1821–26),* ed. Cesare Foligno (Firenze: F. Le Monnier, 1953), p. 73.

43. Alfred Jean François Mézières, *Pétrarque: Etude d'après de nouveaux documents* (Paris: Didier, 1868). In the chapter "Restaurateur des lettres," Mézières took note of Petrarch's geographical interests: "Geography interested him no less than history. He loved to know places as well as men. His traveler's temperament would have drawn him to undertake, he confesses, distant expeditions and veritable voyages of discovery had he been able to take his books everywhere with him and were Latin spoken everywhere. He consoled himself for not being able to visit unknown places by stimulating others to undertake investigations. He wrote to an Englishman, Richard of Bury, to engage him in seeking the position of the island of Thule, and by means of his *Itinerarium syriacum*, the first work in its genre among the moderns, he resuscitated geographical studies" (p. 127).

44. See de Nolhac, *Pétrarque et l'humanisme*, pp. 149–52; and Billanovich, *Petrarca letterato,* pp. 219–26.

45. See, for example, the special issue of *Annali d'italianistica* 14 (1996): *L'Odeporica / Hodoeporics: On Travel Literature,* ed. Luigi Monga; Mario Pozzi, *Ai confini della letteratura: Aspetti e momenti di storia della letteratura italiana* (Alessandria: Edizioni dell'Orso, 1998); Daria Perocco, *Viaggiare e raccontare: Narrazione di viaggio ed esperienze di racconto tra Cinque e Seicento*

(Alessandria: Edizioni dell'Orso, 1997); S. Benso, L. Formisano, J. Guérin Dalle Mese, M. Guglielminetti, M. Masoero, M. Pregliasco, and A. Rossebastiano, *La letteratura di viaggio dal medioevo al rinascimento: Generi e problemi* (Alessandria: Edizioni dell'Orso, 1989); *La letteratura di viaggio: Storia e prospettive di un genere letterario,* ed. Maria Enrica D'Agostini (Milano: Guerini, 1987).

46. Francis Petrarch, *Itinerario in terra santa 1358,* ed. Francesco Lo Monaco (Bergamo: Lubrina, 1990).

47. Francis Petrarch, *Volgarizzamento meridionale anonimo di Francesco Petrarca* Itinerarium Breve de Ianua usque ad Ierusalem et Terram Sanctam, ed. Alfonso Paolella (Bologna: Commissione per i Testi di Lingua, 1993).

48. Noteworthy in the context of humanistic reception of the *Itinerarium* is Benvenuto da Imola's reference to the work in a gloss on Dante's Acheron at the threshold of the *Inferno,* canto 3, in connection with a discussion of the Neapolitan Virgilian sites reputed to correspond to the entrance to the underworld: "Est etiam aliquis locus ibi, ubi terra sine igne visibili, sine aquis, producit salutarem vaporem et fumum medicinalem corporibus infirmorum. Ideo bene novissimus poeta Petrarca in quadam Epistola sua, quam *Itinerarium* vocat, dicit: sic dicere potes quod in eisdem locis convenerint remedium vitae et horror mortis" (*Comentum super Dantis Aldigherij Comoediam,* ed. Jacobo Philippo Lacaita [Firenze: Barbèra, 1887], vol. 1, p. 125).

49. Nelli was also known as Simonides, prior of the Church of the Holy Apostles in Florence; he was Petrarch's principal addressee in the *Familiares* (twenty-seven letters) and later was the dedicatee of the *Seniles.*

50. That the letter *Fam.* 19.6 refers to Giovanni Mandelli was established and first developed by Billanovich (*Petrarca letterato,* pp. 219–26); Arnaldo Foresti also takes the letter as recommending Mandelli to Nelli ("Il carme proemiale alle 'Metriche,'" in *Aneddoti della vita di Francesco Petrarca,* ed. Antonia Tissoni Benvenuti [Padova: Antenore, 1977], chapter 50, pp. 374–75). Ernest Hatch Wilkins, on the other hand, believed the addressee of *Fam.* 19.6 to be an unidentified "man of short stature called Giovannolo who had been a member of the household of Cardinal Giovanni Colonna" and objected that "Petrarch's references to their companionship in service ["we have served in the same army"], to the death of their leader ["our commander has been killed"], and to the court of Avignon ["who has left behind the court's deafening roar"] seem . . . to preclude identification of this Giovannolo with Giovannolo da Mandello" (*Petrarch's Eight Years in Milan* [Cambridge: Medieval Academy of America, 1958], p. 113). Yet it is not clear how Petrarch would have still considered himself "not yet discharged" from "the army" of Giovanni Colonna, from whom the poet had first become estranged in 1347 (cf. Eclogue 8, *Divortium*) and who had died in 1348, several years before Petrarch wrote *Fam.* 19.6 in 1355. In 1355 both Giovanni Mandelli and Petrarch (who had already completed a mission to Venice on behalf of the Visconti in early 1354) were in the service of the Visconti, whose leading figure, Archbishop Giovanni Visconti, was recently deceased (5 October 1354). In fact, the letter suggests that the two men share the same public sphere at the same time ("he will be able to tell you something of my private life, and nearly all of my public life").

51. Francis Petrarch, *Le familiari,* ed. Vittorio Rossi (Firenze: G. C. Sansoni, 1968), vol. 3, pp. 322–23: "Hic quem cernis homuncio Cristo devotus, mundi rerumque fugacium spretor ingens et cupidissimus eternarum, idem—perexigua tante laudi accessio, sed quam tuus amor faciet esse permaximam —michi quoque carissimus, Romam petit. Sic eum aspices ut me; bone anime vector est. Novi hominem; in eisdem castris militavimus necdum exautorati sumus, duce quamvis extincto. Si consilio tuo eget ad peregrinationis pie compendium, si favore aliquo, puto, non es orandus ut faveas; oro tamen. Nam quid Cristo cui servis, quid Apostolis eius, hospitibus tuis, acceptius potes, quam si cristianissimum hunc virum cupide, dimissis frementis aule fragoribus, ad illorum quietisima limina gradientem iuveris atque direxeris? De me siquid explorare libuerit—libebit autem plurima—etsi diversitas studiorum nosse hunc omnia non sinat, tamen quod ad intimum vite mee modum pertinet, fortasse aliqua, quod ad extimum, pene cuncta narrabit. Hec tibi raptim scripsi in extremo angulo Mediolani, ambrosiane domus in parte remotissima, ea luce eaque lucis hora qua mundo tenebris presso cecisque mortalibus, de terra olim viva lux orta est. Vale, nostri memor."

For different perspectives on Mandelli, see Novati's positivistic and erudite study of Petrarch's Milanese years ("Il Petrarca e i Visconti," in *Francesco Petrarca e la Lombardia* [Milano: Hoepli, 1904], pp. 42–45) and more recently the suggestive pages that Billanovich dedicated to Mandelli's relationship to Petrarch in connection with the *Itinerarium* (*Petrarca letterato,* pp. 218–29). F. Novati published *Dispersa* 69 for the first time in *Petrarca e la Lombardia,* p. 50. It was written 6 July 1368 to Giovannolo Mandelli (it follows a copy of *Fam.* 20.4 in a manuscript at Bergamo, Biblioteca Comunale). Novati's interest in the political context for the Petrarch-Mandelli connection contrasts with Billanovich, who barely makes reference to this letter. Billanovich's treatment amplifies the characterization of Mandelli as "a true despiser of the world and transitory things" and neatly issues into a discussion of the work's earliest reception and the mediation of that reception by Petrarch's "greatest disciple" Boccaccio (a trajectory of reception to which we shall return below). What is somewhat overlooked in Billanovich's discussion is Mandelli's "engaged" political career, which is overshadowed by Billanovich's marshaling of testimonies to Mandelli's piety. In this regard Billanovich cites (p. 221), for example: Franceso Nelli's response (*Epist.* 5) to Petrarch (*Fam.* 19.6), in which Nelli characterizes his guest's religiosity (see Henry Cochin, *Un ami de Pétrarque: Lettres de Francesco Nelli à Pétrarque* [Paris: 1982], pp. 60–61); and a portrait of Mandelli by his "familiare, notaio e domestico," Pietro Azario: "Erat autem iste Johannolus de ferro . . . reductus cum prefato domino archiepiscopo tamquam legalis homo et qui carebat mendacio ad sua magnalia gubernanda et exequenda, pompas et tributa odiens et honestissime et cum caritate vivens...; de quo prefatus dominus archiepiscopus ultra alios confidebat et merito" (Petri Azarii, *Liber gestorum in Lombardia,* ed. F. Cognasso, *Rer. Ital. Script.* 16, P. 4 [Bologna: Zanichelli, 1926–39], pp. 63 and 77). Billanovich notes that Azario's sketch falls under Petrarch's shadow: "Vediamo dunque giungere l'ombra del Petrarca, subito al di là del magnate lombardo, fino sul piccolo cronista Azario" (*Petrarca letterato,* p. 221).

The Billanovich and Novati versions of the Mandelli-Petrarch connection are in a kind of tension with one another, for the most part due to the different contexts that the scholars emphasize. Billanovich emphasizes the pious aspects contained in *Familiares* 19.6 and Novati gives greater weight to the political-biographical background that is so pertinent to *Dispersa* 69. These different versions recapitulate a tension in the object of study.

52. See Nancy Struever, "Petrarchan Ethics: Inventing a Practice," in *Theory as Practice: Ethical Inquiry in the Renaissance* (Chicago: University of Chicago Press, 1992), p. 11: "Epistolary discourse specifies writer as well as reader; the addresser is defined in part by his solicitude for the addressee, since it is by this solicitude that he cultivates the solidarity of his cenacle, of his devoted group with its patrons, supporters and family ambiances. And, indeed, we find in the letters many instances of Petrarch's confection of his own authority and status by means of his clever delineations of regard for his correspondent."

53. See Struever, "Petrarchan Ethics," p. 12: "Petrarch's considerations of addressee are often marked by specific negotiating postures, by reader-writer contracts, to use modern terminology. Just as the letters are both spontaneous and fictional, historical and collected, private and public, Petrarch's contract is a double contract, with the first reader, the addressee, which can be a contact of intimacy, fiction or fact, and with the second reader, posterity—a contract which he stipulates as his submission to objective, public judgement that carries with it the possibility of fame."

54. Billanovich, *Petrarca letterato*, pp. 223–24.

55. Nori, "La corte itinerante," p. 235. Fernand Braudel discusses the travel times of German pilgrims from Venice to the Holy Land on thirty trips between 1507 and 1608. The average length of time for the trip to Jerusalem required forty-three days while ninety-three days were necessary on average for the return voyage (*The Mediterranean and the Mediterranean World in the Age of Philip II* [Berkeley: University of California Press, 1995], vol. 1, pp. 264–65).

56. *Itinerario*, ed. Lo Monaco, p. 16: "Non si hanno notizie se il Mandelli abbia poi effettivamente realizzato il pellegrinaggio" (There is no record as to whether Mandelli actually went on the pilgrimage).

57. Piero Camporesi, *Le belle contrade: Nascita del paesaggio italiano* (Milano: Garzanti, 1992), pp. 110–11.

58. Anderson, *Imagined Communities*, pp. 53–65.

59. Francis Petrarch, *Lettere Disperse*, ed. Alessandro Pancheri (Parma: Guanda, 1994), *Dispersa* 68, var. 27, pp. 454–57; quote is from pp. 455–56.

60. Foresti, *Aneddoti*, chapter 50, p. 453.

61. In this sense Petrarch's pilgrimage narrative addressed to a Viscontean military administrative functionary was more relevant to the lay national purposes of Petrarch's program than to the literature of crusade for which he offered, according to Cardini, only lukewarm and conventional expressions of support. On Petrarch's national program, see Ugo Dotti, "L'ottavo libro delle *Familiari*: Contributo per una storia dell'umanesimo petrarchesco," *Belfagor* 28 (1973), pp. 273–74: "Tra l'universalismo cattolico e l'eventualità di uno stato nazionale italiano, Petrarca sceglieva quest'ultimo" (Between Catholic universalism and the possibility of an Italian national state, Petrarch opted for the latter). The crusade had

limited appeal for Petrarch insofar as it depended upon and represented the constitution of a supranational unification of Christendom.

For example, following the peace treaty of 1 June 1355, a newly united Christendom had turned its attention again to the Turkish threat, and at the end of that year, thanks to the direct intervention of John V Palaiologos with Innocent VI, a crusade was called "della quale il Petrarca fu, almeno formalmente, zelatore entusiasta"(of which Petrarch was, at least formally speaking, a zealous enthusiast) (Cardini, "Viaggiatori medioevali in Terrasanta," p. 337). The crusade, formally announced in Avignon in November of 1356, came to nothing, and Petrarch's role—letters to the doges of Venice and Genoa and invectives in the *Trionfi* against the Christians who would consume one another while the sepulcher of Christ is in the hands of the enemy—seem to Cardini to be "es-tremamente conformistico e debole"(extremely conventional and lacking conviction).

62. Petrarch's letter to Mandelli from Pavia, 6 July 1368, is the only extant testimony of Mandelli's estrangement from the Visconti (he ceases to appear in Milanese documents after 1364). See *Lettere Disperse*, ed. Pancheri, pp. 456–63. Another possible trace of Mandelli in the epistolary is in *Dispersa* 53, dated 9 December 1362, to Moggio da Parma which refers to "Giovannolo da Cuma" serving as a courier of books, in this case the clean copy of the *Vita Solitaria* (see Billanovich, *Petrarca letterato*, p. 221). An archival doc-ument attesting to a payment of 10,000 lire from Bernabó Visconti to Giovanni Mandelli dated 1 June 1364 suggests that Mandelli's exile came after that date (see F. Novati, *Petrarca e la Lombardia*, p. 45).

63. Petrarch gives a full account of the incident in *Familiares* 21.10, to Neri Morando of Forlí, and it is a recurrent theme in his letters (see also *Dispersa* 46). Foresti, *Aneddoti*, p. 382, thought that Petrarch was referring in *Dispersa* 69 to his having fallen from a horse dur-ing his escape from Parma (*Fam.* 5.10).

64. *Lettere Disperse*, ed. Pancheri, p. 456: "Credo et hoc et alia que me angunt ad exercitium mihi celitus data esse, ut mee me conditionis admoneant et animum vagum frenent."

65. *Lettere Disperse*, ed. Pancheri, p. 458: "Vere enim ad hoc nascitur, quamuis in adversum nitens et quietem somnians inanem hic, ubi minime reperitur, quietem exardenter in-quirat."

66. Petrarch describes himself in Pavia as "repaired here, as if in a port, protected from the waves" (in hunc cupide quasi portum ex procellis commigraverim). He arrived in Pavia from Milan, the travel having aggravated his injury so that "that which was the source of pleasure [the horseback ride] I experience today as a cause of pain." The letter em-phasizes the physical aspects of Petrarch's travel and the reflections they inspire. Floating downstream on the rivers of northern Italy—especially the "King of Rivers," the Po—perfectly suited Petrarch's particular subjectivity as well as his political purposes. River travel satisfied the poet's desire for a form of mobility that allows the traveling subject to occupy a position of stasis. To the extent that simultaneous progress and immobil-ity represented his aspiration or ideal mode of being, river travel must have seemed par-ticularly congenial. Two other noteworthy examples of this signature theme in Petrarch's writing include the *De Suis Ipsius et Multorum Ignorantia* (*On His Ignorance and That of Many Others*), which he wrote, according to the fiction (cf. chapter 6), while floating on the Po;

and *RVF* 180, "Po, ben può tu portartene la scorza" (Po, you can bear my body easily). See also below, note 103.

67. *Lettere Disperse,* ed. Pancheri, p. 460: "Humillimam atque abiectam sue particulam creationis, laboriosum anxiumque animal . . . quod idcirco dixerim ne qua ex parte uobis lateat amici status, qui non stat, sed uento ocior ducitur."

68. *Petrarch: The Canzoniere or Rerum Vulgarium Fragmenta,* trans. Mark Musa (Bloomington: Indiana University Press, 1996), pp. 460–61. *Francesco Petrarca Canzoniere,* ed. Marco Santagata (Milano: Mondadori, 1996), *RVF* 331.22–24: "Nebbia o polvere al vento, / Fuggo per più non esser pellegrino: / Et così vada, s'è pur mio destino."

69. Petrarch's reception by Francesco da Carrara in Padua is described in *Sen.* 11.2, addressed to Francesco Bruni: "When I finally arrived in Padua the day before yesterday in the evening during a continuous heavy downpour, the lord of the city, your friend, a man of great power but of still greater virtue [Francesco da Carrara], expecting me earlier and happy at my return, came to meet me at the city gate. Nightfall and the rain drove him home, but he left some of his men to keep the gate open for me. I cannot tell you if I wanted to, or if I could, will you believe how much honor and love he showered upon me that evening, not only by sending his servants loaded with all kinds of gifts, but finally by coming to me in person with a few people, and sitting with me as I ate, and after dinner keeping me company in my library with conversation and storytelling on and on until bedtime" (*Letters of Old Age,* vol. 2, p. 398).

70. Billanovich, *Petrarca letterato,* p. 224. Billanovich promised to illustrate in his critical edition of the *Itinerarium* the branch of the manuscript tradition of the work that derived from Boccaccio's copy. Boccaccio's involvement in the transmission of the work led to its misattribution to him (see D. Manni, *Istoria del Decameron* [Firenze, 1742], p. xvii). In addition, Billanovich believed Boccaccio's *De Montibus* to have been written at least in part under the influence of the *Itinerarium.* That view was later corrected by Manlio Pastore Stocchi in his study of the *De Montibus* (*Tradizione medievale e gusto umanistico nel* De Montibus *del Boccaccio* [Firenze: Olschki, 1963], p. 89). Pastore Stocchi found that "un indizio non trascurabile per la cronologia del dizionario boccaccesco è che in essa non compaiono derivazioni dall'*Itinerarium*" (not insignificant evidence for the dating of Boccaccio's dictionary is the fact that there do not appear in it any derivations from the *Itinerarium*).

The relationship between Boccaccio and the *Itinerarium* is nevertheless intriguing in light of a dramatic passage from the epilogue of Boccaccio's *De Montibus,* in which the author speaks of his having interrupted his work at the news that his master Petrarch was undertaking a work similar to his own: "et vidi insignem atque venerabilem virum Franciscum Petrarcham inclitum preceptorem meum honesta facie et laurea virenti conspicuum per idmet stadium lento tamen incedentem gradu." While Boccaccio went on to finish his work, he averred that anything in it found to be inconsistent with the work his master was preparing should be condemned, since "he (if I know him well) has written and will write everything with many sage considerations distributing all matters with weighty judgment" (cited in Pastore Stocchi, *Tradizione,* p. 31: ipse autem, si mores novi suos, omnia multiplici trutinatione digesta, omnia ponderoso librata iudicio scripsit scribetque).

The passage from the *De Montibus* has given rise to the notion that Petrarch had at one time planned a major geographical work that he never completed or was lost. Pastore Stocchi has emphasized the rhetorical nature of the passage in the context of a humility topos, commonly evoked by Boccaccio, that figures Petrarch as the teacher and master and Boccaccio as the unworthy and ignorant disciple (cf. *De Casibus* 8.1; *Ep.* 2; and *Genealogia Deorum Gentilium*, ed. V. Romano [Bari: 1951], p. 4). But while rhetorical, the passage could not be completely without a genuine pretext. Pastore Stocchi, *Tradizione*, pp. 88–89, did not believe that Boccaccio was refering to the *Itinerarium* ("l'opuscolo a Giovanni di Mandello non era tale da competere col *De Montibus*" [The little book for Giovanni di Mandello was not such as to compete with the *De Montibus*]) but rather to "qualche vaga intenzione espressa dal Petrarca e forse sopravvalutata"(some vague intention expressed by Petrarch whose importance was perhaps exaggerated by Boccaccio). Pastore Stocchi speculates that Petrarch may well have planned a work of geographical erudition and considers the marginal annotations to the Ambrosiana library's Virgil and the Bibliothèque Nationale's Pliny to have perhaps been the beginnings of this work since they are "too elaborate to have been simple annotations of an attentive reader" (p. 89: troppo elaborati per essere semplici annotazioni di un lettore attento). Nevertheless, Pastore Stocchi's own chronological reconstruction for the composition of the *De Montibus*—according to which Boccaccio completed the work by 1359 (except for scattered later additions)—would allow for Boccaccio's having had some word of Petrarch's composition of the *Itinerarium* during spring of 1358, when Boccaccio might plausibly have been coming to the end of the *De Montibus*. According to Pastore Stocchi's account, however, the *De Montibus* was already completed when Boccaccio copied the *Itinerarium* in spring of 1359, since "no derivations appear" (non compaiono derivazioni). The only geographical work by Petrarch that fits this particular chronology is the *Itinerarium*. Perhaps some word of Petrarch's *Itinerarium*, without its contents, had reached Boccaccio, and this represented sufficient pretext for his rhetorical expression of hesitation at the conclusion of the *De Montibus*.

71. Giuseppe Billanovich, "Dall' antica Ravenna alle biblioteche umanistiche," *Annuario dell' Universitá cattolica del S. Cuore* (1955–56 / 1956–57), pp. 91–106. In this article, Billanovich discusses the reception of the minor Roman geographical authors, such as Pomponius Mela (*De situ orbis*) and Vibius Sequester (*De fluminibus*), as well as other minor geographical texts found in a manuscript (Milano, Biblioteca Ambrosiana, manuscript Ambrosiana H 14) that Petrarch studied and annotated and that, via Petrarch, informed Boccaccio's *De Montibus*, Domenico Silvestri's *De Insulis* (where Pomponius Mela is widely used), and Coluccio Salutati, who put together Laurenziano XXX 21, which included a copy of Vibius Sequester and three treatises on Gaul from Petrarch's book (Ambrosiana H 14 "del Corvino"). Alongside Salutati, Domenico Bandini integrated his encyclopedia *Fons Memorabilium Universi* with citations from Pomponius Mela, Vibius Sequester, and Censorino; and some parts were modeled on Vibius's format as well.

72. Studies of Petrarchan landscape have been relatively well developed. See Karlheinz Stierle, *Petrarcas Landschaften: Zur Geschichte ästhetischer Landschaftserfahrung* (Krefeld : Scherpe Verlag, 1979); and more recently, Giorgio Bertone, "Il monte: Gli occhi di Laura, i passi

di Francesco," in *Lo sguardo escluso: L'idea di paesaggio nella letteratura occidentale* (Novara: Interline, 1999), pp. 95–147.

73. Cited in Mary Campbell, "'The Object of One's Gaze': Landscape, Writing, and Early Medieval Pilgrimage," in *Discovering New Worlds: Essays on Medieval Exploration and Imagination*, ed. Scott D. Westrem (New York: Garland Publishing, 1991), p. 4.

74. Carla Maria Monti, "Mirabilia e geografia nel *Canzoniere*: Pomponio Mela e Vibio Sequstre (*RVF* CXXXV and CXLVIII)," *Studi petrarcheschi* 6 (1989), pp. 91–123.

75. The cosmic menagerie gathers together from all the parts of the world *mirabilia* expressing the diversity of God's creation within the unifying perspective of the emperor's gaze. The key is to constitute a harmonious whole from the diversity of the world. For the concept, see Yi-fu Tuan, *Cosmos and Hearth: A Cosmopolite's Viewpoint* (Minneapolis: University of Minnesota Press, 1996), pp. 27–29; and M. W. Helms, who discusses the same notion in a section entitled, "The Emperor's Zoo," in *Ulysses' Sail*, pp. 163–71.

76. Michele Feo, "Inquietudini filologiche del Petrarca: Il luogo della discesa agli inferi (storia di una citazione)," *Italia medioevale e umanistica* 27 (1974), pp. 115–83.

77. Spelunca hec in latere montis est,... ubi ego ipse ante paucos annos fui.... Cited by Feo, "Inquietudini filologiche," p. 121.

78. Tertia (scil. Sibilla), nomine Amalthea, cuius locum nuper prope Cumas Campanie vidimus. Cited by Feo, "Inquietudini filologiche," p. 122.

79. Descriptio loci quem ante annos paucos diligentissime contemplatus sum oculata fide. Cited by Feo, "Inquietudini filologiche," p. 123.

80. Lyell Asher, "Petrarch at the Peak of Fame," *Publications of the Modern Language Association of America* 108/5 (Oct. 1993), pp. 1050–63, has recently read the "Ascent of Mt. Ventoux" as a text that "tells a story that figuratively censures what the text itself literally enacts— Petrarch's implacable desire to attract and hold the attention of posterity. Petrarch sins first and most flagrantly in the ascent itself but again, and perhaps more profoundly, in making that sin a pretext for his epistolary self-revelation" (p. 1052).

81. Petrarch is explicit about how the *Itinerarium* constitutes a portrait of himself when he writes in the proem to Mandelli, "You have followed the usage of lovers, asking of me, whom you will miss, the image with which you will be able to console yourself during your absence, not the image of the face which changes daily but rather the more stable effigy of my soul and my intellect, which, however small it may be, is surely the best part of me" (*Itin.* Pr. 7). On the face of it, Petrarch establishes at the outset an incongruous program whereby the *Itinerarium*, which he later terms a "description of places"—and therefore of an objective world "out there"—will constitute at the same time a portrait of the self. The trope is common in Petrarch and is perhaps most explicitly expressed at the conclusion of the preface to the *Vita Solitaria*, where he urges the dedicatee of the work, Philippe de Cabassoles, but also posterity: "Lend your attention therefore: you will hear my idea on this solitary style of life in all its aspects. It will amount to few things among many, but that you may be able to recognize in them, as in a small mirror, the entire figure of my soul and the entire image of my serene and tranquil spirit" (*The Life of*

Solitude, trans. Jacob Zeitlin [Urban: University of Illinois Press, 1924], p. 102; original in Francis Petrarch, *Prose,* ed. G. Martellotti [Milano: R. Ricciardi, 1955], p. 294).

82. See Giles Constable, "Opposition to Pilgrimage in the Middle Ages," in *Melanges G. Fransen,* ed. Stephan Kuttner, Alfons M. Stickler, E. Van Balberghe, and D. Van den Auweele, Studia Gratiana 19–20 (Roma: Libreria Ateneo Salesiano, 1976), pp. 125–46.

83. Constable, "Opposition," p. 145.

84. Petrarch's concern with his final resting place is perhaps most tellingly expressed in the poet's *Testament* (*Petrarch's Testament,* ed. and trans. Theodor E. Mommsen [Ithaca: Cornell University Press, 1957], pp. 73–75):

> 6. As to the burial place I do not care greatly. I am content to be laid to rest wherever it shall please God and those who shall deign to assume this task. If, however, it is felt desirable that I should express my will more explicitly on this point, I stipulate the following:
>
> > a) If I should die in Padua where I am now, I should wish to be buried in the church of S. Agostino, which the Dominicans now hold....
> >
> > b) If, however, I should end my days in Arquà, where my country-place is, and if God will only fulfill my strong desire to build a small chapel there in honor of the most blessed Virgin Mary, then I choose to be buried there, otherwise farther down in some appropriate place near the parish church;
> >
> > c) If, though, I should die in Venice, I wish to be laid to rest at S. Francesco della Vigna, in a place in front of the entrance of the church;
> >
> > d) If in Milan, in front of the church of S. Ambrosio near the outer-entrance which faces the walls of the city;
> >
> > e) If in Pavia, in the church of S. Agostino wherever it may be agreeable to the Friars;
> >
> > f) If, however, in Rome, either in the church of S. Maria Maggiore or in St. Peter's, whichever may be more suitable, or close outside either the one or the other, as may seem good to the canons;
> >
> > g) I have named those places which I have been wont to frequent in Italy;
> >
> > h) But if I should die in Parma, [I wish to be buried] in a church of the Franciscans if there should be one; if not, in some other church in the neighborhood of the place of my death;
> >
> > i) May these remarks concerning my burial place—more extended, I confess, than becomes a learned man—be as though made by an unlearned man.

85. Petrarch's misadventures at sea go back to a violent tempest experienced during the journey of his family from Pisa to Marseilles when he was eight years old, recalled by the poet in the dedicatory letter of the *Familiares.* During his 1337 trip to Rome he encountered such storms that he memorialized the experience in a series of prose and poetic

passages, including the triptych of *Canzoniere* 67–69 and in *Fam.* 4.6. In *Epystola* 1.7 he describes these storms at length. The most terrifying tempest Petrarch experienced was in Naples in November 1343, and he depicted it under the heading "Description of tempest without equal" in *Familiares* 5.5.

At the time of the tempest in Naples Petrarch first swore he would never again trust himself to the waves, leaving the air to the birds and the sea to the fish: "as a terrestrial animal I choose a terrestrial journey" (*Fam.* 5.5). This biographical theme of fear of the sea and of shipwreck is carried forward throughout Petrarch's life and motivates what Michele Feo has identified as one of a handful of redactional variants in the *Itinerarium*, where the poet added the intensifying phrase, probably at some time during the late 1360s, that his fear of the sea "has increased as I have grown older" (*Itin.* Pr. 6).

86. "And so, like a man on dry land and out of danger, you will look upon the shipwreck of others, and from your quiet haven hear the cries of those wrestling with the waves, and though you will be moved with tender compassion by that sight, yet even that will be the measure also of your thankfulness and joy at being in safety" (*Petrarch's* Secret, p. 104; original in *Secretum*, ed. Enrico Fenzi [Milano: Mursia, 1992], pp. 197–98). For the development of this Lucretian topos in the history of philosophy, see Hans Blumemberg, *Shipwreck with Spectator: Paradigm of a Metaphor for Existence,* trans. Steven Rendall (Cambridge: MIT Press, 1997). For the theme in Petrarch, see Theodore J. Cachey, Jr., "'Peregrinus (quasi) ubique': Petrarca e la storia del viaggio," *Intersezioni: Rivista di storia delle idee* 27 (December 1997), pp. 369–84.

87. *Letters on Familiar Matters*, vol. 3, p. 150. *Le familiari*, ed. Rossi, vol. 4, p. 33: "Me autem versa vice noveris in periculis securum—o fereum caput—et in mediis tempestatibus quiescentem usque—adeo ut nisi alios circumiactatos equoreo turbine viderem et fragore nautico undique pulsarer, in pelago esse me nesciam. Clavum regentis ad pedes sedeo, et fluitantem puppim non immotus certe sed intrepidus teneo et exitum operior eo animo, ut omnis prope iam ventus meus sit et in litore quolibet portus michi."

88. See Dotti, *Vita di Petrarca*, pp. 320–24, on the "opere continuate, completate o rielaborate" in this period: "the poet reported that he was increasingly detaching himself from the things of the world and finding in his solitude an ever greater sense of security" (p. 324: il poeta disse di venire via via staccandosi dalle cose del mondo trovando nella propria solitudine una sicurezza in sé sempre maggiore).

89. Turner, "Pilgrimage as Social Processes," p. 177.

90. According to Turner, pilgrimage tends to surface as a visible social phenomenon in periods "of destructuration and rapid social change, such as in the waning of the Roman Empire and in the waning of the Middle Ages" (ibid., p. 172). Certainly, Petrarch was writing in the autumn of the Middle Ages and more specifically in a period of crisis and political reorganization in Italy, where regional state structures were emerging within a profoundly altered international political context characterized by the increasing marginalization of imperial and papal influence. Petrarch's claims for a lay literary authority not subservient to any political authority—and for the freedom of the poet-humanist above and beyond the university, the court, and the chancery—are made within the frame of this sociopolitical transition.

Petrarch's pilgrimage narrative can be seen within the broader anthropological context of a renewed interest in pilgrimage in Italy during the Trecento, which continued during the Quattrocento up until the Renaissance Age of Discovery and Exploration (discussed and documented by Pastore Stocchi in "Itinerari in Terrasanta nei secoli XIV–XV," in *Dizionario critico della letteratura italiana* [Torino: UTET, 1986], vol. 2, pp. 520–23). Pilgrimages emanating from the principal regional zones of the Italian Tre-Quattrocento were acts of superogatory devotion because of their voluntary origins; their social function was different from that of the penitential pilgrimages—determined by the force of obligation—that characterized large sectors of medieval pilgrimage.

Turner connected the difference between pilgrimage as obligation and pilgrimage as choice to the difference between societies based on status and those based on contract. As the anthropologist notes, "the notion of voluntariness and contract became established with the diversification of social and economic life" (p. 176). For Turner, pilgrimage left the individual room to "distance himself briefly from inherited social constraint and duty, but only enough room so as to constitute, as it were, a public platform in which he must make by word or deed a formal public acknowledgement of allegiance to the overarching religious, political and economic orders." In this regard, Mandelli's putative pilgrimage can be considered in relation to the exceptional individual enterprises of Trecento pilgrimages as well as to prestigious Italian court pilgrimages of the Quattrocento; the shift from a society of status to a society of contract, taking place in Italy and in the rest of Europe during this period, is reflected by a renewed interest in pilgrimage as a voluntary expression of individual piety.

91. Turner, "Pilgrimage as Social Progress," p. 175.

92. Interea *iter* inceptum *sequar,* non prius vie quam lucis exitum operiens; *et quietis michi loco fuerit dulcis labor.*

93. *Letters of Old Age,* vol. 1, p. 329. The passage from the *Seniles* finds its Renaisssance echo in Ariosto's celebration of virtual travel in the third *Satire* (*Satire e lettere,* ed. C. Segre [Torino: Einaudi, 1976], p. 31):

> Chi vuole andare a torno, a torno vada:
> vegga Inghelterra, Ongheria, Francia e Spagna;
> a me piace abitar la mia contrada.
>   Visto ho Toscana, Lombardia, Romagna,
> Quel monte che divide e quel che serra
> Italia, e un mare e l'altro che la bagna.
>   Questo mi basta; il resto della terra,
> Senza mai pagar l'oste, andrò cercando
> Con Ptolomeo, sia il mondo in pace o in guerra;
>   e tutto il mar, senza far voti quando
> lampeggi il ciel, sicuro in su le carte
> verrò, più che sui legni, volteggiando. (Vv. 55–66)

> Let him wander who desires to wander. Let him see
> England, Hungary, France, and Spain. I am content to live in

my native land. I have seen Tuscany, Lombardy, and the
Romagna, and the mountain range that divides Italy, and the
one that locks her in, and both the seas that wash her. And
that is quite enough for me. Without ever paying an
innkeeper, I will go exploring the rest of the earth with
Ptolemy, whether the world be at peace or else at war.
Without ever making vows when the heavens flash with
lightning, I will go bounding over all the seas, more secure
aboard my maps than aboard ships. (*The Satires of Ludovico
Ariosto: A Renaissance Autobiography,* trans. Peter DeSa Wiggins
[Athens Ohio: Ohio University Press, 1976], p. 61)

94. Dante, *Inferno* 26.94–98: Nè dolcezza di figlio, nè la pieta / Del vecchio padre, nè 'l de-
    bito amore / lo qual dovea Penelopè far lieta, / vincer potero dentro a me l'ardore / ch'i'
    ebbi a divenir del mondo esperto.

95. Ulysses often appears to be just beneath the surface of Petrarch's evocations of the ship-
    wreck theme, for instance in *RVF* 180 (*Po, ben può tu*) and *RVF* 189 (*Passa la nave mia*). See
    Michelangelo Picone, "Il sonetto CLXXXIX," *Atti e Memorie dell'Accademia Patavina di
    Scienze, Lettere ed Arti,* 102 (1989–90), part 3, Classe di Scienze Morali, Lettere ed Arti,
    pp. 151–67.

    In general, Petrarch's Ulysses has represented an enigma to students of Petrarch. Michele
    Feo, "Un Ulisse in Terrasanta," *Rivista di cultura classica e medievale* 19 (1977), pp. 383–87, re-
    ported that a preliminary study of the passages in which Petrarch speaks of Ulysses had con-
    vinced him that Petrarch had gathered together all of the available sources regarding Ulysses,
    including Dante, and had sought to reconcile them in order to extract a plausible account
    but was "unable to districate the wheat from the chaff." According to Feo, Petrarch attempted
    a kind of philological reconstruction of Ulysses. For Feo, Petrarch's humanistic Ulysses is
    "philologically a hybrid and ideologically a moral exemplum" (p. 387), and thus any incon-
    sistencies or incoherence in that construction reflect a kind of philological failure. On the
    other hand, Piero Boitani has more recently dedicated a synthetic paragraph to Petrarch's
    Ulysses in *The Shadow of Ulysses: Figures of a Myth* (Oxford: Oxford University Press, 1994).
    Boitani interprets Petrarch's use of Ulysses in the first of the *Familiares* as a figure of cultural
    innovation, "as a new Ulysses, with more wanderlust than the first" (p. 48). Petrarch's praise
    of Ulysses later in the *Familiares* is filled with Homeric and Dantean references. Boitani con-
    cludes, however, that "just when Ulysses seems to be re-emerging as the model of the 'noble
    soul aspiring to noble deeds,' the echo of *Inferno* XXVI qualifies the praise," and "in the *Trionfo
    della fama* Petrarch celebrates Ulysses as he who 'longed to see *too much* of the world.'" Boitani
    appears to credit a palinodic reversal in Petrarch's thinking about Ulysses in the *Trionfo della
    fama* and in Petrarch generally, to uncertainties "that soon cease, and the change becomes
    radical" when "by the fifteenth century Ulysses becomes not only a new model, but a posi-
    tive one." From my point of view, Petrarch's view of Ulysses is consistent: the poet admires
    the heroic aspect of the hero's quest while recognizing the ultimate futility of the journey, the
    inevitability of shipwreck.

96. See Notes to the Text and Translation, note 7.

97. Erik Cohen, "Pilgrimage and Tourism: Convergence and Divergence," in *Sacred Journeys: The Anthropology of Pilgrimage*, ed. Alan Morinis, foreword by Victor Turner (Westport: Greenwood Press, 1992), pp. 47–61; quote is from p. 51.

98. Ibid., p. 51.

99. See Teodolinda Barolini, "Ulysses, Geryon, and the Aeronautics of Narrative Transition," in *The Undivine Comedy: Detheologizing Dante* (Princeton: Princeton University Press, 1992), pp. 48–73.

100. In this sense, Petrarch's Ulysses should be distinguished from the Ulysses of the fathers of the church, who had interpreted the hero's travels as a type of the Christian's journey through terrestrial life. See H. Rahner, "Odysseus at the Mast," in *Greek Myths and Christian Mystery* (London: Burns and Oates, 1963).

101. Weber, cited in Cohen, "Pilgrimage and Tourism," p. 52.

102. Cohen, "Pilgrimage and Tourism," p. 52.

103. Camporesi, *Le belle contrade*, pp. 110–11, called attention to this passage, noting that Petrarch "was the first among the moderns [there is the precedent of Rutilius] to describe the Ligurian and Tyrrhenian coasts observing them from the sea, from a point of view that was at that time unusual." The view was, I would add, paradigmatically Petrarchan, in the way that it combined the immobility of the stationary subject, who observes the passing coastline, with the mobility of the subject's perspective as a passenger on a moving ship (see above, note 66). The coastline described in the *Itinerarium* has an intertextual history that Petrarch explicitly refers to, going back to the verses from *Africa* immediately preceding the dying lament of Mago, as Camporesi has it, "where the lapping of the surf, the foam of the waves, the dangers of the reefs, the blowing of the wind give to the voyage of the dying Mago an exalting breath of final adventure" (p. 110: dove lo sciabordio della risacca, la schiuma delle onde, i pericoli degli scogli, il soffio dei venti danno al viaggio di Magone morente un esaltante respiro d'ultima ventura).

104. See Tom Conley's book on the French Renaissance, *Self-Made Map*, pp. 1–23. For examples from Roman literature, see Eleanor Winsor Leach, *The Rhetoric of Space: Literary and Artistic Representations of Landscape in Republican and Augustan Rome* (Princeton: Princeton University Press, 1988), especially pp. 73–196 (chapter 2, "*Loci et Imagines:* The Development of Topographical Systems in Roman Landscape"; and chapter 3, "Spatial Patterns in Virgil's *Georgics*").

105. Petrarch's contact with the Pizzigani in Parma was first hypothesized by Franz Friedersdorff in *Franz Petrarcas poetischen Briefen* (Halle: M. Niemayer, 1903), p. 140.

106. Leach, *Rhetoric of Space*, p. 78. Leach makes the further point, relevant for Petrarch's *Itinerarium:* "The depiction of space in coherent topographical patterns fixes a relationship between the spectator and his environment that indicates man's confidence in his capacity for organization and control, capacity to be exercised not only on a practical or political plane, but also on an intellectual plane" (p. 79).

107. Leach, *Rhetoric of Space*, p. 78.

108. For the Ciceronian art of memory, see Frances Yates's classic study, *The Art of Memory* (Chicago: University of Chicago Press, 1966).

109. For the concept of the *tourist marker,* see MacCannell, *Tourist,* pp. 109–17 and 119–33.

110. The precise itinerary focused on Virgil's sepulcher, the cave of the Sibyl, Baiae, Lake Lucrinus, Avernus, and the mouth of the inferno. The project was realized, and Petrarch had the joy of seeing the entire northern coast of the bay of Pozzuoli and the Campi Flegrei, accompanied by illustrious guides, Giovanni Barrili and Barbato. The poet was unable to visit the ruins of the villa of Scipio at Literno.

Feo, "Inquietudini filologiche," p. 117, notes that Petrarch's failure to visit the ruins of Scipio's villa had a particular significance for the poet, given the fact that he was well aware (*Fam.* 2.9, 25) that Seneca had thought of a visit to the place as a significant pilgrimage (*Ad Lucilius* 86). Petrarch compared Seneca's desire to visit that place to his own desire to visit Rome: "I desire to see that city though deserted and but a reflection of ancient Rome, a city that I have never seen, for which I accuse my laziness if it were indeed laziness and not necessity that was the sure cause. Seneca seems to me to be rejoicing when he writes to Lucilius from the very villa of Scipio Africanus, nor did he take it lightly to have seen the place where such a great man was in exile and where the bones lay which he had denied to his homeland. If this affected so worldly a Spaniard what would you think that an Italian like myself would feel not only about the villa at Literno or the tomb of Scipio, but even about the city of Rome where Scipio was born, educated and where he triumphed in glory both as conqueror and as an accused; where lived not he alone but innumerable others about whom fame will never be silent" (*Letters on Familiar Matters,* vol. 1, p. 103). Moreover, as Feo notes, p. 115: "Titus Livy had allowed himself to mention within the sacred austerity of his *Histories* (XXXVIII 56, 3) his private journey to the home of the exiled hero."

Petrarch makes it clear in *Fam.* 5.4, in the midst of a discussion of the pleasurable luxurious life of the hills of Baiae disdained by Scipio, who chose to live out of sight of that place at Literno, that he did not visit Literno: "He therefore avoided even a view of the place and preferred to live in Literno rather than in Baiae. I know that his small villa is not far from here, and there is nothing that I would look upon more eagerly if I could visit with some guide places renowned because of so great an occupant" (*Letters on Familiar Matters,* vol. 1, p. 240).

Feo notes that Petrarch added a passage to his life of Scipio in the final redaction—"haud procul Campanie Cumis; quam ipse olim, dum loca illa peregrinus inviserem, ab amicis ostensam non sine quadam animi voluptate prospexi" (*De viris* 12.29, lines 243–45, ed. G. Martellotti [Firenze, 1964], vol. 1, p. 307)—a passage in which the poet clearly aspires to emulate Seneca and Livy in their pilgrimages to the place. Feo notes the echo of this in the *Itinerarium* 9.0: "In this stretch there is Formia, or Formiano, and Literno, or better to say, there used to be; the first was renowned for the shameful assassination of Cicero, the second for the unjust exile of Scipio and for his ashes that were denied to his homeland. Still you will visit these two places more in thought than with the eyes: the first in fact is closed in by rocks, the other is also hidden, except for near Formia, where rise two or three large dunes."

111. *Afr.* 1.30–31: Nutu quam simplice dignum / Effecisse potes quod non erat.

112. Feo, "Inquietudini filologiche," p. 139.

113. Ibid., p. 151. For Petrarch's revisions of his lyric poetry, see the classic essay by Gianfranco Contini, "Saggio d'un commento alle correzioni del Petrarca volgare," in *Varianti e altra linguistica* (Torino: Einaudi, 1970), pp. 5–31. See also A. Schiaffini, "Il lavorio della forma in F. P.," in *Momenti di storia della lingua* (Roma: Editrice Studium, 1953).

114. See above, note 24.

115. See M. Feo, "Di alcuni rusticani cestelli di pomi," *Quaderni Petrarcheschi* 1 (1983), pp. 23–75, and especially pp. 23–24. Feo has called attention to Petrarch's geographical sensitivity in his critical edition and study of *Epyst.* 2.11 and makes note of and emphasizes Petrarch's geographical erudition as the source for the poet's invention of this figure. An early modern analogy for Petrarch's cartographic writing is provided by Benedict Anderson's discussion in the chapter, "Census, Map, Museum," in *Imagined Communities,* where he speaks of the role of the "map-as-logo" as a powerful emblem of anticolonial nationalism: "In this shape the map entered an infinitely reproducible series, available for transfer to posters, official seals, letterheads, magazine and textbook covers, tablecloths, and hotel walls. Instantly recognizable, everywhere visible, the logo-map penetrated deep into the popular imagination, forming a powerful emblem for the anticolonial nationalisms being born" (p. 175).

116. For example, see *Itin.* 19.1, where the Nile, described as "the great border between Africa and Asia," is situated "adversum Thanay," that is, "opposite to the Tanaïs" (Don) river, precisely as it stereotypically appeared on the T-O type of the mappamundi. See Notes to the Text and Translation, note 169; see also Illustrations 10 and 11.

117. Greene, "Petrarch's *Viator*," p. 46.

118. Conley, *Self-Made Map,* p. 2.

119. See Greenblatt, *Renaissance Self-Fashioning: From More to Shakespeare* (Chicago: University of Chicago Press, 1980), especially pp. 1–9.

120. Giuseppe Mazzotta, *The Worlds of Petrarch* (Durham: Duke University Press, 1993), p. 101.

In addition to the manuscript that appears in facsimile in this book (see About the Text and Translation), approximately forty other manuscripts of Petrarch's *Itinerarium* attest to the dissemination of the work in the fourteenth and fifteenth centuries, both in Latin and in vernacular translations. The history of the transmission of the text tells us about the work's reception far beyond its first readers, Mandelli and Boccaccio (see Introduction, Earliest Reception), about its considerable renown, and about its place within Italian literary culture and the traditions of humanistic Italian travel.

An important late-Trecento *miscellanea* of Petrarch's Latin writings, Firenze, Biblioteca Medicea Laurenziana, manuscript Strozzi 91,[1] illustrates how the *Itinerarium* occupied a special niche within the Petrarchan canon from the time of the earliest dissemination of Petrarch's works following his death in 1374. This manuscript, authoritative for its antiquity (it appears in part dependent upon Firenze, Biblioteca Medicea Laurenziana, manuscript Pluteo XXVI sin. 9, written in Padua by Tedaldo Della Casa in 1378), is also distinguished by the discriminating selection of the Petrarchan texts it contains. The codex includes the *Secretum* (ff. 1r–8r), followed by *Seniles* 11.11 (ff. 38r–39r), which is Petrarch's famous "description of this life," a rhetorical exploit that takes the form of a long catalogue of oxymoronic and stereotypical tags. The *Itinerarium* (ff. 39r–48v) comes next and is followed by the famous anthologized passage from the *Africa*, Mago's lament, *Afr.* 8.885–919 (ff. 48v–49r). The moral-historical *Rerum Memorandarum Libri* (ff. 49r–142r), the most substantial work included in the anthology, is followed by the polemical *Invectiva Contra Eum Qui Maledixit Italie* (ff. 143r–164r) as well as by Petrarch's widely disseminated Latin translation of Boccaccio's Griselda story, *Seniles* 17.3 (f.164–170v). A varied and well-calibrated selection of "greatest hits," Strozzi 91 suggests something other than the marginal status for the *Itinerarium* that one might expect given the relative neglect the work has endured in later periods of Petrarchan reception. Instead, alongside other anthologized celebrated shorter pieces like Mago's lament and the Griselda story, Petrarch's *Itinerarium* enjoyed a noteworthy prominence.

The circulation of the *Itinerarium* among the first generation of Florentine humanists is further documented by another manuscript, written by Antonio Corbinelli (1377–1425)—Firenze, Biblioteca Nazionale Centrale, manuscript Conv. Soppr. A 3.

2610—that contains the *De Vita Solitaria* and the *Itinerarium*. Corbinelli had studied under Giovanni Malpaghini, Chrysoloras, and Guarino da Verona and was on close terms with such prominent humanists as Ambrogio Traversari, Niccolò Niccoli, Giovanni Aurispa, and Francesco Barbaro, among others. Corbinelli, who possessed one of the best collections of classical manuscripts in Europe at the time, carefully annotated and corrected the text of the *De Vita Solitaria* in his manuscript against another manuscript of superior quality and then copied out the *Itinerarium*, evidently from the same source.

The superior testimony upon which Corbinelli based his copy was closely related to Città del Vaticano, Biblioteca Apostolica Vaticana, manuscript Vat. Lat. 3357, which contained both *De Vita Solitaria* and the *Itinerarium*. This codex later came into the possession of Bernardo Bembo and was long believed to be an autograph of Petrarch's. Modern scholarship has recently determined that Vat. Lat. 3357 was in fact copied from a text that Petrarch had personally given to a friend, "who was probably Donato degli Albanzani."[2]

The grammarian Donato Albanzani (Apenninigena; b. before 1326, d. after 1411) is perhaps best known as the dedicatee of Petrarch's *On His Own Ignorance* (*De Sui Ipsius et Multorum Aliorum Ignorantia*), as well as numerous of the *Letters of Old Age* (*Rerum Senilium Libri*).[3] Petrarch and Albanzani first met in 1357 in Venice and became close friends. In a letter to Boccaccio, Petrarch speaks affectionately of "our Donato who voluntarily gave himself to us, the successor to that Donatus of old both in profession and in name; no one is more pleasant, no one more faultless, no one more devoted to us" (*Sen.* 3.1).[4] Indeed, Albanzani was godfather to Petrarch's grandson, Franceschino da Brossano (1366), and custodian of Petrarch's library when the poet was away from Venice in 1367. Albanzani enjoyed close relations with Boccaccio and, after 1383, with Coluccio Salutati. In 1382 Albanzani entered the service of the Este family in Ferrara and served as the preceptor of Alberto V's son, Niccolò III, at least until 1392, according to archival documents. The relationship with Niccolò III led to Donato Albanzani's vernacular translations of Petrarch's *De Viris Illustribus* and of Boccaccio's *De Claris Mulieribus*, both dedicated to Niccolò III on the occasion of his marriage in 1397 to Giliola, daughter of Francesco Novello da Carrara.

Donato Albanzani appears to have been a principal conduit for the dissemination of both Latin and vernacular versions of the *Itinerarium*, through his connection with Vat. Lat. 3357 and through his probable authorship of a vernacular translation of the *Itinerarium* that appears to have originated from the court of Niccolò III. In light of Donato's activity as a translator of other Petrarchan works at the Este court, he is highly likely to have been the author of the vernacular translation of the *Itinerarium* that circulated at the court of Niccolò III and is recorded in a 1436 inventory of the marquis's library, where it is described as a "libro chiamado lo itinerario de messere Francesco Petrarcha al sepolcro, coverto de chore roso, in membrana cum doe colone dorade su le aleue." This *volgarizzamento* shares stylistic affinities with Albanzani's translations of the *De Viris Illustribus* and the *De Claris Mulieribus*, according to the editor of the Neapolitan vernacular tradition of the text, Alfonso Paolella.[5]

The link established between Petrarch's *Itinerarium* and Niccolò III is highly suggestive in light of the fact that in 1413 Niccolò III undertook one of the most important and high-profile Italian pilgrimages to the Holy Land of the Quattrocento. The journey was made in the company of a prestigious courtly retinue and carefully memorialized in all its chivalric glory by the court's chancellor, Luchino dal Campo. G. Nori has studied this pilgrimage and has shown how it contributed to a consolidation of Este power. Travel to the Holy Land was always as much about constituting and consolidating an identity back at home as it was about traveling to the Holy Land.[6] In this sense, Niccolò III's pilgrimage found an ideal source in Petrarch's *Itinerarium*. Moreover, the vernacular Tuscan translation of the *Itinerarium*, probably authored by Donato Albanzani, had an impact beyond Ferrara. It survives today in a vernacular codex prepared for Ferrante I of Aragon—Barcellona, Biblioteca de Catalunya, manuscript 948, the text of which has also been made available by Paolella in his recent critical edition of the *Volgarizzamento meridionale anonimo* of the *Itinerarium*.

Before taking up the distinctive Neapolitan vernacular reception of the work, at least two further testimonies of the reception of the Latin text are worthy of note. Firenze, Biblioteca Medicea Laurenziana, manuscript LXXXIX sup. 73, dated around 1473, is attributed to Niccolò Ugolini and was likely written on the island of Chios. The codex presents only two texts of Petrarch: an early redaction of *Seniles* 9.1, "To Pope Urban V, congratulations for having led the Church back to her See, and an exhortation to persevere" (ff. 27r-38r), followed by the *Itinerarium* (ff. 38v-46v). Besides these, the codex contains Ambrogio Traversari's translation of Aeneas of Gaza's *Theophrastus* and poetic compositions and epistles by Filippo Buonaccorsi (Callimachus Experiens) and Marco Antonio Romano (Franceschini), both of whom had sought refuge on the island of Chios following the Roman conspiracy against Pope Paul II, in which they were implicated in 1468. They were guests of Niccolò Ugolini on the island in the summer of 1469. While an interest in papal politics may explain the inclusion of *Seniles* 9.1, the *Itinerarium*'s presence in this codex reflects the eastern Mediterranean extension of Petrarchan travel as a model for Italian humanism. The geographical displacement is intriguing and suggests that Petrarch's travel guide, which describes travel through the Aegean and stops at the island of Chios, was recognized and circulated as a prestigious source among Italian humanists operating in the eastern Mediterranean no less than it was appreciated by archeological tourists in the Kingdom of Naples.

The presence in this manuscript of a work by Ambrogio Traversari, author of a celebrated travel narrative, the *Hodoeporicon*, reminds us that during the Quattrocento travel became one of the most characteristic genres of humanist writing.[7] Traveling in the wake of Petrarch, the anxious tourists of Italian humanism produced a brilliant legacy of travel writing—including the travel letters of Poggio Bracciolini, Ciriaco d'Ancona's *Itinerarium*,[8] and parts of the *Commentarii* of Aeneas Silvius Piccolomini (Pope Pius II, 1405–64)—that finds its source in Petrarch's *magistero* in this class of writing.[9] Meanwhile, in the eastern Mediterranean during the first decades of the Quattrocento, Cristoforo Buondelmonti created an innovative genre for recording his antiquary and literary travels in the Greek archipelagoes, that of the *isolario* or "Book of Islands," which included island maps together with the narrative of his travels. The genre derives its literary origin as first-person travel writing from Petrarch's antiquary tourism in the *Itinerarium.*

The reception of Petrarch as a culturally prestigious exemplar of humanistic Italian travel undoubtedly explains in large measure the *Itinerarium's* success during the fifteenth century, including its presence in Firenze, Biblioteca Medicea Laurenziana, manuscript LXXVIII 2,[10] an anthology of Petrarchan writings from the 1490s very likely prepared for Lorenzo il Magnifico that Feo describes as "culturally . . . a document of the first order" of Laurentian interest in the Tre Corone (he links it to contemporary codexes dedicated to Dante and Boccaccio). This deluxe codex includes *De Vita Solitaria, Invective Contra Medicum, Seniles* 2.1 (the letter to Boccaccio in which Petrarch defends the *Africa's* lament of Mago against its critics), *Seniles* 17.3 (Griselda), *Seniles* 11.11 (a description of this life), *Rerum Memorandarum Libri,* the *Itinerarium, De Ignorantia Sui et Aliorum, Liber Sine Nomine,* and *Invective Contra Eum Qui Maledixit Italie.* This prestigious anthology prepared for the Medici court further demonstrates that the *Itinerarium,* far from forgotten, had established a secure niche within a constellation of frequently anthologized texts. Moreover, as the Neapolitan reception of the *Itinerarium* demonstrates, Petrarch's guide to the Holy Land was considered suitable for export within the context of a general program of Florentine promotion of its literary and linguistic leadership, which found its most famous expression in the *Raccolta Aragonese* of 1476.

Perhaps the most interesting and frequent testimonies of the reception of the *Itinerarium* during the Quattrocento are found in the Neapolitan kingdom, which was especially attracted to Petrarch's treatment of characteristic Neapolitan tourist and classical archaeological sites including Baiae, Mt. Falernus, the Neapolitan Crypt, and Virgil's tomb, among many others.[11] No less distinguished a reader than Jacopo Sannazaro possessed a copy of the *Itinerarium* and utilized it as a guidebook for aristocratic tourists at the end of the fifteenth century.[12] But the *Itinerarium* did not have to wait for Sannazaro or even the Aragonese court to enjoy some currency in and around Naples. Already in 1451, an otherwise unknown copyist named Vinciguerra del Poggio di Marsico copied a codex that contained a *volgarizzamento* of the *Itinerarium* characterized , according to Paolella's analysis, by the same distinctively Neapolitan linguistic patina that distinguishes four other Neapolitan manuscripts of the work found in miscellaneous collections that appeared between 1451 and the first decade of the sixteenth century. The *Itinerarium* was included with other typically Neapolitan works like the *Cronaca di Partenope* and a vernacular prose translation of Pietro da Eboli's *De Balneis.* According to the critical edition of the *volgarizzamento meridionale* prepared by Paolella, the better part of this Neapolitan tradition derives from a Neapolitan transcription, sometime before 1451, of an examplar of Donato Albanzani's original Tuscan translation.

A no less significant document for a history of the Neapolitan reception of the *Itinerarium* is manuscript 948 of the Biblioteca de Catalunya of Barcelona, mentioned earlier, which contains a highly faithful copy of that original Tuscan translation. This codex was prepared and illuminated in Florence at the request of Ferrante I of Aragon, whose arms decorate the book. It was created most likely during the 1470s, during the same period as the *Raccolta Aragonese*. In this source Petrarch's *Itinerarium* appears alongside vernacular versions of Leonardo Bruni's life of Cicero and his life of Sertorius. The *Itinerarium* appears together with other prestigious Florentine-Tuscan classics imported to the Neapolitan court in their vernacular versions as exemplars of the classic Tuscan vernacular. The arrival of a copy of the original Tuscan *volgarizzamento* during the 1470s is thus distinguishable from the independent Neapolitian vernacular tradition of the work and historically may be connected, as Paolella suggested, with both the general background of the Aragonese court's maritime ambitions in the east and more symbolically, but perhaps more directly, with the projected 1474 pilgrimage to the Holy Land of Ippolita Sforza (wife of Ferrante's son, Alfonso II, duke of Calabria).

Notes

1. For this and other Florentine manuscripts discussed in Appendix 1, see *Codici latini del Petrarca nelle biblioteche fiorentine*, ed. Michele Feo (Firenze: Le Lettere, 1991), pp. 306–7.

2. N. Giannetto, *Bernardo Bembo umanista e politico veneziano* (Firenze: Olschki, 1985), p. 323.

3. Letters addressed to Donato Albanzani include *Seniles* 5.4, 5.5, 5.6, 8.6, 10.4, 10.5, 12.5, and 15.9.

4. Francis Petrarch, *Letters of Old Age, Rerum Senilium Libri,* trans. Aldo S. Bernardo, Saul Levin, and Reta A. Bernardo (Baltimore: Johns Hopkins University Press, 1992), p. 90.

5. *Volgarizzamento meridionale anonimo di Francesco Petrarca* Itinerarium Breve de Ianua usque ad Ierusalem et Terram Sanctam, ed. Alfonso Paolella (Bologna: Commissione per i Testi di Lingua, 1993), p. xxi. See also A. Capelli "La biblioteca estense nella prima metà del sec. XV," *Giornale storico della letteratura italiana* 7 (1889), part 2, p. 13; G. Rotondi, "Un volgarizzamento inedito quattrocentesco del *De Otio Religioso*," *Studi petrarcheschi* 2 (1950), p. 48.

6. For discussion, see G. Nori, "La corte itinerante: Il pellegrinaggio di Niccolò III in terrasanta," in *La corte e lo spazio: Ferrara estense*, ed. Giuseppe Papagno and Amedeo Quondam, vol. 1 (Rome: Bulzoni, 1982), pp. 233–46. For the text of Luchino dal Campo's report of the pilgrimage, see G. Ghinassi, "Viaggio a Gerusalemme di Niccolò da Este," in *Miscellanea di opuscoli inediti o rari dei secc. XIV e XV*, vol. 1 (Torino, 1864), pp. 99–160.

7. Ambrogio Traversari, *Hodoeporicon*, ed. Vittorio Tamburini, with an introduction by Eugenio Garin (Firenze: Le Monnier, 1985).

8. *Cyriacus of Ancona's Journeys in the Propontis and the Northern Aegean, 1444–1445*, ed. Edward W. Bodnar and Charles Mitchell (Philadelphia: American Philosophical Society, 1976).

9. Feo describes Petrarch's historical geography as "a conscious capacity to see and to understand the earthly landscape as a human environment, that is, as the theater and testimony of the activity of man over the centuries, as a stratification of civilization" ("Inquietudini filologiche del Petrarca: Il luogo della discesa agli inferi (storia di una

citazione)," *Italia medioevale e umanistica* 27 [1974], p. 118). Feo sees Petrarch in this regard as the "most authentic teacher" of the mature humanism of Aeneas Silvius Piccolomini, "who produced with his magnificent description of Mt. Amiata perhaps the most convincing page of historical geography mediated through literature" (p. 118). See Aeneas Silvius Piccolomini, *Commentarii Rerum Memorabilium que Temporibus Suis Contigerunt, ad Codicum Fidem nunc Primum,* ed. Adriano van Heck (Città del Vaticano: Biblioteca Apostolica Vaticana, 1984). See also *Travels in Italy: Selections from the* Commentarii *of Pope Pius II,* ed. Andrew Hutchinson (Bedminster: Bristol Classical, 1988). For a serviceable edition of Buondelmonti, see Cristoforo Buondelmonti, *Description des îles de l'archipel,* ed. and trans. Emil Legrand, L'Ecole des Langues Orientales, ser. 4, 14 (Paris: Leroux, 1897). An abbreviated text dated 1422 was published in 1824: *Christop. Buondelmontii, Florentini, Librum Insularum Archipelagi, e Codicibus Parisinis Regiis nunc Primum,* ed. Babr. Rud. Ludovicus de Sinner (Leipzig and Berlin: G. Reimer, 1824).

10. Described by Feo in *Codici latini del Petrarca,* pp. 310–11.

11. For more about the Neapolitan vernacular translations of the *Itinerarium,* see Introduction, Early Reception of the *Itinerarium.*

12. See Paolella, *Volgarizzamento meridionale anonimo,* p. xix.

The historical record, insofar as it presents the dedicatee of the *Itinerarium*, Giovanni Mandelli, as a man of action engaged in a remarkably intense military and political career on behalf of the Visconti regime, is somewhat at odds with Petrarch's idealized portrait of a pious pilgrim (a perspective amplified by Billanovich).[1] Son of one of Matteo Visconti's daughters (Florimonda), Mandelli served as general captain of Milan in 1340, as podestà of Piacenza in 1346, and as podestà of Pavia in 1351. He oversaw the construction of the first five spans of the bridge across the Ticino in Pavia, and still today his name and family arms can be found inscribed on the bridge. In 1353, according to the Milanese chronicler Azario, Mandelli played a key role in establishing Milanese dominion over Genoa. Petrarch's friend appears to have facilitated in some unspecified manner the installation of Simone Boccanegra as doge of Genoa; Mandelli was in contact with Boccanegra while he was in exile in Milan.[2] During this period (1351–54) Mandelli also served as captain general on behalf of the Visconti in Piedmont and defended territory there against the competing claims of the lords of Savoia and Monferrato. Between the summer of 1354 and the summer of 1355 he served as podestà of Bergamo.

At the end of 1355, during a "break from heavy political responsibilities,"[3] Mandelli undertook the pilgrimage to Rome, recorded by *Familiares* 19.6. In a letter that directly follows the commendation letter to Nelli (*Fam.* 19.7, written at the beginning of March 1356, according to Foresti), Petrarch states that he would have followed Mandelli and undertaken his own pilgrimage to Rome but that "I am unable to follow him, as he led you to hope, because of the riots in Liguria. I shall wait and see whether the autumn is more peaceful; stormy weather certainly threatens this region, and flight is the only kind of remedy against it" (*Fam.* 9.7).[4] In fact, "the early months of the new year" (1356), as Wilkins has it, "were filled with troubles for the Visconti brothers."[5] Bologna was in revolt against the Milanese governor Giovanni Oleggio while the marquis of Monferrato was seeking to make good his claim on the vicarate of Pavia, which had been granted by the emperor Charles IV; at the same time the marquis was attacking Milanese holdings in the Piedmont, which Mandelli had had a role in pacifying for the Visconti a few years earlier.[6] By the end of 1356, the doge Simone Boccanegra in Genoa had turned on the Visconti and allied himself with the marquis of Monferrato against the Milanese.

Petrarch's own pilgrimage to Rome during Lent was blocked by the difficult political situation in Liguria; he was employed by the Visconti on a diplomatic mission to the emperor in Prague "pro ligustica pace" (*Sen.* 17.2) during the summer of 1356. Petrarch achieved a personal triumph at the court of the emperor, but by the end of 1356 the Visconti had lost Novara, which had come under the control of the marquis of Monferrato. Early in 1357 the marquis gained control of Pavia, which he ruled, in effect, through the Augustinian monk, Jacopo Bussolari.[7] Meanwhile, at the beginning of 1357 Bernabò Visconti, convinced that Petrarch's admirer and friend, the captain Pandolfo Malatesta, had been interfering with one of his amours, threw Malatesta into prison. Upon his release, Malatesta fled Milan and passed over to the imperial side.[8] On 18 December 1357, Petrarch wrote *Familiares* 20.3, dated in Milan, to Galeotto Spinola, an aged leader of the Genoese exiles, to urge him to take leadership of an effort to oust Boccanegra.

Nothing is known about Giovanni Mandelli's movements during this period of renewed Viscontean political crisis following his return from Rome in February 1356. Neither Novati nor Billanovich provide information about Mandelli's activities during the two years between his return from the pilgrimage to Rome and the spring of 1358, when Petrarch addressed the *Itinerarium* to him on the eve of his friend's putative pilgrimage to the Holy Land.[9] There can be little doubt, however, that Mandelli played an important role in Visconti political action, a role that in some way or another can be seen to parallel Petrarch's on behalf of the Visconti "pro ligustica pace" in this period.

Wilkins observes that the "indecisive warfare that had prevailed during 1357 had come to an end by the beginning of 1358, and peace negotiations were carried on during the first half of the year";[10] formal peace was finally declared on 8 June 1358. From the chronology of these events, it is evident that the *Itinerarium,* which was delivered to Mandelli on 4 April 1358, according to the subscription of the Cremona manuscript, was written when the tensions of war appeared to be waning, that is, when Mandelli might plausibly have entertained the idea of a journey to the Holy Land with his famous friend. One would like to have details of Mandelli's political activities between 1356 and 1358, but the proposed pilgrimage to the Holy Land appears to be like Mandelli's earlier pilgrimage to Rome at the end of 1355—a kind of penitential punctuation to an intense season of political activity. In both 1355 and 1358, Mandelli's and Petrarch's ritual "journeys" (virtual or actual) and their roles as "pilgrims" can be seen in counterpoint to their participation in the Viscontean political and public sphere.

Whatever occupied Mandelli during the crisis of 1356–1358, his reappearance alongside Petrarch at the Viscontean reacquisition of Novara in June of 1358 is suggestive, to say the least.[11] In 1947 Giuseppe Billanovich authoritatively cast Mandelli according to the spiritual guise favored by Petrarch in his presentation of his friend, but Novati, at the beginning of the century, presented Mandelli in a more political light, as third in a triumvirate of important political and military friends of Petrarch who were ministers in the service of Galeazzo and Bernabò Visconti, including Giovanni de' Pepoli and Pandolfo Malatesta.[12]

Pandolfo Malatesta was a well-known military commander whose feats earned him a high reputation throughout Italy. His interest in humanistic studies so attracted him to Petrarch that Malatesta commissioned at least two painters to attempt portraits of the poet. Petrarch reciprocated the esteem, and toward the end of his life had what became known as the seventh form of the *Canzoniere* prepared for him, the "Raccolta Malatesta." This was accompanied by *Sen.* 13.11, which is key for understanding the poet's methods, and Pandolfo is also immortalized in the *Canzoniere* (*RVF* 58, 98, 102, and 104). As mentioned earlier, Pandolfo Malatesta would be run out of Milan by the Visconti in 1358, with Petrarch as witness to these events.[13]

Giovanni de' Pepoli had been in Bologna at the height of his powers when Petrarch was there as a young man. Following de' Pepoli's exile the two met again in Milan. De' Pepoli was Galeazzo's most powerful minister by the time Petrarch first frequented him around 1355. The poet lamented de' Pepoli's passing in *Dispersa* 68 (*Var.* 27), dated August 1367.

The formal peace between the Visconti and the imperial league at the beginning of June 1358 had included the Viscontean recovery of Novara from the marquis of Monferrato, and the military and administrative aspects of that transfer featured the participation of none other than Giovanni Mandelli on 17 June 1358. Petrarch's celebrated oration, delivered in the cathedral's cloister the following day, was a prestigious rhetorical flourish to the event and an ideal complement to Mandelli's role.[14] The "two soldiers in the same army" converged in Novara to perform their appointed roles in the reestablishment of Viscontean hegemony according to the peace accord brokered by the emperor between the Visconti brothers and the league of Italian powers arrayed against them.

Yet another period of crisis for the Visconti in late 1368, caused by the entrance into Italy of the emperor Charles IV, "with a considerable body of troops in agreement with the enemies of the Visconti,"[15] provided the political context for Petrarch's last letter to Giovanni Mandelli, *Dispersa* 69. In April of that year Petrarch had accompanied his latest patron, an opponent of the Visconti, the lord of Padua, Francesco da Carrara, on a trip to Udine to greet the emperor. Upon returning to Padua, Petrarch received an urgent request from Galeazzo Visconti that he should come to Pavia to participate in peace negotiations. The poet went there with the permission of both the emperor and Francesco da Carrara and with the promise to return to Padua. In June he attended the festivities celebrating the wedding of Galeazzo's daughter Violante to Lionel, duke of Clarence. During his return to the Veneto, Petrarch wrote Mandelli, while immobilized in Pavia due to the aggravation caused to his ulcerated leg by a horseback ride from Milan to Pavia.

Notes

1. See Giuseppe Billanovich, *Petrarca letterato*, vol. 1, *Lo scrittoio del Petrarca* (Roma: Edizioni di Storia e Letteratura, 1947), pp. 218–29. See also above, Introduction, the section on Earliest Reception: Mandelli and Boccacio.

2. See Petri Azario, *Liber Gestorum in Lombardia,* ed. F. Cognasso, Rer. Ital. Script. 16, part 4 (Bolgna: Zanichelli, 1926–39), pp. 63 and 77. Note that Mandelli's relationship with the new lord of Genoa is ignored by the Genoese chroniclers (see *Dizionario biografico degli Italiani,* ed. Alberto M. Ghisalberti [Roma: Istituto della Enciclopedia Italiana, 1960–], vol. 11, p. 39).

3. Billanovich, *Petrarca letterato,* p. 221.

4. All translations of the *Familiares* are from Francis Petrarch, *Letters on Familiar Matters, Rerum Familiorum Libri,* trans. Aldo S. Bernardo, 3 vols.: vol. 1, *Fam.* 1–8 (Albany: State University of New York Press, 1975); vol. 2, *Fam.* 9–16 (Baltimore: Johns Hopkins University Press, 1982) vol. 3, *Fam.* 17–24 (Baltimore: Johns Hopkins University Press, 1985); quote is from vol. 2, p.89. Cf. Arnaldo Foresti, *Aneddoti della vita di Francesco Petrarca,* ed. Antonia Tissoni Benvenuti (Padova: Antenore, 1977), pp. 374–75.

5. Ernest Hatch Wilkins, *Petrarch's Eight Years in Milan* (Cambridge: Mediaeval Academy of America, 1958), p. 151.

6. Ugo Dotti, *Vita di Petrarca* (Roma and Bari: Laterza, 1987), p. 313.

7. Wilkins, *Eight Years,* p. 135.

8. Francesco Novati, *Francesco Petrarca e la Lombardia* (Milano: Hoepli, 1904), suggests that from that point on, given Petrarch's close relation to Malatesta, the poet "began to find unbearable his stay in Milan" (p. 47: abbia cominciato a prender in uggia il soggiorno di Milano).

9. Billanovich, *Petrarca letterato,* p. 221, offers the bald transition, "two years later," while Novati, *Petrarca e la Lombardia,* pp. 44–45, provides no information beyond Mandelli's term as podestà of Bergamo in 1354–55.

10. Wilkins, *Eight Years,* p. 159.

11. Actually, Billanovich documents Mandelli's presence in Pisa as early as 6 June 1358 but oddly persists in the belief that Mandelli took the pilgrimage. Novati thought it unlikely that Mandelli completed the trip (and Novati was only aware of Mandelli's presence in Milan in 1358 when he was named captain there). Billanovich says Mandelli was in Pisa "because he disembarked there" and that since he was a legal expert he went to see the Pandects, the digest of Roman civil law. His visit is attested to by a document in the archives of the cathedral of Pisa (cod. B 5, ff. 25r–v), which gives an account of the expenses associated with hosting "Ioanni Mondelli de Mediolano qui venit in Palatium dominorum antianorum pro videndo Pandectam" (cited in Billanovich, *Petrarca letterato,* p. 223). One wonders whether or not there might have been a more immediate political concern that brought Mandelli to Pisa. Billanovich's account leads one to believe that Mandelli was simply concluding "in bellezza" his tour/pilgrimage with a final classical-legal flourish in Pisa. But if in fact he never did go on the pilgrimage, what business might he have been attending to in Pisa at that time?

    Novati did not know about Mandelli's appearances in Pisa or Novara but only of a report that Giovanni Mandelli was nominated on 8 December 1358 by Galeazzo Visconti "suo luogotenente in Milano" (*Petrarca e la Lombardia,* pp. 45–46). While admitting that the pilgrimage in that time was possible, Novati was skeptical that Mandelli could have departed in May and have returned and been ready to assume a new office in December. We can imagine that Novati's skepticism would have grown considerably had he known that Mandelli was in Pisa in June of 1358, and one wonders how Billanovich accepted, apparently without hesitation or reservation, that the pilgrimage was in fact completed. He merely opines that "Giovannolo partì subito per usufruire intera la buona stagione e per essere presto ancora presente alle gravi vicende di Lombardia" (p. 222) and somewhat unconvincingly argues from the fact of Mandelli's presence in Pisa that he must have really gone on the pilgrimage: "Anche la ricomparsa a Pisa conferma che, nonostante la brevità del tempo entro cui bisognava chiuderlo, il pellegrinaggio per il quale era stato preparato l'*Itinerarium* fu realmente compiuto" (p. 224, n. 1).

12. Another significant military and political figure with whom Petrarch came into contact at this time, not mentioned by Novati but relevant in this context, was Luchino dal Verme. Luchino dal Verme, a condottiere, later suppressed on behalf of the Venetians a revolt in Candia, and in that context Petrarch addressed several letters to him (*Sen.* 4.1, 4.2, 4.3). Luchino dal Verme presented to Petrarch a richly illuminated world map; see *Lettere disperse*, ed. Alessandro Pancheri (Parma: Guanda, 1994), *Disp.* 31, p. 256: "totum mihi terrarum orbem in membranis descriptum insigne quidem artificio remisistis."

13. See the letter written by Petrarch on behalf of Bernabò Visconti accusing Pandolfo (*Lettere disperse*, ed. Pancheri, *Disp.* 37, pp. 296–304); see also Giovanni Rao, "Bernabò Visconti, Pandolfo Malatesta e una nuova lettera del Petrarca," in *Codici latini del Petrarca nelle biblioteche fiorentine*, ed. Michele Feo (Firenze: Le Lettere, 1991), pp. 459–73.

14. For the text of this oration, see Conrad H. Rawski, "Petrarch's Oration in Novara: A Critical Transcription of Vienna, Österreichische Nationalbibliothek, MS Pal. 4498, fols. 98r–104v," *Journal of Medieval Latin* 9 (1999), pp. 148–93. For an Italian translation, see *Francesco Petrarca a Novara e la sua aringa ai novaresi, fatta in italiano,* trans. Carlo Negroni (Novara: Miglio, 1876), which is based on the text of the Vienna manuscript first published by Attilio Hortis in *Scritti inediti di Francesco Petrarca* (Trieste: Tipografia del Lloyd Austro-Ungarico, 1874). See also Raoul Manselli, "Petrarca nella politica delle signorie padane alla metà del Trecento," in *Petrarca, Venezia e il Veneto,* ed. G. Padoan (Firenze: Olschki, 1976), pp. 9–22. Mandelli's presence in Novara is documented by Pietro Azario (*Liber Gestorum in Lombardia,* ed. Cognasso, pp. x and 107).

15. Wilkins, *Eight Years,* pp. 215–16.

ABOUT THE TEXT AND TRANSLATION

Although Giuseppe Billanovich reported nearly fifty years ago that a critical edition of the *Itinerarium* prepared for the Edizione Nazionale of Petrarch's works was ready, none has appeared.[1] Since that time, three editions have been published in Italy: Altamura (1979), Lo Monaco (1990), and Paolella (1993).[2] Each of these in its own way sought to improve access to the work, whose only modern edition, by G. Lumbroso (1888), is widely acknowledged to be inadequate.[3]

The most important contribution to the philological reconnaissance of the text to date, short of a critical edition, is contained in an appendix to Michele Feo's 1974 study, "Inquietudini filologiche del Petrarca."[4] Feo identified the elegant codex of Cremona, Biblioteca Statale, Deposito Libreria Civica, manuscript BB.1.2.5, as presenting "only the slightly distorted mirror image of the original of 1358."[5] This fourteenth-century parchment manuscript—consisting of folios AB plus 22 folios, 13.6 x 18 cm (the writing space, 8.3 x 12.3 cm)—contains only the text of the *Itinerarium* (ff. 1r–20r). The booklet was discovered at the beginning of the last century by Novati, who utilized it in his research of Petrarch's Milanese years,[6] but the philological importance of the manuscript has only recently been established by Feo.

The fundamental value of this codex for our knowledge of Petrarch's original intentions, in the absence of a critical edition of the work, emerges clearly from Feo's precise study. The manuscript is, according to the explicit declaration of the scribe, a copy of Petrarch's autograph of 1358 (f. 19v: "extractum ab originali manu sua scripto"). According to Feo, the distinct gothic textura and foliation appear to be inspired "by a Petrarchan graphic ideal," as exemplified at this stage in the poet's career by the 1357 autograph of the *Bucolicum carmen,* Città del Vaticano, Biblioteca Apostolica Vaticana, manuscript Vat. Lat. 3358 (see Illustration 1).[7] Of particular importance for the present edition and translation is Feo's affirmation that the "division of the text is itself certainly that of the author" and that "the varying length of the chapters corresponds to a logical and not a quantitative partition of the text that the author better than anyone else was able to judge."[8]

While the provenance of the Cremona manuscript is not clear, a note at the beginning of the codex, from between the fifteenth and sixteenth centuries, gives the name of the owner of the book as Gerolamo Mandelli, no doubt a member of the same

Lombard family as Giovanni Mandelli, the work's dedicatee (f. Av: HIER[ONIM]I MAN-DELLI. / et Amicor[um]). One can easily imagine that a book by the famous poet laureate dedicated to a distinguished ancestor would have represented a precious legacy. Another note, given on the last folio, provides further testimony of the manuscript's proximity to the original date of the text's completion and its delivery to the dedicatee: "given to Lord Giovanni Mandelli or rather his messenger 4 April 1358" (In cuius fine sic notatum erat. Datus domino Iohanni / de Mandello seu nuncio eius iiii° Aprilis 1358). The reader should refer to Feo's contribution for further codicological and philological details regarding the manuscript.

The Cremona manuscript has been taken as the basis for the present edition and translation because of its authority. The manuscript is reproduced in facsimile at its original size.[9] The goal is to provide reliable access, in the absence of a critical edition, to a work whose special character within the Petrarchan canon is expressed by the original format of the Cremona manuscript. The guidebook takes the form of an elegant little pamphlet prepared at the request of a friend, a graceful souvenir and refined self-portrait of the author that the pilgrim might easily have taken along with him, as was the poet's explicit intention: "I shall be with you in spirit, and . . . will accompany you with this writing, which will be for you like a brief itinerary" (*Itin.* Pr. 7).

A transcription of the text that resolves abbreviations and gives modern punctuation is provided to facilitate reading the Latin original. The transcription corrects banal errors identified by Feo—for example, "sicut" for "situs"(*Itin.* 2.1); "infine" for "infinite"(2.3); "regnum" for "regum" (6.0); "Meliora" for "Meloria" (7.3), etc.—and signals the correction by enclosing it in brackets.[10] Variant spellings and oscillations in spelling in the manuscript have been kept intact.

Seven redactional variants identified by Feo have been integrated into the transcription and translation. These variants were most likely introduced by Petrarch during the late 1360s and clearly emerge from a collation of the Cremona manuscript with the posthumous tradition of the work, including Città del Vaticano, Biblioteca Apostolica Vaticana, manuscript Vat. Lat. 3357,[11] which has been consulted for the present edition. Given the relatively secure authorial status of these variants, they have been included in the transcription and translation of the work in order not to sacrifice the drama and poignancy of Petrarch's late interventions.

The chapter numbers of both the transcription and the translation follow the Cremona manuscript. For ease of reference, paragraph numbering has been given to the proem and the twenty-one chapters into which Petrarch originally divided the text following the proem.

Feo stressed in his study that a complete resolution of all the philological questions surrounding the *Itinerarium* will have to await the critical edition of the work. The question of the title is perhaps the most delicate of these, and rather than venture into this uncharted territory, I adopt the title of the work according to the Cremona manuscript.

In this, the first English translation of Petrarch's *Itinerarium,* I have sought in as straightforward a manner as possible to achieve a clear and accurate English rendering of Petrarch's Latin. I have depended upon and been greatly aided in this task by the commentaries and translations of Lo Monaco and Paolella. Regarding several passages that I found particularly challenging, I have been ably supported by the expert assistance of Ilaria Marchesi and Simone Marchesi. I would like to acknowledge my debt to them here in the same place where I assume my own responsibility for any lapses, flaws, and misunderstandings that remain.

Notes

1. Giuseppe Billanovich, "Dall' antica Ravenna alle biblioteche umanistiche," *Annuario dell' Università Cattolica del Sacro. Cuore* (1955–56 / 1956–57), p. 94.

2. Francis Petrarch, *Viaggio in Terrasanta, volgarizzamento inedito del Quattrocento,* ed. A. Altamura (Napoli, 1979); Francis Petrarch, *Itinerario in Terra Santa 1358,* ed. Francesco Lo Monaco (Bergamo: Lubrina, 1990); and *Volgarizzamento meridionale anonimo di Francesco Petrarca,* Itinerarium Breve de Ianua usque ad Ierusalem et Terram Sanctam, ed. Alfonso Paolella (Bologna: Commissione per i Testi di Lingua, 1993).

3. G. Lumbroso, "L'itinerarium del Petrarca," *Atti d. Accad. dei Lincei,* s. 4, Rendiconti 4 (I° semestre 1888), 390–403; reprinted in *Memorie italiane del buon tempo antico* (Torino, 1889), pp. 16–49. Altamura's edition includes a fourteenth-century vernacular version of the *Itinerarium* with Lumbroso's edition on the facing page. Lo Monaco offers what he calls a "vulgata editorum in usum" with some improvements with respect to Lumbroso. Lo Monaco's edition is based on two mansucripts: Cremona, Biblioteca Statale, Deposito Libreria Civica, manuscript B.1.2.5 (upon which the present edition is based); and Firenze, Biblioteca Medicea Laurenziana, manuscript Pluteo XXVI sin. 9, ff. 104r–111v (which was copied from Petrarch's papers by Tedaldo Della Casa shortly after the poet's death). See the critical review of Lo Monaco's procedure and his edition by Vittore Nason in *Studi petrarcheschi,* new series 8 (1991), pp. 303–15. Paolella is primarily concerned with the linguistic characteristics of early Neapolitian vernacular translations of the work, which he has carefully edited; for purposes of comparison, he also includes a transcription of the Latin original of the *Itinerarium* according to Città del Vaticano, Biblioteca Apostolica Vaticana, manuscript Vat. Lat. 3357, which does not have any particular textual authority, as well as the fourteenth-century Tuscan vernacular translation attributed to Donato Albanzani.

4. Michele Feo, "Inquietudini filologiche del Petrarca: Il luogo della discesa agli inferi (storia di una citazione)," *Italia medioevale e umanistica* 27 (1974), pp. 115–83.

5. Ibid., p. 181.

6. Francesco Novati, "Il Petrarca ed i Visconti: Nuove ricerche su documenti inediti," in *Francesco Petrarca e la Lombardia* (Milano: Hoepli, 1904), pp. 44–46.

7. For discussion of Petrarch's graphic ideal in this period, see A. Petrucci, *La scrittura di Petrarca* (Città del Vaticano: Biblioteca Apostolica Vaticana, 1967), pp. 73–75. Other illustrations of Città del Vaticano, Biblioteca Apostolica Vaticana, manuscript Vat. Lat.

3358 can be found in in Petrucci, *La scrittura*, illustrations 22–26; in A. Avena *Bucolicum carmen* (Padova, 1906), illustrations 1–3; and in *Laurea Occidens: Buccolicum Carmen X*, ed. and trans. Guido Martellotti (Roma: Edizioni di Storia e Letteratura, 1968).

8. Feo, "Inquietudini filologiche," p. 181. Lo Monaco's edition had altered the paragraphing of the work with respect to Cremona, Biblioteca Statale, Deposito Libreria Civica, manuscript BB.1.2.5, on the basis of his study of Firenze, Biblioteca Medica Laurenziana, manuscript Pluteo XXVI sin. 9; his apparatus is ambiguous as to which divisions of the text are found in the Cremona manuscript and which in Pluteo XXVI sin. 9. For criticism of this ambiguity, see Nason's review in *Studi petrarcheschi*, p. 305. My examination of Pluteo XXVI sin. 9, which was intended to clarify ambiguities in Lo Monaco's description of the paragraphing in the two manuscripts, revealed that Pluteo XXVI sin. 9 has fifty-four paragraphs, marked in red, against the twenty-one of BB.1.2.5, and barely half of the paragraph breaks in the Cremona manuscript correspond to those in Pluteo XXVI sin. 9. The authority of the paragraphing—and the title, *Itinerarium domini Francisci Petrarche de Ianua usque Ierusalem et Alexandriam*—given in Pluteo XXVI sin. 9 will have to be dealt with in a critical edition. The proliferation of new paragraph breaks in Pluteo XXVI sin. 9 and their lack of correspondence with the Cremona manuscript (as well as a note by the copyist of Pluteo XXVI sin. 9, Tedaldo Della Casa, that he copied the text in a rush and it is very incorrect) do not argue for their authority.

9. In photographing the manuscript, the extreme outer edges were lost, thus the dimensions of the manuscript page in the facsimile vary slightly from the original. The text area remains unchanged.

10. There are only two additional corrections made in the transcription that do not appear in Feo's list: "pessumdedit" for "possumdedit" at f. 5r; and "Romani" for "Romanorum" at f. 15v.

11. Published by Paolella in *Volgarizzamento meridionale anonimo*, pp. 54–116.

ILLUSTRATIONS

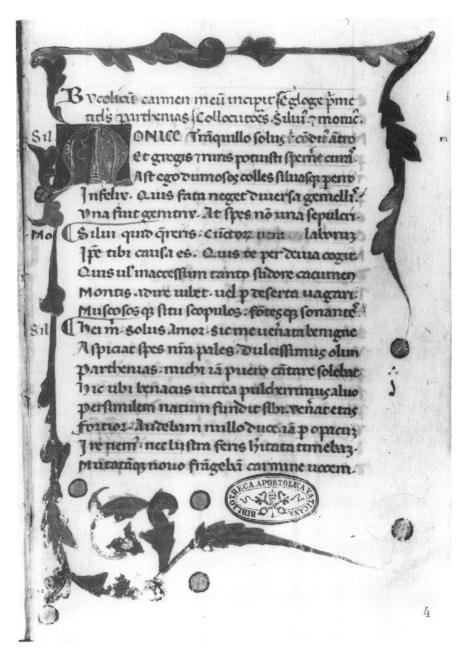

ILLUSTRATION 1   Autograph manuscript page of Petrarch's *Bucolicum Carmen*

Written Petrarch in 1357, the autograph of the *Bucolicum Carmen* illustrates the poet's script and his graphic ideal around the same time as the composition of the *Itinerarium*. The style of the script and the graphic ideal are reflected in Cremona manuscript of the *Itinerarium* (Biblioteca Statale, Deposito Libreria Civica, manuscript BB.1.2.5), which was, according to the explicit declaration of the scribe, a copy of Petrarch's autograph of 1358 (f. 19v: "extractum ab originali manu sua scripto"). Città del Vaticano, Biblioteca Apostolica Vaticana, manuscript Vat. Lat. 3358, f. 20r. (*By permission of the Biblioteca Apostolica Vaticana, Città del Vaticano.*)

ILLUSTRATION 2   Ulysses in the dress of a medieval pilgrim

"Nearby is Astura, thereafter a mountain of a certain height to which it is believed the sorceress Circe, powerful for her incantations, gave the name. In fact, it is said that she lived there and there she transformed the companions of Ulysses into beasts, a metamorphosis whose significance is known to you. The place is famous for its name and for the descriptions of writ-

ers" (Petrarch's *Intinerarium*, paragraph 8.1). Ulysses in the dress of a medieval pilgrim, together with his companions and the sorceress Circe on the island of Aeaea. From a fourteenth-century manuscript of Boethius's *De consolatione philosophiae*, Paris, Bibliothèque Nationale, manuscript Lat. 11856, f. 93v. (*By permission of the Bibliothèque Nationale, Paris.*)

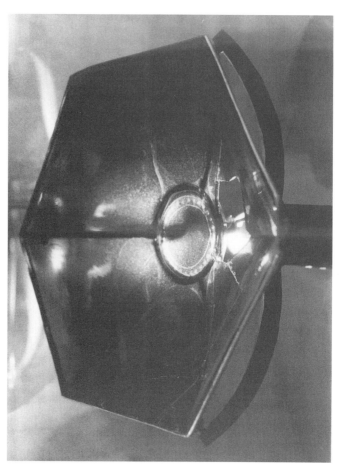

ILLUSTRATION 3

The *sacro catino* (Holy Grail)

"Even if your traveling companions are
hastening and the sailors are untying the
ropes from the shore, do not leave before
you have seen that precious and noble
vase of solid emerald which Christ, for the
love of whom you are traveling so far from
your country, is said to have used as a
dish–an object worthy of devotion (if what
is said is true) and also celebrated for its
craftsmanship" (*Itin. 2.5*). Genoa,
Museum of the Cathedral of St. Lorenzo.

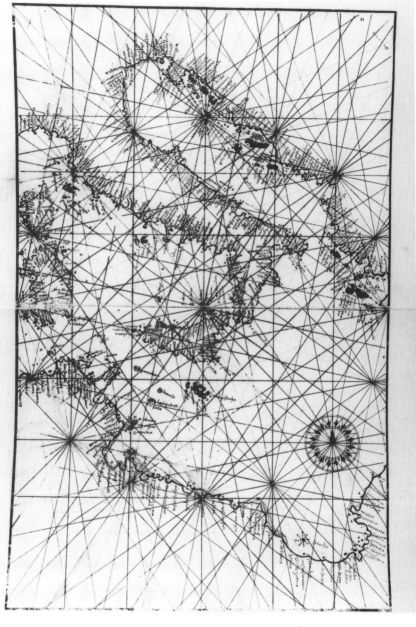

ILLUSTRATION 4

Portolan chart of Italy

"From here I hope that you will
reach the ends of Italy as easily
brought by favorable winds and
smooth sailing, as I am by a
simple and swift style" (*Itin.*
12.0). Italy with the Tyrrhenian
and Adriatic Seas, the islands of
Sicily, Sardinia, and Corsica,
with the opposite coast of Africa,
from an anonymous portolan
atlas, c. 1550s, with all the characteristics of the work of
Baptista Agnese. (*By permission of
the Newberry Library, Chicago,
Illinois.*)

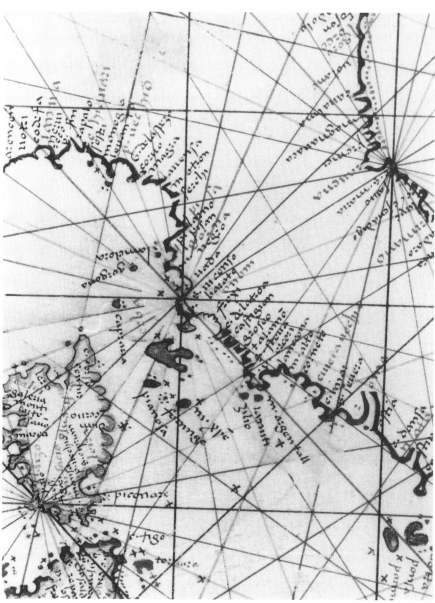

ILLUSTRATION 5

Portolan chart of Italy depicting the
northern Tyrrhenian coast

"After twenty miles, if I am not mistaken, you will find yourself before a
promontory extending into the sea
called Capo di Monte, and the port of
Delfino, or as the sailors call it, Alfino,
tranquil and hidden among smiling
hills. Thereafter come Rapallo, Sestri,
and the famous port named for Venus,
sheltered from all winds and capable
of receiving all of the fleets under
heaven" (*Itin.* 4.0–5.0). From an
anonymous portolan atlas, c. 1550s,
with all the characteristics of the work
of Baptista Agnese. See Illustrations 6
and 9 for other segments from the
same chart. (*By permission of the
Newberry Library, Chicago, Illinois.*)

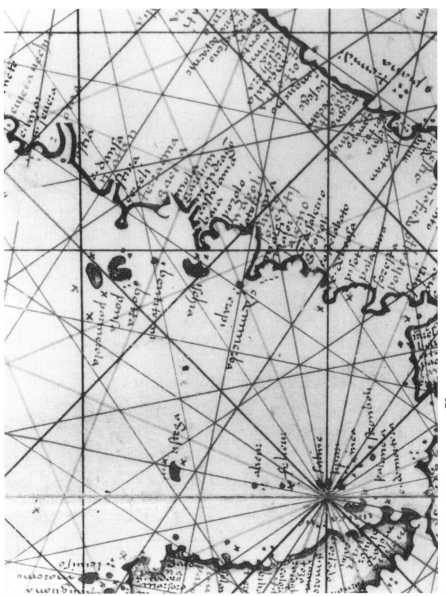

ILLUSTRATION 6

Portolan chart of Italy depicting the central Tyrrhenian coast

"After the mouth of the Tiber appears the Cape of Anzio, as the sailors call it. There the city of Anzio rose, capital of the Volsci, which, after numerous wars against the Romans, was finally conquered and subdued, together with all its people. Nearby is Astura, thereafter a mountain of a certain height to which it is believed the sorceress Circe, powerful for her incantations, gave the name. In fact, it is said that she lived there and there she transformed the companions of Ulysses into beasts, a metamorphosis whose significance is known to you. The place is famous for its name and for the descriptions of writers. On the right is the small island of Ponza, where illustrious persons were once confined" (Itin. 8.1). From an anonymous portolan atlas, c. 1550s, with all of the characteristics of the work of Baptista Agnese. See Illustrations 5 and 9 for other segments from the same chart. (By permission of the Newberry Library, Chicago, Illinois.)

Facciata, e Veduta della Grotta di Napoli che forma la strada per andare a Pozzuolo

Car. Ceccarini d. et f.

ILLUSTRATION 7A   The Grotto of Naples

"In the middle there is an extraordinary path open to all, that has a nearly sacred aspect, unviolated even in times of war, if it is true what the people say, and it appears immune to acts of brigandage. They call it the 'Neapolitan crypt,' and Seneca mentions it in the letters to Lucilius" (*Itin.* 10.1). 7a: Facade and view of the Grotto of Naples that forms the road to go to Pozzuoli; Engraving from Carlo Ceccarini, *Avanzi delle antichità di Pozzuoli, e luoghi vicini già pubblicati, e descritti in foglio atlantico dal P. Paolo Antonio Paolilucc[i] al presente per comodo de' viaggiatori disegnatii* (Naples, 1775), p. 4. (By permission of the Special Collections Research Center, the University of Chicago Library, Chicago, Illinois.)

Pianta dell' ingresso nella grotta

della Grotta

Veduta interiore

Pianta dell'interno

della Grotta

Scala di palmi Napoletani
50   100   150   200.

ILLUSTRATION 7B

The Grotto of Naples

Plan of the entrance to the grotto and
plan of the interior of the grotto.
Engraving from Ceccarini, *Avanzi delle
antichità di Pozzuoli*, p. 5 (see Illustration
7a). (By permission of the Special
Collections Research Center, the University
of Chicago Library, Chicago, Illinois.)

77

ILLUSTRATION 8

Virgil's tomb

"Towards the end of the dark passage,
when one begins to see the light of the
sun, one can see on another prominent
height the tomb of Virgil, surely very
old, and from which probably derives
the belief that he excavated the mountain" (*Itin.* 10.1). *Virgil's Tomb*, 1782, by
Joseph Wright (1734-97), oil on canvas
40 x 50 in (101.6 x 127 cm). (*By permission of the Derby Museum and Art
Gallery, Derby, Derbyshire.*)

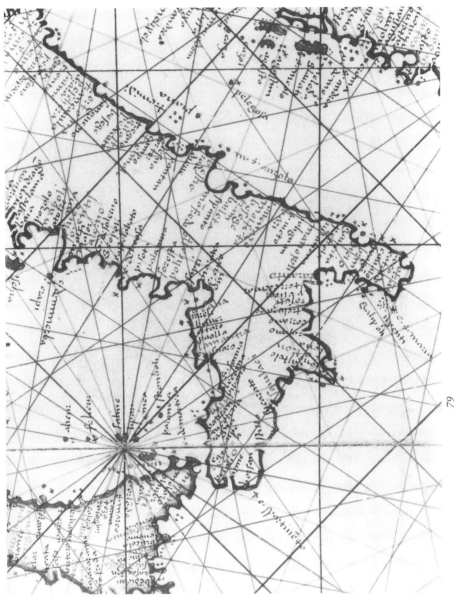

ILLUSTRATION 9

Portolan chart of Italy
depicting the southern Tyrrhenian
and Ionian coasts

"Leaving behind then Scalea, the
course to Reggio is due south.

Thereafter the route turns to the east,
leaving behind in the distance to the
right Mt. Etna, the prince of volcanoes.
Then with a brief course to the north,
avoiding Squillace which is ill-famed
for shipwrecks, you will come to
Crotone, a city that was once unsurpassed among the peoples of Italy for
the vigor of spirit and body of its populace, for beauty, wealth, and fame:
now (what is it that the passage of
time cannot do?) it is barely known
even to the inhabitants of Italy" (*Itin.*
13,0).From an anonymous portolan
atlas, c.1550s, with all of the characteristics of the work of Baptista
Agnese. See Illustrations 5 and 6 for
other segments from the same chart.
(*By permission of the Newberry Library,
Chicago, Illinois.*)

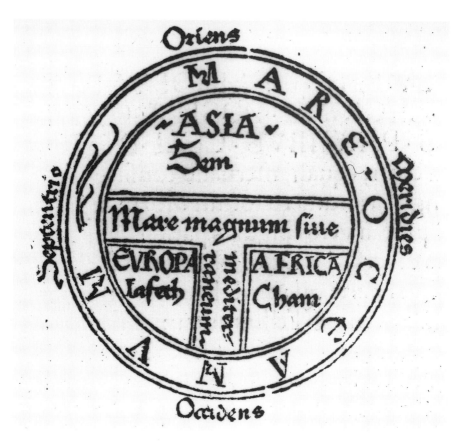

ILLUSTRATION 10   Medieval mappamundi, T-O map

"A *T* in an *O* gives us the division of the world into three parts. / The upper part and the greatest empire take nearly the half of the world. / It is Asia; the vertical bar is the limit dividing the
third from the second, Africa, / I say, from Europe; between them appears the Mediterranean
Sea" (Leonardo Dati [1365–1424], *La Sfera*, c. 1420). In Petrarch's account of the Holy Land, the
cartographical model for his writing turns to the ideological and cosmographical perspective of
medieval maps of the world. From the 1532 Augsburgh edition of Isidore of Seville's
Etymologiae (Inc. fol., 1532). (*By permission of the Newberry Library, Chicago, Illinois.*)

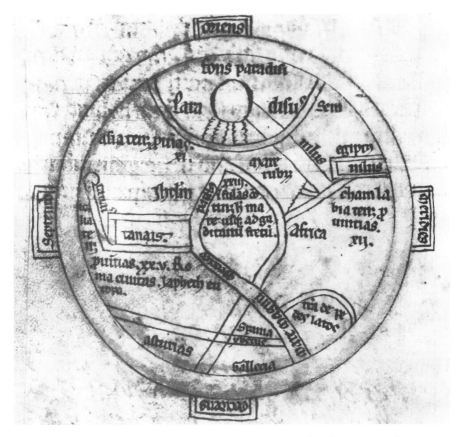

ILLUSTRATION 11   Medieval mappamundi, Y-O map

"You will see the great border between Africa and Asia, opposite to the Tanaïs, a large and stupefying river, concerning which philosophers, poets, and cosmographers have expressed divergent opinions (Aristotle dedicated an entire book to the problem); it is a river with an extraordinary high water mark in the summer, very fertilizing floods, an endless river bed, and an unknown source that Egyptian, Persian, and Macedonian kings and finally even Roman emperors sought to discover but all in vain. The source remains still today unknown and the well-read will know the numerous hypotheses, expeditions, and narrations regarding the problem" (*Itin.* 19.1). Tenth-century T-O map, in a variant form sometimes called a Y-O map, with clear labels of the Tanaïs (Don) and the Nile. Florence, Biblioteca Medicea Laurenziana, manuscript Laur. Plut. 27 sin. 8, f. 64v. (*By permission of the Ministero per i Beni e le Attività Culturali, Biblioteca Medicea Laurenziana, Florence.*)

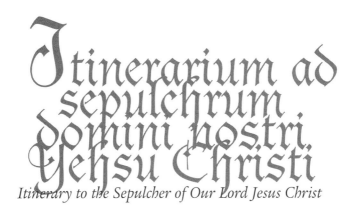

Itinerarium ad sepulchrum domini nostri, Yehsu Christi

Itinerary to the Sepulcher of Our Lord Jesus Christ

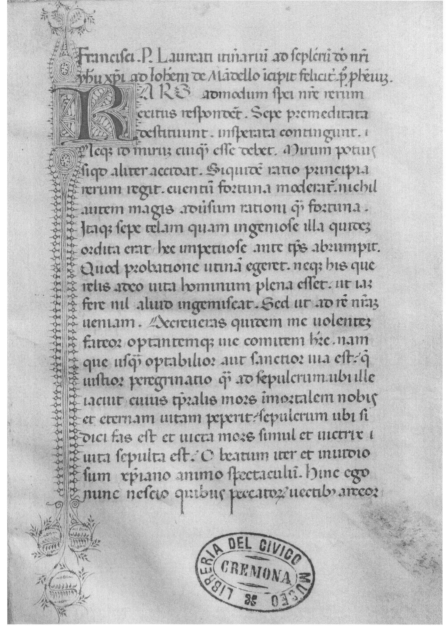

f. 1r

Francisci Petrarche Laureati itinerarium ad sepulcrum domini nostri yehsu christi ad Iohannem de Mandello incipit feliciter. Primo prohemium.

$\mathcal{R}$ARO admodum spei nostre rerum exitus respondent. Sepe premeditata destituunt, insperata contingunt. Neque id mirum cuiquam esse debet. Mirum potius si quid aliter accidat. Siquidem ratio principia rerum regit, eventum fortuna moderatur, nichil autem magis adversum rationi quam fortuna. Itaque sepe telam quam ingeniose illa quidem ordita erat, hec impetuose ante tempus abrumpit. Quod probatione utinam egeret neque his querelis adeo vita hominum plena esset, ut iam fere nil aliud ingemiscat.

Proem 1

Francis Petrarch the Poet Laureate's *Itinerary to the Sepulcher of Our Lord Jesus Christ* to Giovanni Mandelli begins auspiciously.

Proem 1

ℛARELY do things come out according to our hopes. Often what is planned does not take place and the unhoped for happens. Truly no one should wonder at this; rather, it would be a wonder if it were otherwise. Even supposing reason rules the beginning of things, Fortune governs the outcome; nothing, moreover, is more contrary to reason than Fortune. Thus it often impetuously tears apart before its time the cloth reason has ingeniously fashioned. Would that this fact needed proving, since then the life of men would not be filled with so many lamentations that it almost seems they weep for nothing else.[1]

Pr. 2

But to come to our subject: you had conceived the idea of having me as a willing and desirous traveling companion. Does there exist in fact any more desirable and holy route? What more just pilgrimage is there than to go to the sepulcher where he lay, whose temporal death brought forth immortality and eternal life for us? The sepulcher where, if one may say so, defeated death and triumphant life are buried together.[2] O blessed journey and sight to be coveted by the Christian soul! I do not know by what burdens of sin I am weighed down and by what hooks I am now held back.

Sed ut ad rem nostram veniam. Decreveras quidem me volentem, fateor, optantemque vie comitem habere. Namque usquam optabilior aut sanctior via est? Que iustior peregrinatio, quam ad sepulcrum ubi ille iacuit, cuius temporalis mors immortalem nobis et eternam vitam peperit? Sepulcrum ubi, si dici fas est, et victa mors simul et victrix vita sepulta est. O beatum iter et invidiosum cristiano animo spectaculum! Hinc ego nunc nescio quibus peccatorum vectibus arceor

uncisque detineor. Infans quidem ut flaccus t
ait pudor loqui phibet. sed imperiosa ueritas
fari iubet et ut paream cogit. Cum multe t
igitur me teneant cause. nulla potentior q̃
pellagi metus. non q̃ aut uite cupidior aut
timidior mortis sim q̃ ceteri mortales. aut
terrestrem mortem maritime preferendam
rear. neq̃ enim in loco sed in animo e q̃d fe
lices facit et miseros Et cum ũq̃ moriendũ
sciam ubi sit mori melius ignoro. frustra bel
lum et maria uitamus. frustra labores fugi
mus. perituroq̃ parcimus corpusculo. i me
dias uoluptuosorum latebras. inq̃ ipos regũ
thalamos inuisa mors penetrat. et sepe quã
forte labor et exercitiu₃ distulissent. iners lux̃
anticipat. Semel utiq̃ moriendũ est. et hãc
mortem ut arcessere uetitum: sic euitare uel
le dementia est. procrastinare mollities. at t
equanimit́ expectare tanq̃ ubiq̃ proxima₃
et horis omnibṣ affuturã̃/ea uirtus eximia
est. ueriq̃ uiri opus. Secunda mortẽ omĩ
nixu fugẽ ̃filiu₃ erat. Sed ita se res ht. Ad
ipossibilia studiũ õĩe ̃uersu₃ est. Non ᴀ

uncisque detineor.

Infans quidem, ut Flaccus ait, pudor loqui prohibet, sed imperiosa veritas fari iubet et ut paream cogit. Cum multe igitur me teneant cause, nulla potentior quam pellagi metus. Non quod aut vite cupidior aut timidior mortis sim quam ceteri mortales, aut terrestrem mortem maritime preferendam rear: neque enim in loco sed in animo est quod felices facit et miseros, et cum ubique moriendum sciam, ubi sit mori melius ignoro. Frustra bellum et maria vitamus, frustra labores fugimus perituroque parcimus corpusculo: in medias voluptuosorum latebras

Certainly, "speechless shame," as Flaccus says, "stops me from speaking," but imperious truth commands that I speak and compels me to testify.[3] Although numerous causes hold me back, none is more powerful than fear of the sea: It is not that I am more greedy for life or more fearful of death than all other mortals, or that I believe death on land is preferable to death at sea. In fact, that which makes men happy or miserable is not to be found in any place but in the soul, and knowing that we must die in some place, I do not know where is better.[4] In vain we avoid war and the sea, and in vain we flee from labors and trouble, and we seek to preserve the wretched body that is destined to pass away. Despised death penetrates into the midst of pleasure's retreats and into the bedrooms of kings; and often lazy luxury brings an early death to some whose lives might perhaps have been prolonged by work and exercise.[5]

Pr. 3

Eventually it is necessary to die, and just as it is forbidden to hurry death, so to want to avoid it is madness, and to want to delay it weakness; rather, to expect it with a tranquil soul, as if it were in every place nearby and about to arrive at any time is high virtue and behavior worthy of a man.[6] To flee with every effort the second death would be good counsel.[7] But here is what happens: Men dedicate all their study to achieving the impossible.

inque ipsos regum thalamos invisa mors penetrat et sepe quam forte labor et exercitium distulissent, iners luxus anticipat.

Pr. 3

Semel utique moriendum est et hanc mortem ut arcessere vetitum, sic evitare velle dementia est, procrastinare mollities, at equanimiter expectare, tanquam ubique proximam et horis omnibus affuturam, ea virtus eximia est verumque viri opus. Secundam mortem omni nixu fugere consilium erat. Sed ita se res habet: ad impossibilia studium omne conversum est. Non

f. 2r

mori, non egrotare, non laborare, non dolere, non servire, non egere volunt omnes, non peccare vult nullus, cum ea vera et maxima mortis et egritudinis et laboris et doloris et servitutis et penurie causa sit.　Pr. 4

Michi vero nunc forte dicat aliquis: "Si mortem ergo non metuis, quid metuis?" Longam mortem et peiorem morte nauseam, non de nichilo quidem sed expertus, metuo. Quotiens putas illud monstrum retentavi, si forte naturam consuetudo vel vinceret vel leniret? Si quid profecerim queris? Non metum minui, sed geminavi potius cum navigatione supplicium. Hoc forsan animo vago et rerum novarum visione inexplebili oculo frenum posuit natura.　Pr.5

And while all men want not to die, not to fall ill, not to toil, not to feel pain, not to serve, and not to be needy, no one wants not to sin, even though sin is the worst cause of death and infirmity, of toil and pain, of servitude and want.

Pr. 4

Now someone will perhaps say to me: "So, if not death, what then makes you afraid?" I fear slow death and nausea worse than death itself, not without reason but from experience.[8] How many times do you think I have challenged that monster in the hope that habit would defeat or soften nature? You ask if it did me any good? I tell you I have not reduced my fear but rather by sailing redoubled the torment. Perhaps nature has put this bridle on a vagabond soul and on an eye insatiable for new things.[9]

Pr. 5

Therefore I now fear going to face my familiar enemy, and although I did not fear it so when younger (although I always feared it) the fear has increased as I have grown older;[10] and it is amazing how much it pleases me to gaze upon something with which I nevertheless abhor coming into contact. This fear keeps me here now. Fortune begrudges that I should be a member of your group, as I would like to be. And if you ask whether love will eventually overcome this fear, it is difficult to say.

Pr. 6

Therefore you will go without me[11] and will see many things whose memory will delight you as long as you live. Meanwhile I will limit myself until your return

---

Congressum itaque nunc noti hostis exhorreo [Vat. Lat. 3357: quem sic non iunior horruissem, (horrui autem semper), sed in dies magis], cuius prospectu tamen adeo delector ut quem [Vat. Lat. 3357: vel] tangere abominor quam cupide videam stupor ingens sit. Iste me nunc metus hic detinet. Exoptatum michi comitatum tuum invidet fortuna. An unquam vero posthac metum hunc victura sit caritas subdifficilis coniectura est.   Pr. 6

Ibis ergo sine me et multa conspicies quorum tibi, dum vixeris, memoria voluptatem renovet. Ego interim dum tu

redis, quod ut celeriter feliciterque sit cupio, Europe Italieque finibus contentus agam.
Nichilominus te animo comitabor et, quoniam ita vis, his etiam comitabor scriptis, que tibi
brevis itinerarii loco sint. Morem enim secutus amantium, cuius presentia cariturus es,
imaginem flagitasti, qua utcumque tuam absentiam solareris, non hanc vultus imaginem,
cuius in dies mutatio multa fit, sed stabiliorem effigiem, animi ingeniique mei que,
quantulacumque est, profecto pars mei optima est. Hic tibi ergo non amici domicilium corpus
hoc (quod videntes quidam totum se hominem vidisse falso putant), sed amicum ipsum
internis spectare luminibus licebit, quoniam, ut ait Cicero, "Mens cuiusque is est quisque, non
ea figura que digito demonstrari potest." Pr.7

(which I hope will be rapid and trouble free) to travel within the confines of Europe and of Italy. Nevertheless I shall be with you in spirit, and since you have requested it, I will accompany you with this writing, which will be for you like a brief itinerary. You have followed the usage of lovers, asking of me, whom you will miss, the image with which you will be able to console yourself during your absence,[12] not the image of the face which changes daily but rather the more stable effigy of my soul and my intellect, which, however small it may be, is surely the best part of me.[13] Therefore you will see here not this body, the house of your friend, which some who see it believe falsely to be the whole man, but you will contemplate that friend with inner vision, since, as Cicero says, "The mind of every man and not that figure that one can point at with a finger is the man."[14]

Pr. 7

But I am delaying too long you whom your companions await, whom the tranquil aspect of spring and favorable winds beckon, whom all of us, sighing at your departure, wish were already returning.[15]

Pr. 8

Ⓢ INCE, most excellent man, you cannot have me, you ask to have the company of these little letters in which those things that you yourself will see with your eyes,

Sed iam nimium te moror, quem socii expectant, quem tranquilla veris facies faventesque vocant aure, quem nos omnes, qui te suspiramus abeuntem, iamiam reducem exoptamus.

Pr. 8

Ⓟ OSCIS ergo, vir optime, quoniam me non potes, comites has habere literulas, in quibus que oculis ipse tuis

mox videbis ex me, qui ea certe necdum vidi omnia, nec unquam forte visurus sim, audire
expetis: mirum dictu, nisi quia passim multa que non vidimus scimus, multa que vidimus
ignoramus. Parebo quidem, eoque promptius, quo iustius cupis. Primum scilicet ut que ad
salutem anime, dehinc que ad notitiam rerum et ingenii ornamentum, postremo que ad
memoriam exemplorum excitandumque animum pertinere videbuntur explicem iterque
longissimum brevi stilo metiar. Prima quarum, nisi fallor, religiosi prorsus ac fidelis, alia
ferventis ac studiosi, tertia militaris ac magni animi cura est. Quid vero non possit amor?
Certius te visurum speras que calamus meus hinc quam que oculus tibi tuus inde
monstraverit.

1.0

you would hear from me who never saw those things and perhaps never will. A marvelous thing to say, if it were not for the fact that we sometimes know many things that we have never seen and many things that we have seen we do not know. I will satisfy you then, and all the more promptly because you justly request. First I will discuss what seems to be pertinent to the salvation of the soul, followed by what pertains to the knowledge of things and to the excellence of the intellect, and finally memorable examples that are capable of inspiring courage; and I will complete a very long journey in a concise style. The first of these, if I am not mistaken, directly interests a man of religion and faith, the second a passionate and studious soul, the third a great and martial spirit.[16] But what can love not do?[17] You hope to see here what my pen describes more clearly than what your eyes will show you there.

1.0

Let us finally begin this journey and leave aside the places in between, since they are continually before our eyes and to report them to the ears is superfluous.[18] We come to Genoa,[19] which, as you say, you have not yet seen.

1.1

¶ Thus you will see the imperious city on the side of a rocky hill, proud[20] of its men and its walls, whose very aspect declares her lady of the sea. As already happened with many cities, her power itself, from which continual causes of civil strife are born, hinders her and damages her.

2.0

Ingrediamur vero iam tandem iter hoc et media pretervecti, que assidue subiecta oculis inculcare auribus supervacuum est, nondum tibi visam, ut ais, Ianuam veniamus.   1.1

¶ Videbis ergo imperiosam urbem lapidosi collis in latere, virisque et menibus superbam, quam dominam maris illius aspectus ipse pronuntiat; sua sibi potentia, quod multis iam fecit urbibus, obstat atque officit iugis unde materia civilium simultatum scatet.   2.0

Autorem urbis et nominis Ianum ferunt, primum ut quibusdam placet Italie regem. Quod an ita sit, an ipse [sicut: situs] urbi nomen dederit, quod nostri orbis quasi ianua quedam esse videatur, incertum habeo. Prima ibi celebrior opinio est et in cronicis eorum scripta et publicis insculpta monimentis. Utrique autem illud obstat, quod apud veteres non Ianue sed Genue nomen in usu est.   2.1

Huius sane multa recentia et memorabilia dici possunt, que pretereo, neque enim scribo nunc hystoriam, sed loca describo. Antiqua autem pauciora, quod non semper hoc, sed, quantum intelligere est, caput gentis Albingaunum fuerat. Ipsa quidem de qua loquor

They write that Janus, believed by some to have been the first king of Italy, was the founder of the city and source of its name. I am uncertain whether this is true or if the site itself gave name to the city, which is like a *ianua* (that is to say, "door") to our territory. The former opinion is given the most credit in Genoa, not only in local chronicles but also on public monuments. The fact that in ancient times not "Ianua" but "Genua" was the name in use stands against both opinions.[21]

2.1

I pass over numerous recent events worthy of memory since I am not writing history but a description of places. There are fewer events from classical times, for this was not the most important center; rather, from what we can gather, Albenga was the capital of the population.[22] But the city Genoa of which I am speaking was destroyed by the Carthaginians during the second Punic War and was rebuilt by Roman commanders.[23]

2.2

Here you will therefore see the ways of the people and the situation of the places, the grandeur of the buildings and above all, the fleet, corresponding to what you have seen written of Tyre: terrible and worthy to be feared by all shores.[24] Thereafter you will admire the massive breakwater that opposes the sea, and the manmade port, an inestimable expense and a colossal undertaking, that tempests batter day after day in vain.

2.3

What more can one say? When you will have considered this city and the shore that embraces it from the right and from the left, the mountains plummeting down to

---

Ianua temporibus belli Punici secundi a Cartaginensibus eversa, a Romanis ducibus restituta est.   2.2

In qua tu nunc et populi habitum et locorum situm et edificiorum decus atque in primis classem, quod de Tyria scriptum vides, cunctis terribilem tremendamque littoribus; tum mollem pelago obiectam portumque mirabere manu factum, inextimabilis sumptus, [infine: infinite] opere, quem quotidiane nequicquam feriunt procelle.   2.3

Quid multa? Cum sedulo civitatem hanc et dextra levaque circumfusum littus ac montes fluctibus impendentes, ad hec corpora, mores, animos et victum gentis aspexeris, scito te vidisse cotem illam alteram que Romane virtutis aciem, longo exercitio, multos olim annos exacuit; quod, si quid Livio creditur, nulla provincia magis fecit, ut cui scilicet essent omnia que vigilem atque solicitum Romanum exercitum haberent: locorum montana durities, hostis prompta velocitas, commeatuum difficultas, insidiarum opportunitas, communitio castellorum, labor iugis, periculi plurimum, prede minimum, otii nichil. Itaque cum ubique terrarum cum singulis, hic cum multis difficultatibus uno tempore pugnandum erat.   2.4

Hinc tu, tametsi socii properent et naute de littore funem solvant, non tamen ante discesseris quam preciosum illud et insigne vas solido e smaragdo, quo Christus, cuius te tam procul a

the waves of the sea, and in addition, the persons, customs, the
soul and life of the people, know that you have seen that other
whetstone that once sharpened by long use, over many years, the
point of Roman virtue. For, if one is to believe Livy, no province
made a greater contribution to creating the need for Rome to have
a vigilant and ready army: the mountain ruggedness of the places,
the prompt speed of the enemy, the difficulty of group movement,
the opportunities for ambush, the strong fortifications of its
castles, the continuous labors, the many occasions for danger, few
for booty, none for repose.[25] Thus, while it was necessary
everywhere else to struggle against one difficulty at a time, here
one confronted many all at once.

2.4

Even if your traveling companions are hastening and the sailors
are untying the ropes from the shore, do not leave before you have
seen that precious and noble vase of solid emerald that Christ, for
the love of whom you travel so far from your country, is said to
have used as a dish—an object worthy of devotion (if what is said
is true) and also celebrated for its craftsmanship.26

2.5

⸿ Having departed from there heading east, see that you do not
take your eyes off the land that entire day. Many things will appear
to them that will be much easier for you to admire than for any
man to encompass with the pen: most beautiful valleys, running
streams, hills of momentous ruggedness and remarkable for their
wonderful

patria amor trahit, pro parapside usus fertur, videas devotum si sic est, alioquin suapte specie
clarum opus.   2.5

⸿ Hinc digressus ad levam totum illum diem ne oculos a terra dimoveas caveto. Multa enim
illis occurrent que multo tibi facilius sit mirari quam cuiquam hominum stilo amplecti: valles
amenissimas, interlabentes rivulos, colles asperitate

f. 4v

gratissima et mira fertilitate conspicuuos, prevalida in rupibus oppida, vicos amplissimos; et marmoreas atque auratas domos, quocumque te verteris, videbis sparsas in littore et stupebis urbem talem decori suorum rurium deliciisque succumbere. 3.0

❡ Viginti, nisi fallor, passuum milia emensus extentum in undas promontorium, Caput Montis ipsi vocant, obvium habebis et Delfinis sive, ut naute nuncupant, Alfini portum, perexiguum sed tranquillum et apricis collibus abditum. 4.0

❡ Inde Rapallum ac Siestrum et nomine Veneris insignem portum, securum ventorum omnium et omnium que sub celo sunt classium capacem, nostrum prope Ericem (habet enim alterum Sicilia). In medio sinus est maris, opportunus fatigatis puppibus. 5.0

fertility, strong castles on the cliffs, very large villages. And you will
see scattered along the coast, in whichever direction you turn,
houses adorned with marble and gold, and you will marvel that
such a city is surpassed in splendor and pleasure by its
surrounding country.[27]

3.0

¶ After twenty miles, if I am not mistaken, you will find yourself
before a promontory extending into the sea called Capo di
Monte,[28] and the port of Delfino,[29] or as the sailors call it, Alfino,
small but tranquil and hidden among smiling hills.

4.0

¶ Thereafter come Rapallo, Sestri,[30] and the famous port named
for Venus,[31] sheltered from all winds and capable of receiving all of
the fleets under heaven, not far from our Lerici (there is in fact
another in Sicily).[32] In between Portovenere and Lerici there is a
gulf well suited for receiving tired sailing vessels.[33]

5.0

Here the entire shore, rich with palm trees and cedars, as hostile to
Ceres as it is friendly to Baccus and Minerva, is surely second to
no other place on earth.[34] Therefore I marvel greatly that it was
overlooked by classical authors and above all by the poets. But I
am forced to conclude that the cause of this silence is not to be
found in envy or sloth but because those fertile places had not yet
been explored and were therefore unknown. Thus it was that while
everyone often exalted Meroe,[35] Falernus, and other lands in
illustrious poetry, this one, surpassing them all in praise was
overlooked.[36]

Et hoc quidem littus omne, palmiferum atque cedriferum, ut adversum Cereri sic Bacho
gratissimum ac Minerve, nulli usquam terrarum cedere certum est. Quo magis id priscis
rerum scriptoribus, et presertim vatibus, pretermissum miror. Sed adducor ut extimem non
invidiam neque desidiam causam dedisse silentio, sed quod nondum tentata ideoque nondum
nota fertilitas locorum erat. Hinc est ut, cum claris sepe carminibus Meroen Falernumque
concelebrent

terrasque alias. hanc cunctis hac laude prestante
omnes indictam preterierint. Id me mouit i
omnium q scripserunt et ingenio et stilo et e
tate nouissimi:ut in Affrice mee quondam i
loco conexin nact'occasione loca ista describe;
caractere dicendoiq; genere longe alio. Qui li
ber nisi uel uite breuitas uel ingenij tarditas
uel aliorú librorú unú in tps cura coincidens.
uel quorú nullus é modus fortune impedimta
uetuerint. aliquanto forte sub oculos tuos ue
niens in horú te atq; aliorú que multa nunc
nisurus es locorú memorú reuocabit. Sz mul
tum nobis uie restat. ¶ Non procul hunc ear
ca extremos fines ianuensiú Cornú famosum
scopulum et nomen a colore sortitum ae pau
lulu; prouectus. Macre amnis ostia qui man
tinos ligures ab etruscis dirimit supraq; lit'
maris sinistramq; ripam fluuij ruinas lune i
iacentis aspicies.si fame fides é. Aluo enz hac
in parte nichil habeo magni exempli fugiede
libidinis. que sepe non modo singulorú hoiu;
sed magnarú urbiú et locupletiu; pplorum
ae regnum opes fortunasq; possidedit. licet

---

terrasque alias, hanc cunctis hac laude prestantem omnes indictam preterierint. Id me movit,
omnium qui scripserunt et ingenio et stilo et etate novissimum, ut in *Affrice* mee quodam loco,
idoneam nactus occasionem, loca ista describerem, caractere dicendique genere longe alio.
Qui liber, nisi vel vite brevitas vel ingenii tarditas vel aliorum librorum unum in tempus cura
coincidens vel, quorum nullus est modus, fortune impedimenta vetuerint, aliquando forte
sub oculos tuos veniens, in horum te atque aliorum, que multa nunc visurus es, locorum
memoriam revocabit. Sed multum nobis vie restat: [Vat. Lat. 3357: progrediamur ad
reliqua].

And this inspired me, last in genius, style, and age of all who have
written, to describe these places in a passage of my *Africa*, where the
ideal opportunity presented itself, in a kind of writing very different
from any other.[37] And if the brevity of life or slowness of intellect or
the concurrent distraction of other books or obstacles of fortune
without measure should not keep that work from coming under
your gaze, it will recall to your memory these and other places that
you are now about to see. But a long road awaits us: let us move on.

5.1

¶ Not far from there, near the farthest frontier of the Genoese,
you will see the famous cliff Corvo, which takes its name from the
color of the rock.[38] Penetrating a bit farther, there is the mouth of
the river Magra, which divides the Ligurian coast from that of
Etruria;[39] above the seashore on the left bank of the river, you will
see the ruins of Luni, if one is to believe what is said about the
place.[40] In this area I do not know of any greater example of how
one should flee from lust,[41] which often has been the ruin not only
of individual men but also of great cities and powerful peoples
and of sovereigns, although Troy was a greater and more ancient
example of this very thing.[42]

6.0

¶ Non procul hinc, circa extremos fines Ianuensium, Corvum famosum scopulum et nomen a
colore sortitum; ac, paululum provectus Macre amnis ostia qui maritimos Ligures ab Etruscis
dirimit supraque littus maris sinistramque ripam fluvii ruinas Lune iacentis aspicies, si fame
fides est. Aliud enim hac in parte nichil habeo magnum exemplum fugiende libidinis, que sepe
non modo singulorum hominum, sed magnarum urbium et locupletium populorum ac
[regnum: regum] opes fortunasque p[o:e]ssundedit, licet

buiuisce rei exemplu maius et antiqus troia
fit. ¶ Hunc iam sensim cedentibz montibz
aliquandiu planu et absqz scopulis lene litt?
portus rari. castella procul in collibus. plaga
maris inhospita. Sarçanum paulo siimorum
a littore nouu frequensqz oppidui. Inde Laue
tia uicus ignobilis. Fluui deinde re 7 nomine
frigidus aquis arenisqz plucidus secus Mas
sam amenissima terram descendit in pelagus
Prope oppidum e petram sancta dicit cuius
autor ut audio concivis quidam tuus fuit
illius tunc prouincie pses. et uir domi clar²
ac nobilis. Itaqz familie sue nom transtulit
in suum opus. Vltra iam pret duas pisanoz
arces nichil memorabile. quaru altam Mutro
nem. alteram uo uiam regia appellant. Nec
multo post Sera atqz Arni fluminum fauces
sunt. quoru alter lucam preterlabitur. altez
patrie mee muros primum tande Pisas inte
fluit. Et de Luca qdem dubius sum. Florena
prorsus extra conspectu latet. Pisas autem ex
ipa puppe gubernaculi 7 rector ostendet cui
tatem puetustam sed recenti 7 decora spetie.

f. 5v

---

huiusce rei exemplum maius et antiquus Troia sit.   6.0

¶ Hinc iam sensim cedentibus montibus, aliquandiu planum et absque scopulis lene littus,
portus rari, castella procul in collibus, plaga maris inhospita. Sarçanum paulo summotum a
littore, novum frequensque oppidum. Inde Laventia, vicus ignobilis. Fluvius deinde re ac
nomine Frigidus, aquis arenisque perlucidus, secus Massam amenissimam terram descendit in
pelagus. Prope oppidum est, Petram sanctam dicunt, cuius autor, ut audio, concivis quidam
tuus fuit, illius tunc provincie preses et vir domi clarus ac nobilis. Itaque familie sue nomen
transtulit in suum opus.   7.0

From this point, as the high cliffs begin to descend, the coast grows flatter and free of shoals: harbors for landing become infrequent, fortified cities appear on distant hills, and the seashore is inhospitable. Not far from the shore is Sarzana, a recent and crowded town.[43] Thereafter the ignoble town of Avenza.[44] Beyond there the river Freddo (both in name and in fact), with shining waters and sands, casts itself into the sea near the very beautiful town of Massa.[45] Not far is the village of Pietrasanta, founded, from what I hear, by a fellow citizen of yours when he was governor of that province, a famous man of noble lineage. For this he gave his family name to the place he founded.[46]

Further on there is virtually nothing worthy of memory besides two Pisan forts, one called Motrone and the other Via Regia.[47] Not long after emerge the mouths of the Serchio and of the Arno: one washes up against Lucca and the other passes first the walls of my homeland and thereafter Pisa. I don't know about Lucca, and Florence is certainly too far away to see, but the commander will show you Pisa from the deck of the ship, an ancient city which nevertheless has a modern and pleasant aspect.

Ultra iam preter duas Pisanorum arces nichil memorabile, quarum alteram Mutronem, alteram vero Viam Regiam appellant. Nec multo post Serci atque Arni fluminum fauces sunt, quorum alter Lucam preterlabitur, alter patrie mee muros primum, tandem Pisas interfluit. Et de Luca quidem dubius sum, Florentia prorsus extra conspectum latet, Pisas autem ex ipsa puppe gubernaculi tibi rector ostendet, civitatem pervetustam sed recenti et decora spetie.

et licet in plano sitam non tñ ut magna pars
urbium paucis turribꝰ sed totam simul eminē
tissimus edificiis apparentē quedam quoqꝫ ı
maris potentissimaꝫ donec patrū memoria ñ
modo uires equoreas sed animos nauigandı
qꝫ proposıtı magno uicti prelio ıanuensium
amisere. Post hec paucis passiui milibus port'
et ipẽ manu factus pisanu uocant aderit.ꝫ fere
contiguum liburnuꝫ ubi preualida turris est
cuius in uertice pnox flāma nauigantibꝰ tuti
littoris signū prebet. Hinc si ad dexteram te
deflectas Gorgon atꝗꝫ Capraria pue quedam
pissanoꝛū insule presto erunt. Nec non turris
exigua pelagı medıo qMeliora ulgo dicitur ı
fāīlta illı ıpto qꝫ scilicet illic ıpa cui'paulo añ
memini pugna cōmissa ē. Sin pressi'intēdeꝭꝫ
uıdebis et Corsica inculta insulam et armētis
siluestribꝰ l abundātꝫ. Quinquaginta inde
uel non multo amplius passiui milibꝰ plūbi
num insigne opproui ad leuā fertili sedet in ı
colle portus subest neqꝫ multam capax naui
um et securitatis ambigue. Ad dextrı exigvo
spatıo Hna ē insula exaustis calibum gñosa

f. 6r

et licet in plano sitam, non tamen, ut magna pars urbium, paucis turribus sed totam simul eminentissimi[i]s edificiis apparentem; quondam quoque maris potentissimam donec, patrum memoria, non modo vires equoreas sed animos navigandique propositum, magno victi prelio Ianuensium, amisere.   7.1

Post hec paucis passuum milibus, portus et ipse manu factus, Pisanum vocant, aderit et fere contiguum Liburnum, ubi prevalida turris est, cuius in vertice pernox flamma navigantibus tuti littoris signum prebet. Hinc si ad dexteram te deflectas Gorgon atque Capraria, parve quedam Pisanorum insule, presto erunt, nec non turris exigua, pelagi medio, que [Meliora:

Though located on a plain, Pisa as a whole stands out for its grand edifices, unlike most cities with but a few towers. It was a sea power until the Pisans, within the memory of our fathers, were defeated by the Genoese in a great battle and lost not only their navy but also their spirit and habit of navigation.[48]

7.1

After a few miles there is a manmade port called Pisano and almost adjacent to it Livorno,[49] where there is a solid tower, on top of which a fire is lit at night as a sign for navigators of a safe shore. From this point, if you turn to the right, you will have in front of you Gorgona and Capraia,[50] two small islands under the control of the Pisans, and also a small tower, in the middle of the sea, that the people call Meloria, inauspicious for the Pisans, since that is where the battle I just spoke of took place. If you look carefully you will also see the uncultivated island of Corsica, abundant with herds of wild animals.[51]

7.2

After fifty miles or a little more, on the left side, a noble castle called Piombino[52] rises up on a fertile hill, beneath which is a port that cannot contain too many ships and is not very secure. On the right, not too distant, is the island of Elba, "a generous island with inexaustible metals for the Chalybes," as Virgil says.[53]

Meloria] vulgo dicitur, infausta illi populo, quod scilicet illic ipsa, cuius paulo ante memini, pugna commissa est. Sin pressius intenderis, videbis et Corsicam incultam insulam et armentis silvestribus abundantem.   7.2

Quinquaginta inde, vel non multo amplius, passuum milibus Plumbinum, insigne oppidum ad levam fertili sedet in colle; portus subest neque multarum capax navium et securitatis ambigue. Ad dextram exiguo spatio, Ilva est "insula [exaustis: inexaustis] Calibum generosa

metallis ut Maro ait. perhibent qui longiores
ibi taxerunt moras omnia illic ad uictu optima
prouenire. deniqʒ post Sardiniaʒ amissaʒ pisa
narum opum illaʒ precipuā sedem esse. Haud
procul inde Populonia. Massa marina. Grosseti
Thelamonis portus an ab Aiacis patre an unde
dictus pfitcor me nescire. Inde rursus ad dexte
ram Igilium insula uino ⁊ marmore nobilis.
Ad leuam sci Stephani quē dicut. et mox por
tus herculeus. Argentarie mons medius. Post
Corneti turriti et spectabile oppiduʒ gemino
cinctum muro. et ex alto colle maria longa de
spicies. Hui' in finibʒ Tarqnij fuerūt oliʒ ciuitaʒ
ne nichil. preʒ nudū nomē ac ruinas. Vnd q
Rome regnar Tarqnij peliere. Post hec illa que
ciuitas netus dz deceʒ ñ fallor passiui milibuſ
sita e. Deinde quē Toriani portū uocat opus
inter cuncta mirabile. qd ne int septē illa fa
mosissima nūet nil sibi ñ etas et iactantia
graua defuerit. ❡ His exactis tiberine fau
ces ad leuam sunt ad dextra remanente Sardi
nia. Supra Tiberis ripam Ostia est. Anci Mar
tij colonia quarti romanoʒ regis. qui in ipso

Those who have spent a lot of time there maintain that everything
necessary for life grows very well there. Because of this, since the
loss of Sardinia, that island has become the principal source of
Pisa's wealth.[54]

Not far off are Populonia,[55] Massa Marittima,[56] Grosseto,[57] the
port of Talamone (I admit I don't know if it is named after the
father of Ajax or for another reason).[58] Immediately after, on the
right, is the island of Giglio, famous for its wine and its marble;[59]
on the left, what they call Porto Santo Stefano and, nearly
contiguous to it, Port' Ercole, with Mt. Argentario[60] between
them. After, there is Corneto,[61] a noteworthy city with its towers,
enclosed by two circles of walls and looking down from its high
hill onto the open sea. In this area was Tarquinia, once a city and
now nothing more than a mere name and some ruins, from which
came the Tarquini who ruled Rome. Beyond, after ten miles or so,
if I am not mistaken, is a place called Civitavecchia. Thereafter the
so-called port of Hadrian, without doubt an admirable
construction and not included among the other seven wonders
only because of its recent date and the arrogance of the Greeks.[62]

⨐ Having left behind these places, the mouth of the Tiber is on
the left while Sardinia is still to the right.[63] Ostia is on the banks
of the Tiber, a colony founded by the fourth king of Rome, Ancus
Martius,

nunc nichil preter nudum nomen ac ruinas, unde qui Rome regnarunt Tarquinii prodiere. Post
hec illa que Civitas Vetus dicitur, decem nisi fallor passuum milibus sita est. Deinde quem
Adriani portum vocant, opus inter cuncta mirabile, quod ne inter septem illa famosissima
numeretur nil sibi, nisi etas et iactantia graia, defuerit.   7.4

⨐ His exactis Tiberine fauces ad levam sunt, ad dextram remanente Sardinia. Supra Tiberis
ripam Ostia est, Anci Martii colonia, quarti Romanorum regis, quam in ipso

maris fluminisque confinio posuit, ut ait Florus, iam tum videlicet presagiens animo futurum: "ut totius mundi opes et comeatus illo veluti maritimo urbis hospitio reciperentur." Illic sane cum fueris, scito te a regina urbium Roma non nisi duodecim passuum millibus abesse, de qua si tam parvo in spatio loqui velim, intolerande nimis audacie sim, cuius gestis ac glorie totus terrarum orbis angustus est, cuius nomini libri lingueque omnes non suffitiunt.   8.0

Post Ostia Tiberina Caput Antii apparet, ita enim vocant naute. Civitas ibi Antium fuit, Vulscorum caput, que cum multa olim bella cum Romanis gessisset, capta demum et cum tota gente subacta est. Proxime Astura est. Inde mons prealtus, cui carminibus potens Circe

who built it on the border between the sea and the river, as Florus
writes, almost as if with perspicacious soul he saw what the future
would bring: "that all the riches and traffic of the world would
have been lodged, so to speak, in that maritime quarter of the
city."[64] When you are there, be aware that you are about twelve
miles from the queen of cities, Rome. If I had the intention of
speaking of it in such a brief space I would show myself to be
intolerably too bold, since the entire terrestrial globe is small with
respect to its deeds and fame, and all books and all tongues are
inadequate to its name.

8.0

After the mouth of the Tiber appears the Cape of Anzio,[65] as the
sailors call it. There the city of Anzio rose, capital of the Volsci,
which, after numerous wars against the Romans, was finally
conquered and subdued, together with all its people. Nearby is
Astura,[66] thereafter a mountain of a certain height to which it is
believed the sorceress Circe, powerful for her incantations, gave
the name.[67] In fact, it is said that she lived there and there she
transformed the companions of Ulysses into beasts, a
metamorphosis whose significance is known to you. The place is
famous for its name and for the descriptions of writers. On the
right is the small island of Ponza,[68] where illustrious persons were
once confined.

8.1

❡ Proceeding farther you will find in front of you Terracina, once
called Anxur,[69] then Gaeta, which preserves the name of Aeneas's
nurse,[70]

nomen imposuisse creditur. Ibi enim, ut aiunt, habitavit atque ibi Ulixis sotios [evertit:
convertit] in beluas, que transformatio quid mysterii vellet nosti. Locus est autem et fama
celebris et scriptorum ingeniis. Hic ad dexteram Pontie remanent brevis insula et olim carcer
illustrium.   8.1

❡ Progredienti tibi Terracina nunc, olim Anxur, primum aderit. Mox Caieta, nutricis Eneie
nomen servans ubi, quo prosperior

nauigatio fit facru Herafmi tumuli adire ne
pigeat. cuius opem multis iam in maritimo
difcrimine profuiffe opinio conftans e. Hic i
flexus littorü et pelagi finus ingens. faltusq
lauriferi cedriferiq. et odoratu3 ac fapidum
femp lete uirentiu3 nemus arbufcularü. In hoc
tractu formie feu Formianü et Liternü funt
dicam uerius fuer. alterum Ciceronis infanda
cede. alterum Scipionis indigo exilio nobilita
tum. 7 cineribs patie negatis. Sed hec duo lo
ca extimatione magis aî q oculis affequeris.
Alter enî iacet. aliter et latet. ñ q apud For
mias adhuc due feu tres magne fupeminent
arene. Ipa fed in oculis erit Inarime. que fe fe
obuiam dabit infula poetarü nota promo. Ifclā
moderni uocitant. Sub qua iouis edicto obru
ni Typhei gigante fama e. fecitq loci fabu
le uapor uelut hois anhelantis. 7 ethneo mo
re eftuare foliti incendiu3. Vicina huic Pro
chita eft pua infula. fz unde nup magnus qdā
uir furrexit Iohes ille qui formidati Karoli i
diademata nō iuftus 7 grauis memor iniurie7
maiora fi licuiffz aufurus. ultionis loco huit

navigatio sit, sacrum Herasmi tumulum adire ne pigeat, cuius opem multis iam in maritimo discrimine profuisse opinio constans est. Hic flexus littorum et pelagi sinus ingens, saltusque lauriferi cedriferique et odoratum ac sapidum semper lete virentium nemus arbuscularum. In hoc tractu Formie seu Formianum et Liternum sunt. Dicam verius, fuerunt; alterum Ciceronis infanda cede, alterum Scipionis indigno exilio nobilitatum et cineribus patrie negatis. Sed hec duo loca extimatione magis animi quam oculis assequeris: alter enim iacet, [aliter: alter] et latet, nisi quod apud Formias adhuc due seu tres magne supereminent arene. 9.0

where, in order to have a more favorable navigation, try to visit the sanctuary of St. Erasmus, who according to a well-established belief, has in the past assisted people who encountered dangers at sea.[71] Here the trend of the shoreline and the gulf are ample, the sides of the mountains are rich in laurel and cedars, and the vegetation is odoriferous and pleasant for the presence of evergreen bushes. In this stretch there is Formia,[72] or Formiano, and Literno, or better to say, there used to be; the first was renowned for the shameful assassination of Cicero, the second for the unjust exile of Scipio and for his ashes that were denied to his homeland.[73] Still you will visit these two places more in thought than with the eyes: the first in fact is closed in by rocks, the other is also hidden, except for near Formia, where rise two or three large dunes.

9.0

In any case, before your eyes will be Inarima, which will present itself right in front of you: an island noted for the praise of poets that the people today call Ischia, beneath which, it is said, the giant Typhoeus was buried by the will of Jupiter. The clouds of vapor that rise there, which bring to mind those of a gasping man, give credit to this legend, as do the flames that are used to rising from there as upon Mt. Etna.[74] Procida is near to it, a small island, but from which a great man recently emerged, that Giovanni, who, not concerning himself with the feared crown of Charles, recalling a grave offense, and deciding to dare much more if it were possible, for vendetta took Sicily from the king.[75]

9.1

Ipsa sed in oculis erit Inarime que sese obviam dabit, insula poetarum nota preconio, Isclam moderni vocitant, sub qua, Iovis edicto, obrutum Typheum gigantem fama est; fecitque locum fabule vapor, velut hominis anhelantis, et Ethneo more estuare solitum incendium. Vicina huic Prochita est, parva insula, sed unde nuper magnus quidam vir surrexit, Iohannes ille qui formidatum Karoli dyadema non veritus, et gravis memor iniurie, et maiora, si licuisset, ausurus, ultionis loco habuit

regi Siciliam abstulisse. Simul et ad levam ı
Cumas colle humili Sibille patriam urbeb'
vbi Tarqn'supbus regno pulsus. tandeq; tu
scozu 7 latinozuz destitutus auxilijs exul obyt.
Nam hoc Mediolano proximu Lario iminés
alpibus adiacens Comuz é non cume. qd ne
forte cu uulgo fallereris dixeriz. Hinc iam ı
Misenus collis in mare porrigitur. illic huma
ti tubicinis frigy nom hris. cuius rei méinit
Virgilius. Sunt qui putent Misenü ibi pem
ptuz ab Enea dys infernis sacra factó. que ut
afferunt absq; humana cede fieri nequeunt
atrocitatéq; facinozis maroneo eloquio excu
satam. Illic sane sacrificatu ab Enea narrasse
Virgilium ubi sacrificasse Vlixem Homer'
ante narrauerat pari ritus imanitate esse
aut huuiscemodi sacris apta loca. q' ibi sint
Auernus atq; Acheron tartarea nomina. Ibi
Ditis hostia limen irremeabile et ille facilis
descensus Auerni de quo loqtur poeta. que;
patenté diebз dixit ac noctibз sed laboriosi ı
atqз oposi reditus. de qua re qa qd scriptu é
legisti. si qd ipe preterea uiderim atqз audierı

regi Siciliam abstulisse.   9.1

Simul et ad levam Cumas colle humili Sibille patriam videbis, ubi Tarquinius Superbus, regno pulsus tandemque Tuscorum et Latinorum destitutus auxiliis, exul obiit. Nam hoc Mediolano proximum, Lario imminens, Alpibus adiacens, Comum est, non Cume, quod ne forte cum vulgo fallereris dixerim.   9.2

Hinc iam Misenus collis in mare porrigitur, illic humati tubicinis Frigii nomen habens, cuius rei meminit Virgilius. Sunt qui putent Misenum ibi peremptum ab Enea diis infernis sacra facturo

At the same time, on the left, you will see on a low hill Cuma, the homeland of the Sibyl, where Tarquinius the Proud died in exile after having been deposed and deprived of support by both the Latins and the population of Tuscia.[76] That which is near Milan, on the banks of the Lario, at the foot of the Alps, is Como and not Cuma: I say this so that you should not be misled like the common folk.[77]

9.2

From here the hill of Misenum already juts out into the sea. It gets its name from the Phrygian trumpeter who is buried there, as Virgil recalls.[78] Some maintain that Misenus was killed there by Aeneas as a sacrifice to the gods of the underworld, a sacrifice that cannot be consummated, as they affirm, without the killing of a man, and the atrociousness of the gesture is excused by Virgil's eloquence; and that Virgil has Aeneas sacrifice in the same place where Ulysses had, according to Homer's narration, with the same cruel rite, is maintained by some (in any case the matter is very uncertain).[79] These places are very appropriate for sacrificial rites of this kind, since the infernal names of Avernus and Acheron are found there and the door of Dis is there, a threshold that can be crossed only one time. There is that "easy descent to Avernus" of which Virgil speaks, who describes it open by day and night; but the return is more tiring and difficult.[80] Since you have read all that is written on this topic, if I continued to tell you what I have seen and heard myself, I would exceed the bounds I set myself.[81]

9.3

que, ut asserunt, absque humana cede fieri nequeunt atrocitatemque facinoris Maroneo eloquio excusatam. Illic sane sacrificatum ab Enea narrasse Virgilium ubi sacrificasse Ulixem Homerus ante narraverat, pari ritus immanitate, [Vat. Lat. 3357: ut quidam putant (res enim ambigua est valde);] esse autem huiuscemodi sacris apta loca, quod ibi sint Avernus atque Acheron Tartarea nomina, ibi Ditis hostia, limen irremeabile, et ille "facilis descensus Averni," de quo loquitur poeta, quem patentem diebus dixit ac noctibus, sed laboriosi atque operosi reditus; de qua re quia quod scriptum est legisti, si quid ipse preterea viderim atque audierim

f. 8v

sequar, extra propositi metas eam, Hic Sibille cu
mane domus maxima sup horrentem Auerni
ripam cernit iam senio semiruta. habitatore qde
nullo. sz uariarü uolucrü nidis frequens. In eode
flexu fontes caldi tepentesqz insignius qp i alia
pte nri orbis erumpunt. qdam uo sulphureuz
ac feruente cinerem eructantes. Est ubi terra si
ne igne uisibili sine aquis e se ipa salubre uapo
rem et medente corporibus fumü pfert. deniqz
isdem in locis et humane uite remedui ouenisse
dixeris et mortis horrorem. Et sub Miseno qdem
semper in anchoris romanarü una classiu stabat
ad occurrendü repentinis incursibz. Alia quidez
Rauene erat. Idqz alto consilio Augustus Cesar
instituit. ut mare supum atqz inferuz quibz isule
uistar Italie magna ps cingitur hoc gemino psidio
tuta essent. Intra Misenum Baie sunt. ab illic se
pulto Baio quodaz socio Vlixis appellate. situ i
longe amenissimo. ut non imento hiberne roma
norü delitie uideatur fuisse. qd et marmoree re
studines caldis fontibus supiecte et murorum
reliquie indicant amplissime urbi i satis multe
et scriptorü astipulatur fides. Hic neroniane i

---

sequar, extra propositi metas eam.   9.3

Hic Sibille Cumane domus maxima, super horrentem Averni ripam cernitur, iam senio
semiruta, habitatore quidem nullo, sed variarum volucrum nidis frequens. In eodem flexu
fontes calidi tepentesque insignius quam in alia parte nostri orbis erumpunt, quidam vero
sulphureum ac ferventem cinerem eructantes. Est ubi terra sine igne visibili, sine aquis, e se
ipsa salubrem vaporem et medentem corporibus fumum profert. Denique isdem in locis et
humane vite remedium convenisse dixeris et mortis horrorem.   9.4

Et sub Miseno quidem semper in anchoris Romanarum una classium stabat ad occurrendum

Here one can see, on the steep banks of Avernus, the immense home of the Cumean Sibyl, half ruined by age and uninhabited but full of nests for birds of every kind.[82] In the bay itself hot and warm springs erupt in a more extraordinary manner than anywhere else in our part of the world, and some erupt sulphuric and boiling ashes. There are places where the earth, without one seeing any flame and without water, emits by itself healthful vapors and a smoke that heals the body. In sum, one could say that in the same place are gathered the horror of death and help for the life of man.[83]

9.4

Beneath the promontory of Misenum, there was always anchored one Roman fleet that served for rapid intervention; there was yet another in Ravenna. Augustus Caesar, with the utmost prudence, had established it thus so that the sea above as well as the one below, which together surround the greater part of Italy[84] almost like an island, would be protected by this double guard.[85]

9.5

Inside the cape of Misenum is Baiae, which is thus named because a companion of Ulysses, Baios, is buried there.[86] It is a place of enchanting beauty, such that one understands why it was chosen as the preferred place for winter sojourns of the Romans, as is clear from the marble roofs placed above the hot springs as well as by the remains of constructions, sufficient to match a city of the grandest scale;[87] the testimony of writers also certify it. Here the grandiose beginnings of Nero's pools

repentinis incursibus, alia quidem Ravenne erat. Idque alto consilio Augustus Cesar instituit, ut mare superum atque inferum, quibus insule instar Italie magna pars cingitur, hoc gemino presidio tuta essent.   9.5

Intra Misenum Baie sunt, ab illic sepulto Baio quodam socio Ulixis appellate, situ longe amenissimo, ut non immerito hiberne Romanorum delitie videantur fuisse, quod et marmoree testudines calidis fontibus superiecte et murorum reliquie indicant, amplissime urbi etiam satis multe, et scriptorum astipulatur fides. Hic Neroniane

f. 9r

piscine ingentia monstrant exordia. Nam fu
roris alterius quo fossam ab Auerno usq; Ostiam
tanto terraru spatio. per tot montes no impensa
rei.p. sed iactura. non labore pploru; sed exitio fo
diendas destinarat. ut humano uicta studio na
tuto et libere tantu iter non aperto quide mari s;
marinis aquis ac nauib; ageretur.nulla n i lite
ris uestigia remanserut. Hic angulus 9 Lucinu
ht. et undam illa iulia; atq; equor indignans.
quoru et poeta recordatus e du georgica scbet
opus a Iulio extructu.ab Augusto Cesare imu
tatum.et aut me memoria frustratur.aut mare
mortuu appellant.sic maris ferocia atq; ipetum
compresse hoium manus. ❡ Contra Misenu;
et Baias Puteole tribus aut quatuor passuu;
milib; procul apparent. Hoc maris interualli
Gaius romanoru quart' imparoru. pessimoru uo
post Nerone priu' per manem suptuosaq; iac
tantia terrestri pote onexuit.que ipse ide eque
stri primu bitu.mox triumphantis in morem
magno pceru comitatu fastuq; plusq; cesareo
pmeauit. Non longe a Puteolis Falernus col
lis attollit'famoso palmite nobilis. Int Falnu

piscine ingentia monstrantur exordia. Nam furoris alterius quo fossam ab Averno usque Ostiam, tanto terrarum spatio, per tot montes, non impensa rei publice sed iactura, non labore populorum sed exitio, fodiendas destinarat, ut humano victa studio natura tuto et libere tantum iter, non aperto quidem mari, sed marinis aquis ac navibus ageretur, nulla [Vat. Lat. 3357: que noverim] nisi in literis vestigia remanserunt. 9.6

Hic angulus et Lucrinum habet et undam illam Iuliam atque equor indignans, quorum et poeta recordatus est dum 'Georgica' scriberet; opus a Iulio extructum, ab Augusto Cesare immutatum et, aut me memoria frustratur, aut Mare Mortuum appellant, sic maris ferociam atque impetum compressere hominum manus. 9.7

are on display.[88] Meanwhile, there does not remain any trace, as far as I know, except in the literary sources, of that other mad undertaking of a canal that was supposed to connect the Avernus with Ostia for so long a distance and across so many mountains, to be accomplished not just at the cost of one expenditure but with the collapse of the state, not by the work of the people but with their death, so that, nature having been overcome by the skill of man, one might travel safely and tranquilly, not on the open sea, but on waters and ships of the sea nonetheless.[89]

9.6

This cape also encloses the Lucrine lake, the Julian waters and the indignant sea that Virgil mentions in the *Georgics*.[90] Ordered by Julius Caesar, the work was modified by Augustus Caesar and, if my memory does not deceive me, called the "Dead Sea," to such a great extent were the fury and impetuousness of the sea suppressed by the hand of man.[91]

9.7

⁋ Opposite Misenum and Baia, distant three or four miles, appears Pozzuoli. Caligula, the fourth Roman emperor but worst of the worst after Nero, inspired by inane and presumptuous arrogance, connected these shores across this stretch of sea by a land bridge,[92] which he himself first crossed on horseback, in triumphal pomp, in the company of many important citizens and with a more than imperial accompaniment. Not far from Pozzuoli rises the hill of Falernus, worthy of note for its beautiful vineyard.[93]

⁋ Contra Misenum et Baias Puteole, tribus aut quatuor passuum milibus procul, apparent. Hoc maris intervallum Gaius, Romanorum quartus imperatorum, pessimorum vero post Neronem primus, per inanem sumptuosamque iactantiam terrestri ponte connexuit, quem ipse idem equestri primum habitu, mox triumphantis in morem, magno procerum comitatu fastuque plus quam cesareo permeavit. Non longe a Puteolis Falernus collis attollitur, famoso palmite nobilis. Inter Falernum

et mare mons est saxeus hominu manibus per
fossus, qd uulgus insulsiuz a Virgilio magicis
cantaminibus fctm putat. Ita clarozui fama ho
minum no iis contenta lauoibz sepe q fabulis
uiam facit. oe quo cu me olim Robertus regi
clarus sz preclarus ingenio ac literis qo senti
rem multis astantibz puntat esser humanita
te firtis regia qua non reges modo sz hoies ui
cit iocans nusqz me legisse marmorariuz fuisse
Virgiliuz respondi. qo ille serenissime nutu fro
tis approbans non illic magie sz ferri uestigia
esse confessus est. Sunt aute fauces excauati
montis anguiste sz longissime atqz atre tene
brosa inr et horrifica semp nox. publicii iter in
medio mirum et religioni proximii.belli qz tpzib
immolati si uera populi uox e. et nullis unqp la
trocinys attentati patet. Cuptam neapolitana
dicunt. Cuius et in eplis ao Luciliuz Senecai
mentione facit. Sub finem fusci traminis ubi
primo uioeri celi incipit in aggere edito ipuis
Virgily busta uisuntur puetiisti opis. Vioe
hec forsan ab illo pforati montis fluxit opinio.
Iuxta breue sz oeuotissimii sacellu supra ipsum

---

et mare mons est saxeus, hominum manibus perfossus, quod vulgus insulsum a Virgilio
magicis cantaminibus factum putat. Ita clarorum fama hominum, non veris contenta
laudibus, sepe etiam fabulis viam facit. De quo cum me olim Robertus regno clarus, sed
preclarus ingenio ac literis, quid sentirem multis astantibus percuntatus esset, humanitate
fretus regia, qua non reges modo sed homines vicit, iocans nusquam me legisse marmorarium
fuisse Virgilium respondi; quod ille serenissime nutu frontis approbans, non illic magie sed
ferri vestigia esse confessus est.   10.0

Between Falernus and the sea there is a rocky mountain, excavated by men, a work the common people foolishly believe was performed by Virgil with magic spells.[94] Thus the fame of illustrious men, for whom true praises are inadequate, often encourages the creation of legends. And when King Robert, famous for his kingdom, but still more illustrious for his intelligence and his literary culture, in the presence of many other people, asked me what I thought about it, trusting myself to his regal humanity, in which he surpasses not only other kings but all other men, I answered playfully that I had nowhere read that Virgil was a marble worker. To which he assented with a nod of his serene brow, and confirmed that those were vestiges of iron and not magic.[95]

The entrances to the little caves are very narrow, but the tunnels are very long and dark, within which it is always an impenetrable and fearful night; in the middle there is an extraordinary path open to all, that has a nearly sacred aspect, unviolated even in times of war, if it is true what the people say, and it appears immune to acts of brigandage. They call it the "Neapolitan crypt," and Seneca mentions it in the letters to Lucilius.[96] Towards the end of the dark passage, when one begins to see the light of the sun, one can see on another prominent height the tomb of Virgil, surely very old, and from which probably derives the belief that he excavated the mountain.[97]

Sunt autem fauces excavati montis anguste sed longissime atque atre, tenebrosa intus et horrifica semper nox, publicum iter in medio, mirum et religioni proximum, belli quoque temporibus inviolatum, si vera populi vox est, et nullis unquam latrociniis attentatum patet. Criptam Neapolitanam dicunt, cuius et in epistolis ad Lucilium Seneca mentionem facit. Sub finem fusci tramitis, ubi primo videri celum incipit, in aggere edito ipsius Virgilii busta visuntur, pervetusti operis. Unde hec forsan ab illo perforati montis fluxit opinio. Iuxta breve sed devotissimum sacellum supra ipsum

Capte exitum. et mox ad radicem montis in ł
littore virginis matris templu. quo magnus ł
ipłi magnus assidue pnauigantiu fit xursus.
Proxima sedet ipa in ualle Neapolis . inter urbes
littoreas una quidē ex paucis. Portus hic et
manu factus. Supra portū Regia. Vbi si in tra̅ꝫ
exeas capellam regis intrare ne omisis . in qua
conterrane̅ olim meus pictoꝛii n̅ri eui p̅nceps
magna reliquit manus et ingeniꝯ monime̅ta.
Non audeo te hoꝛtari ut extante̅ in colle urbi
proximo Cartusie domū adeas. Scio ut naui
gatio fatigatice̅ꝫ et fastidiuꝫ parit. At dare
uirginis predaru̅ domicilii q̅uis a littore ł
parump abscesserit uidero . regine senioꝛis
amplissimū opus. Illud nulla festinatio n̅lłꝭ
laboꝛ impediat / qn duos urbis illi uicos N̅ou̅
scilicet et Capuanā uideas . edificiꝭ sup̅ p̅ua
tim modii et ante quā pestis oꝛbē terre suoꝛ
tus exhausissꝫ uix cuiꝗ credibili milicie nu̅o
ac decoꝛe memorabiles . milicie ad milicie ꝑ
lagus . opus professioi tue debiti te muto.
non studiosiuꝫ ueritatis ad fabulas . et wcir
co castru̅ Oui titulo cognicii emin̅ aspexisse

Cripte exitum et mox ad radicem montis in littore Virginis Matris templum, quo magnus populi, magnus assidue pernavigantium fit concursus. 10.1

Proxima sedet ipsa in valle Neapolis, inter urbes littoreas una quidem ex paucis. Portus hic et manu factus. Supra portum regia, ubi si in terram exeas, capellam regis intrare ne omiseris, in qua conterraneus olim meus, pictorum nostri evi princeps, magna reliquit manus et ingenii monimenta. Non audeo te hortari ut extantem in colle urbi proximo Cartusie domum adeas.

At the exit from the crypt, there is a small but very much venerated shrine, and thereafter, at the foot of the hill, on the shore, is a church dedicated to the Virgin, to which a great number of people always flock by land and sea.[98]

Naples itself is situated in the nearby valley, one of few coastal cities. The port here is also manmade and the royal castle overlooks it. If you disembark, don't miss visiting the king's chapel, in which the greatest painter of our times, my countryman, has left great monuments of his skill and his genius.[99] I don't dare urge you to go to the Charterhouse that is on the nearby hill.[100] I know how sailing can be tiring and tedious. Nevertheless, even if it is slightly distant from the coast, you must see the famous abode of the virgin Saint Clare: it is a beautiful work of the elderly queen.[101] No hurry or weariness should keep you from visiting two of the city's neighborhoods, Nido and Capuana, worthy of mention for their extraordinary edifices and, before the plague emptied the entire globe, for their incredible concentration of nobility and wealth. In your role as soldier I send you to that sea of soldiers, which is proper to you, and not, since you love truth, to fables: for this reason it will be sufficient for you to observe from a distance that which is called Castel dell'Ovo.[102]

Scio ut navigatio fatigationem et fastidium parit. At Clare virginis preclarum domicilium, quamvis a littore parumper abscesserit, videto, regine senioris amplissimum opus. Illud nulla festinatio, nullus labor impediat, quin duos urbis illius vicos, Nidum scilicet et [Caprianam: Capuanam], videas, edificiis supra privatum modum et, ante quam pestis orbem terre funditus exhausisset, vix cuiquam credibili militie numero ac decore memorabiles. Militem ad militie pelagus, opus professioni tue debitum, te micto, non studiosum veritatis ad fabulas, et idcirco Castrum Ovi titulo cognitum eminus aspexisse satis fuerit. 10.2

Hec est civitas ubi Virgilius noster liberalibus studiis operam dedit, cum iam ante patria illum tua Mediolanum, tenerioribus annis, discipulum habuisset. Hic se carmen ille georgicum scripsisse, hic se ignobili otio floruisse verecondissime memorat. Hanc dulcem vocat ille Parthenopem, id enim est aliud de nomine conditricis civitati nomen. Demum peregre moriens, inter extrema suspiria sue meminit Neapolis et huc revehi optavit ut, quam vivus amaverat, vita functus incoleret. 10.3

This is the city where our Virgil dedicated himself to liberal studies, after studying during his youth in your city Milan. Here he wrote the *Georgics*, here he recalls, with great modesty, having flourished in inglorious ease.[103] He calls it "sweet Parthenope," which is in fact the other name of the city that derives from the name of she who founded it.[104] Finally, as he lay dying far away, he remembered Naples amid last sighs and hoped to be returned there so that the city he had loved while living should have him after his death.[105]

10.3

¶ Having left there, you will have nearby the double summits of Vesuvius (called "Summa" by the people), and it is usually erupting flames.[106] Pliny the Elder, a master of many sciences and of florid eloquence, went to witness that spectacle desiring experience and knowledge, only to be crushed by wind-driven volcanic ash and flames: what a miserable departure for such a great man![107] Thus on one side Naples guards the bones of a Mantuan and on the other those of a Veronese citizen.[108] The mountain possesses also many other characteristics, but first of all it is marvelously abundant with wine,[109] which is called "Greek," because this part of Italy was possessed by the Greeks and was once called Magna Graecia.[110] From there, on the right hand side one leaves behind the island of Capri, which is surrounded by very steep cliffs,

¶ Hinc tandem digresso, biceps aderit Vesevus (vulgo Summa monti nomen) et ipse flammas eructare solitus. Ad quod olim spectaculum visendum cum experiendi noscendique cupidine perrexisset Plinius Secundus, vir scientie multiplicis et eloquentie floride, vento cinerem ac favilam excitante compressus est: miserabilis tanti viri exitus. Sic Neapolis, hinc Mantuani, inde autem Veronensis civis ossa custodit. Mons est autem multarum rerum, sed in primis vini ubertate mirabilis, quod Grecum ideo dicitur, quia illa pars Italie a Grecis possessa olim Magna Grecia dicebatur. Hic ad dexteram Capree insula linquitur, asperrimis rupibus circunsepta, secessus

infamis senilium Tiberii uoluptatum et officina se
uicie. pulcherrimus terrarum tractus ad leua Po
peios atque herculaneum huit. celebres olim urbes
nunc inania noia. quas terremotibus euersas
Seneca inter ceteros teste diximus. Supest ad
huc Surrentu et ipm mellifluo palmite gñosu.
Tota regio terra laboris hodie / ps olim Campa
nie fuerat. utraque precipue ubertatis appellatio.
quo pretextu Cereris hic Liberique certame
incerta uictoria statue. Post ◡ hoc gremiu
maris ecce mox aliud ex ordine panditur. in
quo Salernu uidebis et Silerim. Fuisse hic me
dicine fonte fama e. Sed nichil est qued no
senio exarescat. ¶ Hic utinaq tu securior ue
nis et cursu tam facili proueharis ut ego ad Ita
lie finem facili pulchar stilo leua utaque pretuo
tractu calabrii littus extendit. dextra autem
longe Trinacria et Vulcanus ac Liparis mi
noresque insule. et ipse fumu flamaque fundentes
uentuoseque adeo ut Eoli uentorii regis hic regi
am fuisse uel fabulosu est uel hystoricu sit. u
truique em lectu e. hic qd conuenit eolie dicte
sunt. Vbi angustissima italia e Scalea uocat

infamis senilium Tiberii voluptatum et officina sevicie. Pulcherrimus terrarum tractus ad levam Pompeios atque Herculaneum habuit, celebres olim urbes, nunc inania nomina, quas terremotibus eversas Seneca inter ceteros teste [didimus: didicimus]. Superest adhuc Surrentum et ipsum mellifluo palmite generosum. Tota regio Terra Laboris hodie, pars olim Campanie fuerat, utraque precipue ubertatis appellatio. Quo pretextu Cereris hic Liberique certamen incerta victoria statuere. 11.0

Post hoc gremium maris ecce mox aliud ex ordine panditur, in quo Salernum videbis et Silerim. Fuisse hic medicine fontem fama est, sed nichil est quod non senio exarescat. 11.1

refuge for the senile desires of the infamous Tiberius and his torture chamber.[111] The beautiful tract of coast on the left held Pompei and Herculaneum, once celebrated cities, now empty names, since, as we know from Seneca among others, they were destroyed by earthquakes.[112] You can still see Sorrento, abundant with sweet vines.[113] All of this area, today called the "land of labor," was in the past part of Campania: both names derive from the extraordinary fertility. Here beneath the cover of this name the competition between Ceres and Liber was resolved without winners and losers.[114]

11.0

Beyond this gulf, behold, there opens up immediately another, within which you will see Salerno and the Sele.[115] It is said that Salerno was the source of the study of medicine, but there is nothing that does not run dry over time.[116]

11.1

⁋ From here I hope that you will reach the ends of Italy as easily brought by favorable winds and smooth sailing, as I am by a simple and swift style.

12.0

Thereafter, continuing on the left for a lengthy tract, the Calabrian coast stretches out. On the right, after a long piece of it, come Sicily and Vulcano and Lipari[117] and other smaller islands that throw off smoke and flames,[118] and they are also windy, so much so that they are said to have been the dominion of Aeolus, king of the winds; thus one reads of them, historically true or fabulous as the case may be. For this reason they are appropriately called the Aeolian Islands. The place where Italy grows most narrow is called Scalea; I do not know how old the castle is but the name is no doubt modern.[119]

12.1

⁋ Hinc utinam tu secundis ventis et cursu tam facili proveharis ut ego ad Italie finem facili provehar stilo!

12.0

Leva itaque perpetuo tractu Calabrum littus extenditur. Dextra autem longe Trinacria et Vulcanus ac Liparis minoresque insule et ipse fumum flammamque fundentes ventoseque adeo ut Eoli, ventorum regis, hic regiam fuisse, vel fabulosum certe vel hystoricum sit, utrumque enim lectum est. Hinc quod convenit Eolie dicte sunt. Ubi angustissima Italia est, Scaleam vocant,

nescio q̄ uetus oppidū .s̄; nomē haud dubie
modernū. Vnde cum ad extremū Italie an
gulū pueñis eum scilicet q̄ ad occasū ūgit;
hinc Regiū Calabrie metropoliz. hinc Sicilie
Messanaz paruo admodū oculoz flexu et fere
simul aspicies. In medio Pharus ē q̄ messane
sis dr̄. In quo sūt infamia illa portenta multū
formidata nauigantibz Scilla. ⁊ Caribdis. ū
Scillam ṃu saxuz esse constat ad leuam
undisonū uu̅ procellosuz. Caribdim contra
aquaz magnā quādam rapidāq; ūtiginem.
Neq; te moueat q̄ libro t̄io diuini poematis
locate aliē a Virgilio uideant̄. Ille enim ueni
entis. ego aūt euntis iter psequor. Causa nō
tante uertiginis apud poetas et hystoricos ⁊
una est. ferunt ei hūc nr̄m qui nos ambit ac di
rimit Apennīnuz ⁊ Trinacriam protendi soliti
donec multis seculis duo maria uelut ex cōdic
to geminii latus montis hinc illinc sine intinif
sione tandēia undis succumbē coegerūt. Ideoq;
illic amoto obice maria suo ipetu acta xurrere.
Apennini aūt ultima sic a toto corpore motus
erecta noie etiam amisso concessisse in nomē

---

nescio quam vetus oppidum sed nomen haud dubie modernum. 12.1

Unde cum ad extremum Italie angulum perveneris, eum scilicet qui ad occasum vergit, hinc
Regium Calabrie metropolim, hinc Sicilie Messanam parvo admodum oculorum flexu et fere
simul aspicies. In medio Pharus est, qui Messanensis dicitur, in quo sunt infamia illa portenta,
multum formidata navigantibus, Scilla et Caribdis. Scillam saxum esse constat ad levam,
undisonum, procellosum, Caribdim contra aquarum magnam quandam rapidamque
vertiginem. Neque te moveat quod libro tertio divini poematis locate aliter a Virgilio
videantur: ille enim venientis, ego autem euntis iter prosequor. 12.2

When you arrive at the farthest cape of Italy, that trends toward the west, from there you will see, with a slight turning of your gaze and almost at the same time, on one side the city of Reggio Calabria and on the other, in Sicily, Messina. In between is a lighthouse that is called the tower "of Messina,"[120] where one encounters those infamous marvels, most feared by navigators, Scylla and Charybdis. Scylla is a rock on the left, very loudly lashed by stormy waves, while Charybdis is instead a great and swift whirlpool.[121] It should not surprise you that Virgil in the third book of the divine poem apparently placed them otherwise. He was describing in fact the voyage of one who was arriving while I the voyage of one who is departing.[122]

Poets and historians give the same reason for this whirlpool. They say in fact that the Apennine mountain chain, those mountains that enclose and divide us, used to extend as far as Sicily until the seas, after centuries of relentlessly battering the mountain on both sides, as if conspiring together, forced it to submit to the waves. Thus having removed the obstacle, the two seas came together forcefully there, and the last extension of the Apennines,[123] separated from the rest of the mountain chain in this way, also lost its name and took on that of the Sicilian mountain Pelorus,

Causa vero tante vertiginis apud poetas et hystoricos una est: ferunt enim hunc nostrum qui nos ambit ac dirimit Apenninum [et: in] Trinacriam protendi solitum, donec multis seculis duo maria, velut ex condicto, geminum latus montis hinc illinc sine intermissione tundentia, undis succumbere coegerunt; ideoque illic, amoto obice, maria suo impetu acta concurrere. Apennini autem ultima, sic a toto corpore montis execta, nomine etiam amisso, concessisse in nomen

montis siculi Pelori unius scilicet ex his tribus
unde Trinacrie appellatio sumpta e. Qui mons
Messane proxim e. Cui qd nomen an fuerit
incertu heo. Hoc enim a Peloro gubnatore u
Hambalis: que ille siue tota cu classe Italiam
linquens ut Varo placet: siue ut alij uolunt
et similius uo e patriaz sua puppe unica ꝗ ro
manos fugiens uictores. propter q̈ locoru an
gustias dum emin exitu non intelligit falli
ratus occiderat. ibiq̈ tande errore recognito
terre mandauat accepisse notissimum est. 1

❡ Et Scalea quide digressis usq̈ Tegiu ferme
rectus in meridie est cursus. Inde rursus ad
oriente relicta procul a dextris Ethna flama
tium principe montiu. Inde breui flexu in sep
tentrione uersus. ꝗ Scyllaceu naufragijs ita
me transiliens Crotone uenies ciuitate quo
dam uir Italie populos et aioz robore et cor
porum et forma et opibus ac gloria ꝓcellere.
nunc quid no ꝑterit longa dies uix ipis ita
licis bene noti. hic Iunonis lacinie templu
fuit toto orbe ꝑcelebre. Inde in intimo quoda
pelagi recessu Tarentum tibi monstrabitur En

montis Siculi Pelori, unius scilicet ex his tribus unde Trinacrie appellatio sumpta est, qui mons
Messane proximus est; cui quod nomen ante fuerit incertum habeo. Hoc enim a Peloro
gubernatore Hanibalis, quem ille sive tota cum classe Italiam linquens, ut [Varo: Valerio]
placet, sive, ut alii volunt, et similius vero est, patriam suam puppe unica et Romanos fugiens
victores propterque locorum angustias dum eminus exitum non intelligit, falli ratus occiderat
ibique tandem errore recognito terre mandaverat, accepisse notissimum est.   12.3

❡ Et Scalea quidem digressis usque Regium ferme rectus in meridiem est cursus. Inde rursus
ad orientem, relicta procul a dextris Ethna, flammantium principe montium. Inde brevi flexu

that is to say, one of the three peaks from which the appellation Trinacria derives, a mountain not far from Messina, and whose previous name is unknown to me.[124] The source of the modern name on the other hand is well known: it is Hannibal's helmsman Pelorus, who was killed by the Carthaginian general either as he was about to leave Italy with his entire fleet (as Valerius Maximus maintains) or, as others say and as seems more likely, on the return trip to his homeland while fleeing from the victorious Romans with only one ship; on account of the narrowness of the passage Hannibal could not see from faraway that there was a passage and believed he had been deceived. After recognizing his mistake, he made a burial place for Pelorus there.[125]

12.3

⁋ Leaving behind then Scalea, the course to Reggio is due south. Thereafter the route turns to the east, leaving behind in the distance to the right Mt. Etna, the prince of volcanoes. Then with a brief course to the north, avoiding Squillace which is ill-famed for shipwrecks,[126] you will come to Crotone, a city that was once unsurpassed among the peoples of Italy for the vigor of spirit and body of its populace, for beauty, wealth, and fame: now (what is it that the passage of time cannot do?) it is barely known even to the inhabitants of Italy. Here there was a temple to Juno Lacinia that was celebrated throughout the world.[127]

13.0

in septentrionem versus et Scyllaceum naufragiis infame transiliens, Crotonem venies, civitatem quondam inter Italie populos et animorum robore et corporum et forma et opibus ac gloria precellentem, nunc (quid non poterit longa dies?) vix ipsis Italicis bene notam. Hic Iunonis Lacinie templum fuit, toto orbe percelebre.   13.0

Inde in intimo quodam pelagi recessu Tarentum tibi monstrabitur, En-

nio natalis. Virgilio fatalis locus. quuis alij
Brundusii dicant. magni q̃ cum romanis
belli causa Pirro rege in Italiã accersito. ad
uitoq̃ armis ac menib; post longũ tempus
Hanibale. quos hostilui ducũ primos roma
ne hystore omnib; seculis nũabũt. ¶ Iam
ad finem orbis italici uentu est in quo ulti
mum cũ Idrunte attigeris pedem hñs ob
uuum adriatici equor emensus primã isula
rum ab aduerso littore Corcyram ignobilesq̃
alias inuenies, donec ad Achaie primũ an
gulum pueneris. Illic equidẽ optabis Hist
nuȝ qõ quibusdã uenit in mentẽ esse pfossũ
quo cum rectior t̃ tum breuior cursus sit. t
mons est duo maria dirimens. qui si loco t
cederet. insula esset. Achaia. cuis in uertice
Chorintus est situ in expugnabili. ro sibi cũ
a romanis capta esset, euersionis prebuit ma
teriã secutis oportunitate loci maxime ut ait
Cicero. ne posȝ aliquando ad belluȝ faciendũ
locus ipe adhortari. Cum uero limes equore'
ille preclusus sit paterioũ nature. et pretinis
sa Chorinto Malee flexus ille longior oberio'

nio natalis, Virgilio fatalis locus, quamvis alii Brundusium dicant, magni quoque cum Romanis
belli causa Pirro rege in Italiam accersito adiutoque armis ac menibus, post longum tempus
Hanibale, quos hostilium ducum primos Romane [hystore: hystorie] omnibus seculis
numerabunt.

13.1

¶ Iam ad finem orbis Italici ventum est, in quo ultimum cum Idruntem attigeris pedem,
habens obvium Adriaticum equor emensus primam insularum ab adverso littore Corcyram
ignobilesque alias invenies, donec ad Achaie primum angulum perveneris. Illic equidem
optabis histmum (quod quibusdam venit in mentem) esse perfossum quo cum rectior tibi tum

Thereafter in a hidden corner of the sea Taranto will appear to you, the birthplace of Ennius and the place where Virgil died, although others maintain he died in Brindisi.[128] The city had a great source of conflict with the Romans when it called King Pyrrhus into Italy, and much later when it gave military help and the protection of its walls to Hannibal, two generals to whom Roman history will give the prize as the greatest enemies of all time.

13.1

❡ Now you have arrived at the end of Italy upon having touched at Otranto, and after crossing with full sails the Adriatic sea, you will find the first island on the opposite side Corcyra and others of little importance, until you reach the first cape of Achaea.[129] There you will wish that the isthmus had really been breached (and the idea had occured to some) in order to have a more direct and therefore shorter route. There is a mountain that divides two seas, and if it gave way, Achaea would have been an island.[130] At the top is Corinth, in an unassailable position. That was the reason why the Romans razed it when they conquered it, given its territorial advantage, lest its inaccessible position should, as Cicero says, encourage the Corinthians to wage war at some later time.[131]

14.0

Since that passage by water is precluded, it is necessary to follow nature, and leaving aside Corinth, travel the longer bend of Malea

brevior cursus sit. Mons est duo maria dirimens, qui si loco cederet insula esset Achaia. Eius in vertice Chorintus est, situ inexpugnabili. Id sibi, cum a Romanis capta esset, eversionis prebuit materiam, "secutis oportunitatem loci maxime," ut ait Cicero, ne posset aliquando ad bellum faciendum locus ipse adhortari.   14.0

Cum vero limes equoreus ille preclusus sit, parendum nature et, pretermissa Chorinto, Malee flexus ille longior obeundus

est. uidendumque littus Achaicum. atque urbes in
littore Motana. Corona et quicqd terrarú mare
illud aluit usque ad extremú regionis angulum.
ut uero alter italiam. sic ille Cretam respicit
nunc possessioné uenetor. ut humana omnia
noluunt olim iouis regnú superstitionú fere óui
fontem atque principiú. Hanc a dextris Eubo
eam quá Nigropontú uocant a sinistris hús
inter Cyclades Egei maris insulas que syder
in moré pelagus illud illustrant crebris portú
bus tutú iter ages. Hic Scyros achillei amo
ris atque adolescentie prima sedes. unde ulixeo
torni astu fulmen illud uenit ad Troiam. hic
Chous Ypocratis. Lesbos Theophrasti. Samo
Pithagore patria quá ille desta in has nostra
terras uenit. et italicus phylosophus dici m
meruit cum phie nomé qd primus inuenerit
súmo studio atque ingenio exornasset. Sz quid
ago? non multo facilius Ciclades oms q celi
stellas enumerem. P has ergo nauigas et pel
a tergo linquens illa duo Grecie lumina Lace
demonem 7 Athenas. Ad leuam uero Hellespó
ti fauces. Sexton qz et Abidon infaustis amo

est videndumque littus Achaicum atque urbes in littore: Motana, Corona et quicquid terrarum
mare illud [aluit: alluit], usque ad extremum regionis angulum.   14.1

Ut vero alter Italiam, sic ille Cretam respicit, nunc possessionem Venetorum (ut humana
omnia volvuntur), olim Iovis regnum, superstitionum fere omnium fontem atque principium.
Hanc a dextris, [Eubocam: Euboeam], quam Nigropontum vocant, a sinistris habens, inter
Cyclades, Egei maris insulas, que syderum in morem pelagus illud illustrant, crebris portibus
tutum iter ages. Hic Scyros Achillei amoris atque adolescentie prima sedes, unde, Ulixeo

and coast the Achaean shore past cities like Modon, Coron, and those the sea washes as far as the farthest cape of that region.[132]

Just as the first cape faced Italy, this one looks toward Crete, which is now (observe the instability of things!) a Venetian possession; it was once the kingdom of Jupiter and was the source of every pagan belief.[133] With Crete on the right and Eubea, which is called Negroponte, on the left, you will travel, safely thanks to the many harbors that are close to one another, among the Cyclades of the Aegean Sea, those that like a constellation dot that sea and render it famous. Here there is Skyros, the first site of Achilles' love and

adolescence, and from which, hurled by Ulysses' craftiness, that lightning bolt was brought to Troy. Here there are Hippocrates' Chios, Theophrastus's Lesbos and Samos, the fatherland of Pythagoras, which he left to come to our land, meriting to be called an Italian philosopher, since he honored the name of philosophy, which he first invented, with great genius and industry.[134]

But what am I doing? I could no more easily name all the Cyclades than all the stars in the heavens. Sailing then among them and leaving behind those two luminaries of Greece that are Sparta and Athens, to the left you will have the mouths of the Hellespont, called Sextus and Abydos, famous for their unhappy loves,[135]

tortum astu, fulmen illud venit ad Troiam. Hic Chous Ypocratis, Lesbos Theophrasti, Samos Pithagore patria, qua ille deserta in has nostras terras venit et Italicus philosophus dici meruit, cum philosophie nomen, quod primus invenerat, summo studio atque ingenio exornasset.   14.2

Sed quid ago? Non multo facilius Ciclades omnes quam celi stellas enumerem. Per has ergo navigans et procul a tergo linquens illa duo Grecie lumina, Lacedemonem et Athenas, ad levam vero Hellesponti fauces Sextonque et Abidon, infaustis amo-

ribus notas. et Bizannon atqz Ylion illuð e
emulatione romani impij. hoc propzijs famo
sum malis. recto tramite Rhoduz petes. oliz soli
nunc xpo uerius scilicet soli sacram. et milite
domicilui Iohis. ¶ Iam hinc Asia minoz
ao leuam iacet. olim prouinciarii mitissima
post Troie ruinam grecis referta cultozibz.nuc
turchozu uen hostiu ferox regio. Hui'ptes ao
austrii uerse et itineri tuo pxime sunt Licia
atqz Cilicia.et caput regionis Isauria. arx
olim oium piratarii. qui sumis tunc uiribus
maria cuncta puasant. ita ut ipis qz romans
classibus apta acie oecertarent. Suma tame
Pompeij magni uirtute ac prouincetia supati
abductiqz maritimis latrocinijs. et terre culti
bz restituit. ac nequa uncp occasio illos ao co
sueta retraherett a conspectu maris procul ab
stracti sunt. ex his inter ceteras Lauoensem
coloniam patrie tue pzoxima constare. et oe
Pompei lauoibus sumptu nom traoitur. q
quioem no tantuz a mari sed a fluminibus
etiam longe erat oonec nup euersa ou resur
geret. ut sibi casus ao aliquio pfuisse uioe

f. 13v

---

ribus notas, et Bizantion atque Ylion, illud e emulatione romani imperii, hoc propriis famosum malis, recto tramite Rhodum petes, olim Soli, nunc Christo, verius scilicet soli, sacram et militie domicilium Iohannis.　　　　　　　　　　14.3

¶ Iam hinc Asia minor ad levam iacet, olim provintiarum mitissima, post Troie ruinam Grecis referta cultoribus, nunc Turchorum veri hostium ferox regio. Huius partes, ad austrum verse et itineri tuo proxime, sunt Licia atque Cilicia et caput regionis Isauria, arx olim omnium

and Byzantium and Troy, the first illustrious for its rivalry[136] with the Roman empire, the second for its own troubles, and on a straight path you will head for Rhodes, once devoted to the Sun and now to Christ, that is to say, to the true sun, and home to the militia of John.[137]

¶ At this point, Asia Minor already stretches out on the left side, once an extremely peaceful province, populated by Greek colonies after the fall of Troy, now instead a ferocious country in the hands of the Turk, enemies of the truth.[138] Parts of this region facing south and near to your route include Licia, Cilicia, and the capital of the region Isauria, once the stronghold of all the pirate bands who, with most powerful forces, had infested the seas, even to the point of openly engaging Roman fleets. They were defeated by the virtue and foresight of Pompey the Great and thereafter forceably dissuaded from maritime thievery and limited to the cultivation of the soil; and so that there would never be the least chance that they might return to their usual ways, they were relocated to places far from the sea.[139] To them among others we owe the construction of the colony Lodi, which is near your fatherland and which is said to have taken its name in "laud" or praise of Pompey. This city was not only far from the sea but also from any river, until, recently destroyed, it was rebuilt, and so that misfortune might lead to something more favorable,

piratarum, qui summis tunc viribus maria cuncta pervaserant, ita ut ipsis quoque Romanis classibus aperta acie decertarent. Summa tamen Pompeii magni virtute ac providentia superati abductique maritimis latrociniis, et terre cultibus restituti, ac ne qua unquam occasio illos ad consueta retraheret, a conspectu maris procul abstracti sunt. Ex his inter ceteras Laudensem coloniam, patrie tue proximam, constare, et de Pompei laudibus sumptum nomen traditur. Que quidem non tantum a mari, sed a fluminibus etiam longe erat, donec nuper eversa, dum resurgeret, ut sibi casus ad aliquid profuisse vide-

retur translatis sedibus ripam pulcerrimi amnis
obtinuit. Sed nondum tempus est in patriam redeu~
di. Ad ea que restant procedam. Ante Cilicie
fronte Ciprus e~. terra nulla re alia q~ inertia ac
delitiis nota. quaru~ merito Veneri sacra~ dixere et
nunc q~ Veneri magis q~ Marti seu Palladi sa
cra est. Raro ibi seu nuq~ uir aliquis clarus fuit.
Neq~ eni~ in molli agro uoluptatis uirtutum
rigida semina coalescunt. libidinem incolar~
terre celiq~ feruor indicat. cum enim regioes
tractu maximo soli uiciniores grata temperie
pfruantur. hec ppe contra natura~ intolerandis
ardorib~ estuat. quasi hoium complexio ad
elementa transierit. Noli ibi multu~ imorari.
non e~ enim militaris certe neq~ uirilis hita
tio. fastus gallicus. syria mollicies. grece blan
ditie ac fraudes una in insulam conuene~. Quod
optimu~ ac preciosissimu~ h~nt illic dissimilli
mis moribus aluntur ueniens iacet Hilarion.
Contra Ciprii~ in extremo maris angulo mi
nor latet Armenia. cui tergu~ puppis obuertes
in dextru~ latus agenda e~. ¶ Sed iam qua
si tecu~ piculi fastidiiq~ princeps ad triam pue

its site was transferred to the banks of a most beautiful river.[140]
But it is not yet time to return home. Let's move on to what
remains.

15.0

In front of Cilicia is Cyprus, a land noted only for leisure and
luxury, and rightly was it called sacred to Venus and even now it is
more sacred to Venus than to Mars or to Minerva.[141] Rarely, if ever,
has it produced an illustrious man, since the sober seeds of virtue
do not grow in the soft fields of pleasure. The heat of the soil and
the sky point to the lustfulness of the inhabitants. In fact, while
regions that are closer to the sun along its longest course can
enjoy a temperate climate, this one boils almost unnaturally with
unbearable heat, just as if the constitution of the inhabitants had
been transferred to the elements. Don't stop there long. It is not
the place for a soldier or even a virile man. There Gallic
extravagance, Syrian ease, and the frauds and enticements of the
Greeks are brought together in a single island. What they do have
there that is very prestigious and precious is the tomb of Hilarion,
who came from another place with different customs.[142]

15.1

Opposite Cyprus, in the farthest corner of the sea is hidden Lesser
Armenia,[143] and turning the back of the ship it will be necessary to
come alongside it from the right.

15.2

⁋ But by now, as if I shared with you in the danger and the
difficulty, I am happy we have reached land.

---

immorari. Non est enim militaris certe neque virilis habitatio: fastus Gallicus, Syra mollities,
Grece blanditie ac fraudes unam in insulam convenere. Quod optimum ac preciosissimum
habent illic, dissimillimis moribus aliunde veniens, iacet Hilarion.   15.1

Contra Cyprum, in extremo maris angulo, minor latet Armenia, cui tergum puppis obvertens
in dextrum latus agenda est.   15.2

⁋ Sed iam, quasi tecum periculi fastidiique particeps, ad terram perve-

nisse gaudeo. In quam ubi descensurus sis ne
scio. neque enim unius tantum portus patet acces
sui. Magistri sententia. comitum consensus. uent
mare. dies. locus. opportunitas quid te agere
oporteat ad dicent. nam ut antiquo puerbio
monemur consilia capiunt ex tempore. Sunt aut
in littore illo ut ab aquilone in austru descenda
maritima opproa. Tortosa. Tripolis. Barut. Sur.
Cesarea. Iaffa. Ascalon. Horumque in medio no
bilis olim nunc euersa et in cinerem uersa iacet
Acon. summum et inexpiabile dedecus. ac tpis
sima cicatrix xpianorum regum. nisi aliquanto i
turpior esset ipsa Ierusalem. Sane si altius desce
das io habebis amplius. ut uideas caput Sy
rie damascu. sic enim uocant eam no qcuiqz
cosmographus. sed clarissim ppharum Vsaias.
quis non ignore apud alios Antiochia Sirie
primam ac metropolim hn. Cui sententie acce
dit Egesippus libro. uii. hystoriarum Iosephum
secutus. Aliquanto tame nobilior ut puto et
certe multo uetustior e Damascus. Videbis ci
uitate et forma spectabile et etate. de q quem
ab ipsis temporibus regu Israel multis seculis

nisse gaudeo. In quam ubi descensurus sis nescio, neque enim unus tantum portus patet
accessui. Magistri sententia, comitum consensus, ventus, mare, dies, locus, opportunitas quid
te agere oporteat dicent. Nam ut antiquo proverbio monemur: "Consilia capiuntur ex
tempore." Sunt autem in littore illo, ut ab aquilone in austrum descendam, maritima oppida
Tortosa, Tripolis, Barut, Sur, Cesarea, Iaffa, Ascalon, horumque in medio nobilis olim, nunc
eversa et in cinerem versa iacet Acon, summum et inexpiabile dedecus ac turpissima cicatrix
Cristianorum regum, nisi aliquanto turpior esset ipsa Ierusalem.   16.0

I don't know where you will disembark since there are many ports available. The opinion of the commander, the consensus of companions, the winds, the sea, the days, the place and opportunity will tell you what is best to do. To say it with an ancient proverb: "decisions are made in accordance with the times."[144] On that shore descending north to south are the coastal cities of Tortosa, Tripoli, Beirut, Tyre,[145] Caesarea, Jaffa, Ascalona, and, in the middle of them, one that was once noble and is now leveled to its foundations and burned, Acre, the greatest and unpardonable dishonor and shameful scar of the Christian kings, if that of Jerusalem herself were not more shameful.[146]

16.0

If you take land farther north, you will see Damascus, the capital of Syria. This title is given it not by any common cosmographer but by the great prophet Isaiah.[147] Although I am aware of the fact that for others the most important center of Syria is Antioch, an opinion shared also by Hegesippus in the third book of his *Histories,* following the lead of Flavius Josephus,[148] I nevertheless believe that Damascus is more illustrious and also much more ancient. You will see a city noteworthy for its aspect and its antiquity, often mentioned in both sacred and profane literature, already from the times of the Kings of Israel, many centuries before the foundation of Rome.

16.1

Sane si altius descendas, id habebis amplius ut videas caput Syrie Damascum. Sic enim vocant eam non quicumque cosmographus sed clarissimus prophetarum Ysaias. Quamvis non ignorem apud alios Antiochiam Sirie primam ac metropolim haberi, cui sententie accedit Egesippus, libro tertio Hystoriarum, Iosephum secutus, aliquanto tamen nobilior, ut puto, et certe multo vetustior est Damascus. Videbis civitatem et forma spectabilem et etate, de qua quidem ab ipsis temporibus regum Israel, multis seculis

ante urbem conditam crebra in utrisqɜ literis ɩ
sacris ac secularibɜ est mentio. Sin infra mag̃
applicueris . quantu spectaculo defuerit tantu
demitur labori . minus tr̃estri calle lassaberis .
q̃ in t̃iam egresso uicina Ierosolima e itineris
propositicɜ tui t̃minus. Itacɜ tametsi multar̃
in medio querenda et uisenda monstrauerim.
que potas improuisus forte soliicɜ uie finem
cogitas preterire / hic quid te moneaɜ non h̃eo.
Omnia enim iam hinc an q̃ pedem domo mo
ueas preconcepta aĩo et diu agitata sut tibi.
quoniaɜ finis reru ut phylosophis placet fic
in execut̃one ultimus / fic in intent̃oe primus e.
Necɜ uero tu aliam ob causam tituu laboris
ac negotii suscepisti . nisi ut ɩ illa morte domini.
sacra urbe . locisɜ finitimis uiderefoculis que
aĩo iam uidebas. Amneɜ scilicet quo lot̃ e xp̃c.
templu / seu templi ruinas . in quo docuit . loci
u fiima cum humilitate passus e corpore ut ɩ
nos an passionibɜ libaret. Sepulcru ubi sacrati
fimuɜ illud corpus substitit / du ille mortis et
inferni uictor . ad regna hostis spolianda desce
deret . unde et̃a reuisus idem corpɜ ia imortale

ante urbem conditam, crebra in utrisque literis sacris ac secularibus est mentio. **16.1**

[Sin: Si] infra magis applicueris, quantum spectaculo defuerit, tantum demitur labori, minus terrestri calle lassaberis, quod in terram egresso vicina Ierosolima est, itineris propositie tui terminus. Itaque tametsi multa tibi in medio querenda et visenda monstraverim, que poteras improvisus forte solumque vie finem cogitans preterire, hic quid te moneam non habeo. Omnia enim iam hinc ante quam pedem domo moveas, preconcepta animo et diu agitata sunt tibi, quoniam finis rerum, ut phylosophis placet, sicut in executione ultimus sic in intentione primus est. **16.2**

If you land farther to the south, you will avoid many difficulties but you will also miss a great many sights; the journey by land will be less trying, however, since Jerusalem, the destination of your journey and of your desire, will be close to the point of disembarkation. In fact, although I have shown you many things to look for and visit along the way that you can perhaps pass over, thinking only of the goal of the journey, here I have no counsel to give you. In fact, already before setting out from home you had considered and frequented every place within your soul, since the end of all things, as the philosophers maintain, is last to be performed but the first to be conceived.[149]

16.2

And you would not have undertaken such an arduous labor for any other reason than to see with your own eyes in that city made sacred by the death of the Lord and in the places nearby the things that you have already seen with your mind:[150] that is to say, the river in which Christ was baptized, the temple (or better, its ruins) in which he taught, the place where he with the highest humility suffered in body in order to free us from the perturbations of our souls, the tomb where that sacred body was placed while he descended to raid the realms of the enemy, that conqueror of death and the underworld, from which he returned and took again the already immortal body and while the guards were pressed by heavy sleep rose from the dead.

16.3

Neque vero tu aliam ob causam tantum laboris ac negotii suscepisti, nisi ut in illa morte Domini sacra urbe locisque finitimis videres oculis que animo iam videbas: amnem scilicet quo lotus est Christus, templum seu templi ruinas in quo docuit, locum ubi summa cum humilitate passus est corpore ut nos animi passionibus liberaret, sepulcrum ubi sacratissimum illud corpus substitit, dum ille mortis et inferni victor ad regna hostis spolianda descenderet, unde etiam reversus idem corpusque iam immortale

recipiens pressis gravi sopore custodibus resurrexit.
Syon preterea . et Oliueti montes . Ad hec et i
unde in celum ascendit . quo ad iudicium reuer
surus creditur. Vbi uentis et fluctibus imparauit.
Vbi cibo exiguo maximam turbam pauit. Vbi i
aquam uertit in uinum . q licet magna conui
uantibus uiderentur facilia erant illi . qui cibu
et uinum et aquam et ipsos de nichilo creauiat
conuiuantes. Vbi deniq elegit indoctos atq i
inopes piscatores quorum hamis ac retibus pi
scaretur imparatores ac reges gentium. Vbi egros
curauit. cecos illuminauit. leprosos mundauit.
paraliticos erexit. mortuos suscitauit. quatri
duanos iam fetentes ubo uiuos exiuit e sepleto.
Qoq his omnibus maius eet nisi qz omnia eque
facilia sunt deo demonibus ac peccatis oppssam
sepultam qz animam restituit libertati. Multa
et que psequi potius longui in q necessarium
ubi est. cui omnia ex euangelio nota sunt. Que
fixa mente cernetis p singulos passus deuota
aiam pius horror inuadet. Vnum qo elabi i
posset admoneo / uidere te urbem illam quaz
uicisse uictores gentiu romanorii tam clarui z

f. 15v

recipiens, pressis gravi sopore custodibus, resurrexit.   16.3

Syon preterea et Oliveti montem, ad hec et unde in celum ascendit, quo ad iudicium
reversurus creditur; ubi ventis et fluctibus imperavit, ubi cibo exiguo maximam turbam pavit,
ubi aquam vertit in vinum, que licet magna convivantibus viderentur, facilia erant illi qui
cibum et vinum et aquam et ipsos de nichilo creaverat convivantes, ubi denique elegit
indoctos atque inopes piscatores, quorum hamis ac retibus piscaretur imperatores ac reges
gentium; ubi [omitted in Vat. Lat. 3357: egros curavit] cecos illuminavit, leprosos mundavit,
paraliticos erexit, mortuos suscitavit, [omitted in Vat. Lat. 3357: quatriduanos iam fetentes

Then we come to Sion and the Mount of Olives, then also to the place from which he ascended to heaven and where it is believed he will return on the day of judgment,[151] where he stilled wind and water, where he fed an immense crowd with very little food, where he changed water to wine, things that while they appeared great to the banqueters, were easy for him who had created food, wine, water, and the banqueters themselves from nothing, where, finally, he chose uneducated and humble fishermen, to fish with their hooks and nets for emperors and kings among the gentiles, where he gave sight to the blind, cleansed the leprous, straightened the paralyzed, brought the dead back to life, and the greatest feat of all, if it were not for the fact that everything is equally easy for God, restored to liberty the soul oppressed and buried by demons and sins.

16.4

There are many other things that would be too long for me to enumerate, and would be unnecessary for you, who are familiar with everything through the Gospel, which is fixed in your mind as you look, while at each step a reverential awe invades your devout soul. I recall to you only one thing that might escape you: you are visiting a city whose conquest was believed by the Romans, conquerors of the world, to be so

verbo vivos eruit e sepulcro] quodque his omnibus maius esset, nisi quia omnia eque facilia sunt Deo, demonibus ac peccatis oppressam sepultamque animam restituit libertati.   16.4

Multa etiam que persequi potius longum michi quam [Vat. Lat. 3357 has: michi longissimum et nequaquam] necessarium tibi est, cui omnia ex Evangelio nota sunt, que fixa mente cernentis, per singulos passus devotam animam pius horror invadet. Unum quod elabi posset admoneo, videre te urbem illam, quam vicisse victores gentium [Romanorum: Romani] tam clarum

opus esse duxerunt .ut Titus tunc exercitus post
impy gubernator . in ipo ingressu menia urbis
admirans tantam uictoriam non humane uir
tutis sed diuine gratie fateret . 7 pfecto sic erat .
xpc ipe que erasisse de terra iuuentui exitimabt
aduersus suos hostes suis merito fauebat ulto
ribus . licet adhuc illis incognitus noscendus
tamen eorum successoribus et colendus . Itaq ei
sepe alias tum in ea uastatione precipue iple
tu e . qd ex psona eius in psalmo di . Resusci
ta me et retribuam eis . Ea hominu strages .
ea fames miseroru tam mesta necessitas . Que
si ex ordine nosse cupis Iosephu lege non
audita f uisa et comuia sibi cum ceais refente .
⁋ Quid uero nunc cogitas . An nondu te de
stderium nri cepit . ut domuz . ut patriaz . ut
amicos inuisere animus sit . Credo ego qdem
imo ne aliter fieri posse certus sum . Sz nullus
est acrior stimulus q uirtutis . ille nunc per
omnes difficultates geñosium auum impellit .
nec consistere patitur . nec retro respice . cogitq
non uoluptatu modo f honestoru pignoruz
atq affectuu obliuisci . nichil aliud q uirtutis

---

opus esse duxerunt, ut Titus, tunc exercitus post imperii gubernator, in ipso ingressu menia
urbis admirans, tantam victoriam non humane virtutis, sed divine gratie fateretur.   16.5

Et profecto sic erat. Christus ipse quem erasisse de terra viventium exitimabant, adversus suos
hostes suis merito favebat ultoribus, licet adhuc illis incognitus, noscendus tamen eorum
successoribus et colendus. Itaque, cum sepe alias, tum in ea vastatione precipue impletum est
quod ex persona eius in psalmo dicitur "resuscita me et retribuam eis." Ea hominum strages,
ea fames miserorum tam mesta necessitas, que si ex ordine nosse cupis, Iosephum lege, non
audita, sed visa et communia sibi cum ceteris referentem.   16.6

great an achievement that Titus, then commander of the army and later emperor, admiring its walls upon entering the city admitted that this victory was not by human virtue but by divine grace.[152]

16.5

And so it was that Christ himself, whom they believed they had canceled from the earth, justly helped the revengers against his killers, although he was as yet unknown to them and was instead destined to become known and worshiped by their successors.[153] Thus, what often happens, took place in the case of that particular destruction, that which is said of him in the psalm: "Raise me up that I may repay them."[154] The massacres of men, the starving of the poor were such a sad necessity that if you want to know about them in full detail, read Flavius Josephus, who recounts not things he only heard but what he witnessed and suffered together with the others.[155]

16.6

¶ But what are you thinking now? Hasn't the desire to see us again taken you yet; hasn't the desire to return to your home, your fatherland, and friends entered your soul yet? I believe so and am sure it could not be any other way. But there is no greater stimulus than virtue. Virtue inspires the generous soul to overcome every difficulty; it does not suffer one to remain in one place, nor that one should look back; it forces one to forget not only pleasures but also more just duties and affections; it does not allow one to choose anything but the ideal of virtue and it does not allow one to desire or think of anything else.

¶ Quid vero nunc cogitas? An nondum te desiderium nostri cepit, ut domum, ut patriam, ut amicos invisere animus sit? Credo id quidem, imo ne aliter fieri posse certus sum. Sed nullus est acrior stimulus quam virtutis. Ille nunc per omnes difficultates generosum animum impellit, nec consistere patitur, nec retro respicere cogitque non voluptatum modo, sed honestorum pignorum atque affectuum oblivisci, nichil aliud quam virtutis

spetiem optare, michil uelle, michil deniqz cogi
tare. hic stimulus qui Vlixem Laertis et Pe
nelopes et Thelemaci fecit imemoré te nunc
nobis uereo: abstrahet diutius qǒ uellemus.
Vitco tibi faciem eé longius euntis. nec im
merito. Vbi enim dimittes Bethleem ciuita
tem Dauid. quam celesti ortu claram fore / di
uini uates presago ore cecinerat ? Illic p̄ma
incunabula nr̄i regis aspiciens cogitab quā
tum deo grata fuerit semp humilitas. quā
in filij sui unigeniti primordijs euidentissie
consecrauit. Cogitabis ineffabilem Saluato
ris originé. qui ante principiu genitus in fi
ne temporu si ad etatum numeru attenditur
natus est. Virginem maré in presepio iacéré
contemplabé. Et diuinu infanté in cunis ua
gienté. Angelos ab ethere concinétes. Pasto
res attonitos stupentesqz. Reges alienigeas
cum muniǒ affusos. Indigenaz uero regem
gladio seuientem. terram innocuo sanguine t
beatorum infantiu et miserarū genitricū lacri
mis madenté. et mestis resonans celi omne
gemitibus. Inter hec monitu angelico scm

This is the stimulus that made Ulysses forget Laertes, Penelope, and Telemachus, and now keeps you far from us, I am afraid, longer than we should like.[156]

17.0

I see that you have the look of one who goes farther, and not unworthily. How can you leave out Bethlehem, city of David, which the sacred poets, foretelling the future, sang as destined to become famous for a heavenly birth? Looking at the cradle of our King, you will meditate upon how much humility has always been pleasing to God,[157] which he most evidently sanctified at the beginning of the life of his only son; you will meditate upon the ineffable origin of the savior, conceived before the beginning and born at the end of time, if one considers the measure of the ages.

17.1

You will contemplate the virgin mother lying in the manger and the divine child wailing in the cradle, the angels that sing in heaven, the stunned shepherds, the stupified foreign kings who prostrate themselves with gifts, while the king of that place raves with the sword, bathing the ground with the innocent blood of blessed babes and with the tears of despairing mothers, and all the heavens resounding with grieving cries.

17.2

Virginem matrem in presepio iacentem contemplabere et divinum infantem in cunis vagientem, angelos ab ethere concinentes, pastores attonitos stupentesque reges alienigenas, cum muneribus affusos, indigenam vero regem gladio sevientem, terram innocuo sanguine beatorum infantium et miserarum genitricum lacrimis madentem et mestis resonans celum omne gemitibus.   17.2

Inter hec, monitu angelico, sanctum

altorem cum intemerata matre celestique alumno clam ex ingrata patria in Egiptum ire tanto pignori tutas latebras querentem, iam tum gentibus [sepe: spe] iniecta, primogenito propter ingratitudinem abdicato, summi patris hereditatem ad minorem filium, hoc est ad populum gentium, esse venturam. 17.3

⫷ Sed tu quoque nunc, ut [auguor: auguror], Ioseph imo Mariam, imo Christum profugum sequi vis. Sacrum profecto teque dignum iter. Sequendus in terris querendusque nobis est Christus ut vel sic eum discamus ad celum sequi et ubi aliquando habitavit diu quesitum, tandem ubi habitat invenire. 18.0

Amidst these events, thanks to an angelic warning, the holy parent with the courageous mother and the heavenly son, by stealth, flee from the hostile homeland toward Egypt, seeking with so much sacrifice a safe hidden refuge, while hope had already been inspired in the gentiles, since, the first son having been disinherited because of his ingratitude, the inheritence of the highest father was to come down to the younger son, that is, to the people among the gentiles.[158]

17.3

¶ But you also now, I hope, will want to follow Joseph, Mary, and Christ in flight, surely a holy journey and one worthy of you. We must follow and search for Christ on earth so that we can, so to speak, learn to follow him to heaven, and having investigated where he lived for a long time, come to where he is now living.

18.0

Not far from here the Jordan flows into what is called the sea of Sodom where there are evident traces of burned down cities destroyed by celestial punishment.[159] The solitude of the desert is nearby.[160]

18.1

The journey is hard, I admit, but for one who is heading toward salvation, no road should seem difficult. Our enemy will set before you everywhere many difficulties, bothersome people and places to make you turn back on the path you have undertaken, or to delay you, or if he does not succeed in either of these, to make you less enthusiastic in your sacred pilgrimage. And besides these things, the enemy combines the natural dryness of the places and the lack of all necessities.

Iam vero non longe hinc, mare quod Sodomorum dicitur, Iordanis influit, ubi consumptarum urbium vindicteque celestis aperta vestigia apparent. His deserti solitudo proxima est.   18.1

Durum iter fateor, sed ad salutem tendenti nulla difficilis via videri debet. Multas ubique difficultates, multa tibi tedia vel hominum vel locorum hostis noster obiiciet, quibus te ab incepto vel retrahat vel retardet vel, si neutrum possit, saltem in sacra peregrinatione hac minus alacrem efficiat; hic vero preter cetera nativam locorum ingeret asperitatem penuriamque

rerum omnium. Sed meminisse conueniet omne
optimum magno precio constare. 7 uirgilianuz
illud in tuos usus transferre ut ait/uicit iter du
rum pietas. et illud Lucani paululu imutare
durum iter ad leges animecq ruentis amorem.
Nichil tam durum/qd uirtus ardens 7 pietas
intensa non molliat. Equidé si per Syrtes libi
cas et arenosa loca fpentiuz. M. Cato mite Ce
saris impuum fugisse laudatur/tu p desertum
non fugies/imite feroxcq uigu Sathane/per
qd tantus olim populus fugit seuitia Phara
onis. et qd senes ac pueri et muliercule potu
erunt/tu uir fortis ac uiuenis non poteris:
deus cum illis erat. et tecum erit. Isis autem
in locis legem datam Moysi. colloquuiz cum
deo habitum. uisioné rubi. delapsuz celo man
na. ceteras cq erga carum sz ingrati populum
duuinas blandutias ac diuina iudicia tecum
uolues. Incider forte cupiditas maris rubri
uidendi. qd proprie a poeta non mare sz littus
rubrum dictu est. non enim ab x aquis sz a co
lore littoris nom hec trahitur. Quo cum pueris
non odores indicos. et eoas merces ill'faucibz

Nevertheless, you should remember that the best things have a great price, and turn to your profit the saying of Virgil, "Devotion conquers a hard journey,"[161] and alter slightly that of Lucan, "Hard is the path to the law and of an enthusiastic soul toward love."[162] Nothing is so hard as not to be softened by ardent virtue and an intense piety.

18.2

Therefore if Cato is praised for having fled the mild dominion of Caesar,[163] crossing the Libyan Syrte and desert expanses full of serpents, will you not flee the cruel and fierce yoke of Satan by crossing the desert that such a great people crossed in order to flee the rage of the Pharaoh? And won't you, a strong man in his prime, be able to do what women and children were able to do? God was with them and he will be with you.[164]

18.3

Consider that in these places the law was dictated to Moses, and he spoke with God, and saw the bush burning, that manna was sent from heaven, among other divine aids and divine judgments that were addressed to a people dear to the Lord but ungrateful.

18.4

Perhaps the desire to see the Red Sea, that literally the poet does not call a sea but the Red Shore,[165] will come upon you. In fact, it does not take its name from the color of the water but from the color of the shore. When you arrive there, don't stand thinking of Indian spices and the merchandise of the East which is brought from there to Egypt and

His autem in locis legem datam Moysi, colloquium cum Deo habitum, visionem rubi, delapsum celo manna ceterasque erga carum, sed ingratum, populum divinas blanditias ac divina iudicia tecum volves.   18.4

Incidet forte cupiditas maris Rubri videndi, quod proprie a poeta non mare sed littus Rubrum dictum est: non enim ab aquis sed a colore littoris nomen hoc trahitur. Quo cum perveneris non odores Indicos et Eoas merces, illis faucibus

in Egiptum atque inde nostrum in mare convectas, sed populum Deo adiutum per medios
fluctus, sicco pede, transvectum meditabere. Illud enim humane cupiditatis et inopie, hoc
divine pietatis ac potentie est. 18.5

Hic Catherine Virginis corpus cernes, ubi angelicis manibus collocatum fertur, nec indignum
fuit, ut que pro lege Dei usque ad mortem decertaverat, in eo ipso monte requiesceret ubi lex
divinitus data erat. 18.6

Per hec loca formidabiles esse solent Arabum incursus, sitis, fames, labor. Sed nichil fere
periculosius errore vie, nullis indiciis ad rectum referentibus. Ideo vigilanter cave ne ulla te
necessitas seiungat a sociis. 18.7

then to our sea, but think of the people helped by God to pass there with dry feet amidst the waves. The former is the work of human cupidity and weakness, the second of piety and divine power.

18.5

Here you will see the body of St. Catherine, placed there, it is said, by the hands of angels, and it is not inappropriate that she who had fought to the death for God's law was buried on the same mountain where divine law was given.[166]

18.6

In these places the Saracen incursions are overwhelming, the drought, lack of food, and difficulties. But nothing is more dangerous than to lose one's way, since there are no points of reference to put one back upon the right road. Therefore be careful not to be separated from your companions for any reason.[167]

18.7

¶ By a difficult and uncertain path you have already come into Egypt. There, on the Nile you will see the New Babylon, the work of Cambyses and Cairo of Egypt, an immense and densely populated city, which reproduces ancient Babylon beyond the Euphrates and Assyrian Cairo.[168]

19.0

You will see the great border between Africa and Asia, opposite to the Tanaïs,[169] a large and stupefying river,[170] concerning which philosophers, poets and cosmographers have expressed divergent opinions (Aristotle dedicated an entire book to the problem);[171]

¶ Iam tandem in Egiptum laborioso et ancipiti calle perventum est. Ibi ergo supra Nilum videbis Babilonem novam, Cambissis opus, et Carras Egiptias, frequentissimam et immensam urbem, que Babilonem veterem ad Eufratem et Carras Assirias representant.   19.0

Spectabis insignem Asie atque Affrice limitem, adversum Thanai, flumen ingens stupendumque, de quo et phylosophi et poete et cosmographi multa sunt opinati (Aristotiles vero libro integro disseruit), flumen

et estuu mirabilis incrementi et in inundationis i
uberrime et infiniti aluei et fontis incogniti .cui
certitudine et egiptiozu . et persarum .7 Macedo
num reges . ad postremu romani quoqʒ impato
res / sʒ frustra omnes quesiere . fon´ hactenus i
gnozatus manet . opiniones atqʒ inquisitioēs
hominum . et hystozie de hoc scripte multa legē
tibus note sunt . Clarum qddam et relatu di
gnium qd ab illustribʒ uiris accepimus / locus
hic exigit . ferunt fontem esse plucidu illic ubi
ab Herodis rabie xpm occultabant . quem puer
omnipotens e terra arida in refrigeriu anxie
matris eduxerit . ex illo xpianos iocundissime
bibere . farracenis absintio amarioze esse . ita ut
degustare illum uel sumis labijs pena sit . nros
qʒ inde tam cupide haurientes / ceu monstrum
aliqd romuentur . Nec sane magnu fuit illi q
fontem fecit . eide quoqʒ quas uoluit leges dare .
et pro uarietate bibentiuʒ ficei uarii saporem
aquis immittere . ⸿ Nil iam restat memozabile .
qd quidem modo meminerim prter Alexandri
am . Alexandri opus . Alexandri nomi . Alexdri
busti . Ad qd Iulius Cesar post thesalicu diem

f. 18v

et estivi mirabilis incrementi et inundationis uberrime et infiniti alvei et fontis incogniti, cuius
certitudinem et Egiptiorum et Persarum et Macedonum reges, ad postremum Romani quoque
imperatores, sed frustra omnes, quesiere. Fons hactenus ignoratus manet, opiniones atque
inquisitiones hominum et hystorie de hoc scripte multa legentibus note sunt.   19.1

Clarum quiddam et relatu dignum, quod ab illustribus viris accepimus, locus hic exigit. Ferunt
fontem esse perlucidum illic ubi ab Herodis rabie Christum occultabant, quem puer
omnipotens e terra arida in refrigerium anxie matris eduxerit. Ex illo Christianos iocundissime

it is a river with an extraordinary high water mark in the summer, very fertilizing floods, an endless river bed, and an unknown source that Egyptian, Persian, and Macedonian kings and finally even Roman emperors sought to discover but all in vain. The source remains still today unknown and the well-read will know the numerous hypotheses, expeditions, and narrations regarding the problem.

19.1

This place requires that a famous detail worth telling be told here, which I have learned from illustrious persons. They hold that the purest source is there where Christ was hidden from Herod's fury, and that the omnipotent child made it flow from the arid soil in order to refresh his tired mother. It is said that the Christians drink very well from it but it is more bitter than absinthe to the Saracens. Therefore, tasting it, even just with the tip of their lips, is like a very hard punishment for them, and they watch marveling, as if it were a miracle, our fellow Christians who drink of it so thirstily. It was not an extraordinary thing for him who caused the fount to flow, to arrange things as he'd wished and to give to the water a flavor differing according to the variety of the religious beliefs of those who drink it.[172]

19.2

❡ Little remains worth recalling besides Alexandria: the creation of Alexander that bears Alexander's name and the tomb of Alexander.[173] When Julius Caesar arrived

bibere, Sarracenis absintio amariorem esse, ita ut degustare illum vel summis labiis pena sit nostrosque inde tam cupide haurientes ceu monstrum aliquod admirentur. Nec sane magnum fuit illi qui fontem fecit, eidem quoque quas voluit leges dare et pro varietate bibentium fidei varium saporem aquis immittere.   19.2

❡ Nil iam restat memorabile quod quidem modo meminerim, preter Alexandriam, Alexandri opus, Alexandri nomen, Alexandri bustum. Ad quod Iulius Cesar, post Thesalicum diem mortemque Pompeii, cum Alexandriam venisset, ambigue turbati vulgi murmure permotus, per speciem religionis descendisse legitur.   20.0

Et Augustus Cesar, post victoriam Acciacam Antoniumque devictum et coactum mori, eodem veniens, Alexandri corpus reverenter aspexit cumque ex eo quereretur an et Ptolomeum vellet aspicere, elegantissime regem ait se videre non mortuos. Cui dicto illa procul dubio sententia inest, virtute animi et rerum gloria non regno, non sceptro, non Dyademate regem fieri.   20.1

Hoc tu dictum eatenus inflectes, ut sanctos cupias spectare, non mortuos. Quia tamen vetustas et fama clarorum hominum non sine quibusdam facibus animos tangunt, poteris et

there, after the battles in Thessaly and the death of Pompey, shaken by the ambiguous murmurings of the turbulent population, one reads that he entered that city almost as if rendering religious devotion.[174]

20.0

And Augustus Caesar, after the victory of Actium and the defeat and forced suicide of Antony, after arriving there, visited reverently the tomb of Alexander. And when he was asked if he wanted also to see King Ptolemy, he elegantly answered that he wanted to see a king and not the dead. And in this answer is contained the saying: "A king is made by the courage of character and by the glory of his deeds, not by a kingdom, a scepter and a crown." [175]

20.1

Adopt this as your own motto, and desire to see the saints and not dead men. Since the ancient fame of illustrious men never fails to touch the soul without being a stimulus, you too will be able to admire this tomb, if it has not been overcome by time, and also the urn which contains the ashes of Pompey.[176] Alexander is called the Great by Greek writers, as is Pompey by the Latin writers (the French apply this appellation to their Charles).[177] One city holds those two: the one sent from the north, the other from the west; the one from Pella, the other from Rome.[178]

20.2

You will see where, engaged and surrounded by iniquitous Mars, Caesar succeeded in accomplishing those magnificent and nearly incredible deeds. You will see the Pharos from which the term *pharos* spread itself to other lands.[179]

hoc bustum, si nondum senio cesserit, spectare, nec minus urnam que Pompei cinerum ostenditur. Illum enim Greci, hunc Romani scriptores magnum vocant (Galli autem hoc cognomen ad suum Karolum transtulere). Illos duos habet una urbs, quorum alterum Arthos, alterum miserat Occidens; illum Pelles, hunc Roma.   20.2

Videbis ubi iniquo Marte preventus et circumventus illa magnalia et vix credibilia gessit Cesar. Videbis Pharum, unde hoc 'phari'

nomen per alias terras usq̃quaq̃ diffusuȝ e.
Spectabis multifidas Hili faces. ubi fortuna
ppli ro. truncum sui ducis et lacerii cadauer ꝑ
absasumq̃ trunco caput flens uictor aspexit.
Sic cum genero partitus orbem ut illi Nilus.
Tybris hunc abluat. O fortune fides. o reruȝ
finis humanarii. certe ut es ingenio prompt̃
ac docilis / facile tantis ac talibus magistris ꝑ
quantii prosperis sit fidendũ disces / perpetuoq̃
memineris. ⸿ Sed iam satis iui. satis est ꝑ
scriptum. hactenus tu remis ac pedibus maria
et terras / ego hanc papirũ / calamo ꝓp̃te sulcariȝ.
et an adhuc tu fessus sis eundo / certe ego iaȝ
scribendo fatigatus sum. eoq̃ magis quo ce
lerius incessi. Qõ enim iter tu tribus forte
uix mensibus / hoc ego triduo consũmaui. h
utriq̃ igit̃ uie modus sit. Tibi domũ / michi
ad mea studia redeundũ e. qõ ego confestiȝ
fecero. tibi uero plusculuȝ negotij supest / per
agendum xp̃i ope feliciter. His spectaculis
et hoc duce / doctior nobis ac sanctior remea
bis. Explicit itinerariuȝ Francisci Petrarce ꝑ
laureati extractũ ab originali manu sua sᵉpto.

---

nomen per alias terras usquequaque diffusum est. Spectabis multifidas Nili [faces: fauces],
ubi fortuna populi Romani truncum sui ducis et lacerum cadaver abscisumque trunco caput
flens victor aspexit, sic cum genero partitus orbem, ut illum Nilus, Tybris hunc abluat. O
fortune fides, o rerum finis humanarum!   20.3

Certe, ut es ingenio promptus ac docilis, facile, tantis ac talibus magistris, quantum prosperis
sit fidendum disces perpetuoque memineris.   20.4

⸿ Sed iam satis itum, satis est scriptum. Hactenus tu remis ac pedibus maria et terras, ego
hanc papirum calamo properante sulcaverim, et an adhuc tu fessus sis eundo, certe ego iam

You will admire the delta of the Nile with its many branches, where the destiny of the Roman people looked upon the shredded and decapitated body of its commander, and the victor weeping viewed the head separated from its trunk, and thus he divided the dominion with his son-in-law, so that the Nile would bathe that one and the Tiber this one. Oh faithless fortune, oh end of human actions![180]

20.3

Surely, since you are of quick and receptive intelligence, you will easily learn from so many and such great teachers how little one has to trust a favorable state of affairs, and you will remember forever.[181]

20.4

¶ But we have already traveled far enough, and enough has been written. You have come this far by oars and by foot on sea and on land: I, plowing this paper with a swift pen. I don't know if you are at this point tired of traveling; certainly I am tired of writing, especially since I have advanced at greater speed. Your journey of three months I have completed in three days.

21.0

And here be the end of the road for both of us. You must return home while I to my studies. What I have done at great speed, it remains for you to accomplish with a little bit more effort, happily with the help of Christ. After you have seen these sights, with his guidance, you will return to us more wise and more holy.

21.1

Here ends the itinerary of the poet laureate Francis Petrarch, taken down from the original in his hand.

scribendo fatigatus sum eoque magis quo celerius incessi. Quod enim iter tu tribus forte vix mensibus, hoc ego triduo consummavi. 21.0

Hic utrique igitur vie modus sit. Tibi domum, michi ad mea studia redeundum est. Quod ego confestim fecero, tibi vero plusculum negotii superest peragendum Christi ope feliciter. His spectaculis et hoc duce, doctior nobis ac sanctior remeabis. 21.1

Explicit itinerarium Francisci Petrarce Laureati extractum ab originali manu sua scripto.

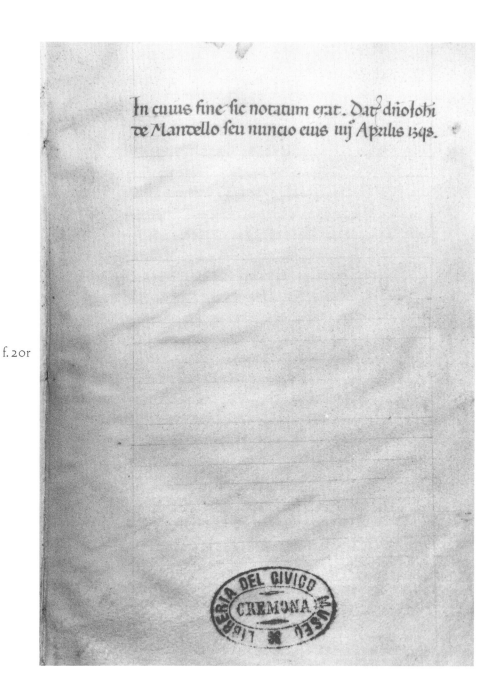

In cuius fine sic notatum erat. Dat͡ dñoſohi ꝛe Manꝺello ſeu nuncio eius iiij Aprilis 1398.

f. 20r

In cuius fine sic notatum erat. Datus domino Iohanni de Mandello seu nuncio eius iiiiº Aprilis 13[4:5]8

At the end of which it was noted: Given to Lord Giovanni Mandelli or his messenger 4 April 1358.

NOTES TO THE TEXT AND TRANSLATION

1. The connection between this opening reflection on the power of Fortune and Petrarch's refusal to join Giovanni Mandelli on a pilgrimage to the Holy Land is made explicitly at *Itin.* Pr. 6: "Fortune begrudges that I should be a member of your group." Cf. *Fam.* 9.8 "To Giovanni da Burnio, attorney": "From our youth to the present time, fortune has begrudged me your face" (Francis Petrarch, *Letters on Familiar Matters, Rerum Familiarium Libri,* trans. Aldo S. Bernardo, 3 vols.: vol. 1, *Fam.* 1–8 [Albany: State University of New York Press, 1975]; vol. 2, *Fam.* 9–16 [Baltimore: Johns Hopkins University Press, 1982] vol. 3, *Fam.* 17–24 [Baltimore: Johns Hopkins University Press, 1985]; quotation here is from vol. 2, p. 26). Cf. also *Fam.* 7.11: "believe me, as I was saying it is fortune that decides the plans of men. Between planning and doing, as the multitude says, there is a high mountain of difference" (*Letters on Familiar Matters,* vol. 1, p. 359). But see *Sen.* 8.3, where despite widespread usage of the name *Fortune,* including by Petrarch in his own writings: "I frankly confess, nor do I fear the taunt of being called an ignoramus, to believing that there is no such thing." In fact, Petrarch claims in this letter not to have written in his *De Remediis* about Fortune but rather "about remedies against what is called Fortune" (*Letters of Old Age, Rerum Senilium Libri,* trans. Aldo S. Berbardo, Saul Levin, and Reta A. Bernardo [Baltimore: Johns Hopkins University Press, 1992], vol. 1, p. 286).

   Indeed, the theme of Fortune had particularly engaged Petrarch during the period leading up to the composition of the *Itinerarium* in 1358. He began work on the *De Remediis Utriusque Fortune* in Milan in 1354 and a first draft was finished toward the end of 1360 (Ugo Dotti, *Vita di Petrarca* [Bari: Laterza, 1992], pp. 293–301). See *Petrarch's Remedies for Fortune Fair and Foul,* trans. Conrad H. Rawski, 5 vols. (Bloomington: Indiana University Press, 1991). For discussion about the dating of the *De Remediis,* see K. Heitmann, "La genesi del *De Remediis Utriusque Fortune* del Petrarca," *Convivium* 25 (1957), pp. 9–30; and the objections of Ernest Hatch Wilkins, *Petrarch's Eight Years in Milan* (Cambridge: Medieval Academy of America, 1958), pp. 69–72. For an analysis of the *De Remediis* and the treatment of the theme of Fortune, see K. Heitmann, *Fortuna und Virtus: Eine Studie zu Petrarcas Lebensweisheit* (Köln and Graz: Bohlau, 1958).

2. A. Paolella has suggested in his edition that this is a paraphrase of a passage from the Easter liturgical sequence *Victimae paschali laudes:* "Mors et vita duello conflixere mirando / dux vitae mortuus regnat vivus" (*Volgarizzamento meridionale anonimo di Francesco Petrarca* Itinerarium Breve de Ianua usque ad Ierusalem et Terram Sanctam, ed. Alfonso

Paolella [Bologna: Commissione per il Teste di Lingua, 1993], p. 118.) The echo corresponds neatly to the Easter season and context for the proposed pilgrimage and for the composition and delivery of the text between March and April 1358.

3.   Horace (Quintus Horatius Flaccus) *Satires* 1.6.57: "infans namque pudor prohibebat plura profari" (for infantile shame stopped me from saying more).

4.   For Petrarch's fear of the sea, see especially *Fam.* 5.5, to Giovanni Colonna, following the description of "a storm without equal" that Petrarch experienced during his second visit to Naples, 24 November 1343: "there is one thing I want to be certain does emerge: that is, I beseech you not ever again to order me to place my trust in winds and seas. This is something in which I would obey neither you, the Pope, or my own father if he were to return to life. I shall leave the air to the birds and the sea to the fish; as a terrestrial animal I shall prefer land trips. Send me where you will, even to the Indies, as long as my foot tramples the soil" (*Letters on Familiar Matters*, vol. 1, p. 247). Cf. *Petrarch's Remedies* 2.54, vol. 3, p. 128, *Gravi naufragio iactatus sum* (Serious shipwreck): Reason: "I cannot see why it should be more terrible to die in the sea than on land, since, indeed, you die in either case—or why it should be more desirable to become food for worms rather than for fish. Yet, as long as you swam out of it, be sure not to commit your life once again to a broken oar or a rotten plank. Learn, earthling, to stick to the land and to think about heaven rather than the sea." On where it is best to die and fear of dying abroad, see *Petrarch's Remedies* 2.125, *Morior extra patrios fines* (Death away from home). Cf. also *Fam.* 2.1.14–19, a consolatoria that treats the theme of facing death. On indifference toward the place of death, see *Petrarch's Remedies* 2.125.

5.   Beyond the generic polemic against luxury, the reference to "early death" when life "might perhaps have been prolonged by work and exercise" may more specifically suggest the deadly effects of the gout that plagued the rich and for which Petrarch recommended on more than one occasion the remedy of work and exercise. Cf. *Fam.* 6.3.43 and *Fam.* 3.13: "Therefore, if you wish to eliminate the gout, eliminate pleasures; if you wish to eliminate all bad things, eliminate wealth" (*Letters on Familiar Matters*, p. 150). Petrarch, in fact, had numerous patrons and friend who suffered from gout, among them Galeazzo Visconti, Emperor Charles IV, Giovanni Colonna di San Vito, Guido Sette, and, perhaps, Azzo da Correggio. See *Petrarch's Remedies* 2.84: *Turpi torqueor podagra* (Gout), and commentary, vol. 4, pp. 304–14. For the *contemptus mundi* theme, cf. *Fam.* 6.3.43, 13.4.20–24, and 21.13. 4.

6.   Cf. *Petrarch's Remedies* 2.117: *Mori timeo* (Fear of Dying), and commentary, vol. 4, pp. 460–75. Cf. *Sen.* 12.1: "In Cicero an excellent man jokes at the point of death" (*Letters of Old Age*, p. 438). On tranquility facing death, cf. *Fam.* 2.1.7–8, *Fam.* 23.21.8, and *Petrarch's Remedies* 2.117.

7.   Fame is usually described by Petrarch (after Boethius *De consolatione philosophiae* 2.7.23–26) as a "second" death insofar as it extends for a more or less brief period mortal life which, considered from a Christian perspective, represents in reality a "first" death; cf. *Africa* 2.431–32, *Secretum* 3.202, and *Triumphus Temporis* 142–45: "Chiamasi Fama, et è morir secondo" (Men call it Fame; 'tis but a second death) (Francis Petrarch, *Trionfi, rime estravaganti, codice degli abbozzi*, ed. Vinicio Pacca and Laura Paolino, introduction by Marco Santagata [Milano: Mondadori, 1996], pp. 503–4).

Michele Feo, "Un Ulisse in Terrasanta," *Rivista di cultura classica e medievale* 19 (1977), p. 384, noted in Petrarch's atypical use of "second death" here, in the sense of "damnation," an echo of Dante's "Ch' a la seconda morte ciascun grida" (*Inferno* 1.117: Each of whom proclaims the second death). The phrase was often used in this sense by theologians (cf. Revelations 21.8—"the lake which burneth with fire and brimstone: which is the second death"—and Rev. 20.14). Cf. Dante *Epistola* 6.2 (*Tutte le opere*, ed. Luigi Blasucci [Firenze: Sansoni, 1981]), p. 327: "Vos autem divina iura et humana transgredientes ..., Nonne terror secunde mortis exagitat?" (And you who transgress human and divine laws . . . does not the terror of the second death [damnation] torment you?).

8. Fear of stormy seas represents an important theme of Petrarch's life and writings. His experience of sea tempests, according to *Fam.* 1.1, went as far back as to when he was seven years old and his exiled father embarked with the family in Pisa for a journey to the south of France and Avignon: "We were almost shipwrecked by winter winds not far from Marseilles and once again I was not very far from being denied a new life on its very threshold" (*Letters on Familiar Matters*, vol. 1, p. 8). A second experience of storm at sea was during Petrarch's first journey to Rome at the end of 1336, memorialized by *Fam.* 4.6, addressed to Giacomo Colonna, who was in Rome: "As you saw, I finally came to you despite the rigors of winter, of the sea, and of war. Love does indeed overcome all difficulties, and as Maro says, 'devotion conquered the difficult journey.' While my eyes sought their venerable and delightful object, my stomach felt no disturbance from the sea (although naturally very impatient about the uncomfortable condition), the body felt no rigor of winter or of the land, and the mind felt no threats of danger" (*Letters on Familiar Matters*, vol. 1, p. 191). This same storm is evoked in *Epyst.* 1.6.64–66 (also addressed to Giacomo Colonna) and in the triptych of sonnets treating this journey, *RVF* 67–68 (in particular 67.2 and 68.10). For these fragments of the poet's *cahier de voyage*, see Rosanna Bettarini, *Lacrime e inchiostro nel* Canzoniere di Petrarca (Bologna: CLUEB, 1998), pp. 145–50; and Paolo Cherchi, "Il sonetto LXVII," *Lectura Petrarce* 11 (1991), pp. 237–58. Another storm at sea that found its way into Petrarch's prose and poetic memorializations of the travels of his youth occured during his embassy to Naples in 1343 on behalf of Cardinal Giovanni Colonna. He reports in *Fam.* 5.3 that he boarded a ship in Nice: "The next day we raised anchor in a dangerous storm, and after being tossed about for the entire day by large waves, we arrived at the port of Moritz during the stormy night" (*Letters on Familiar Matters*, vol. 1, p. 232). From there he elected to continue his journey by foot (cf. also *Epyst.* 2.15.1–5, 19–24). Attilio Hortis, *Scritti inediti di Francesco Petrarca* (Trieste: Tipografia del Lloyd Austro-Ungarico, 1874), includes some prayers against tempests attributed to Petrarch (pp. 294–98 and 367–68). For the connection between Petrarch's fear of the sea and the poetic theme of the tempest, see T. J. Cachey, Jr., "Peregrinus (quasi) ubique: Petrarca e la storia del viaggio," *Intersezioni: Rivista de storia delle idee* 27 (December 1997), pp. 369–84.

9. On Petrarch's passion for travel, see the letter to Andrea Dandolo, *Fam.* 15.4, "a justification for his frequent moves": "At present, like a man on a hard bed, I toss and turn, not finding the desired repose despite all attempts; and so, because I cannot relieve my weariness with a soft bed, I do so with constant change; and thus I wander and seem to be an eternal pilgrim" (*Letters on Familiar Matters*, vol. 1, p. 259). The idea that nature (or heaven)

has placed a bridle on Petrarch's immoderate desire to travel and to see the world also appears in *Dispersa* 69, addressed to Giovanni Mandelli; there Petrarch credits the wound he received from a codex of Cicero's, which limited the poet's mobility, with "making me aware of my condition and cooling my vagabond soul" (see above, Introduction, pp. 15–17). For a parallel situation, see Petrarch's discussion of Giovanni Colonna's gout in *Fam.* 6.3: "Examine, dear father, your journeys since your youth and your propensity not to stay still; you will see that like the bridle for the untamed horse a gout was required for you. Perhaps it ought to be required for me too so that I might now learn to stay in one place and settle down" (*Letters on Familiar Matters,* vol. 1, p. 309).

10. The phrase referring to Petrarch's fear of the sea ("and although I did not fear it so when younger [although I always feared it] the fear has increased as I have grown older") is a late authorial variant from the 1360s, according to Michele Feo, "which is explained psychologically as a reflection in which Petrarch focuses on the space of time that has passed between 1358 and the present moment: at that time he had recognized his fear of the sea; now, if he considers the time which has passed, he can see that his fear has not diminished but only increased with age" ("Inquietudini filologiche del Petrarca: Il luogo della discesca agli inferi [storia una citazione]," *Italia medioevale e umanistica* 27 [1974], p. 183).

11. According to Paolella, *Volgarizzamento meridionale anonimo,* p. 119, this phrase is probably on the model of Tibullus's elegy 1.3.1: "Ibitis Aegaeas sine me, Messalla, per undas." But for Petrarch's knowledge of Tibullus, see B. L. Ullman, "Petrarch's Acquaintance with Catullus, Tibullus, Propertius," in *Studies in the Italian Renaissance* (Roma: Edizioni di Storia e Letteratura, 1955), pp. 181–200: "On the question of Petrarch's acquaintance with Tibullus there is far less evidence (than for Propertius). There are no direct quotations at all. Nolhac rejects various vague reminiscences that have been pointed out and almost concludes that Petrarch knew Tibullus only by name" (p. 192).

12. Marco Ariani notes that the *Itinerarium* "has the specific function of healing an absence according to the 'fashion of lovers' which is singularly evoked as presiding over the writing of the text itself. The humanistic faith in the erudite apparatus as a substitute for experience connects the *Itinerarium* to the imaginative world of the *amor de lonh* upon which Petrarch was constructing, precisely in those years, the book of lyric fragments, as the sign of a philology that was perfectly capable of constituting complete universes of sense independent of any obligation or correspondence with empirical reality" ("Petrarca," in *Storia della letteratura italiana,* ed. Enrico Malato [Roma: Salerno Editrice, 1995], vol. 2, pp. 632–33). Perhaps the most famous example of Petrarch's construction of an image of the desired other as a means of consolation was his commissioning of Laura's portrait by Simone Martini. See the sonnets he dedicated to this theme, *RVF* 77 and 78; and see Giuseppe Mazzotta, "Antiquity and the New Arts," *The Worlds of Petrarch* (Durham: Duke University Press, 1993), pp. 14–32.

13. Petrarch alludes to a work that will be a true portrait of himself in similar terms in *Fam.* 1.1.37: "That other work I have been polishing with great care, though not a Phidean Minerva, as Cicero asserts, but a true portrait and likeness such as it is of my talent [sed qualemcunque animi mei effigiem atque ingenii simulacrum] if ever I shall be able to give it the last touches, that work, I say, when it reaches you, you may set up without con-

cern at the summit of whatever stronghold you please" (*Letters on Familiar Matters,* vol. 1, p. 11). See also the foreword to the *De Vita Solitaria:* "I shall set down but a few of the many thoughts that occur to me, but in these, as in a little mirror, you shall behold the entire disposition of my soul, the full countenance of a serene and tranquil mind" (*The Life of Solitude,* trans. Jacob Zeitlin [Urbana: University of Illinois Press, 1924], p. 102). Hans Baron, *Petrarch's* Secretum: *Its Making and Its Meaning* (Cambridge Mass.: Medieval Academy of America, 1985), pp. 14–15, argues that the work alluded to in *Fam.* 1.1 was the *De Vita Solitaria.* With respect to the implementation of this Petrarchan topos here in the *Itinerarium,* it is remarkable, from the point of view of the genre, that an itinerary or "description of places" (cf. *Itin.* 2.2) should also constitute a self-portrait of its author (see above, Introduction).

14. The citation is from Cicero's "Dream of Scipio," *De re publica* 6.24: "For it is not your outward form which constitutes your being, but your mind; not that substance which is palpable to the senses, but your spiritual nature."

15. Note the signature Petrarchan ambivalence, situated somewhere between coming and going—in this case, between departure and return.

16. Here Petrarch lays out the program for the work, in accordance with the character of the addressee Giovanni Mandelli, who was not only pious but well read, as evidenced by the text's many references to classical literature and Roman history (see, for example, the discussion of the vexed question concerning the death of Misenus at *Itin.* 9.3). Mandelli's primarily military-administrative role in the "army" of the Visconti (cf. *Fam.* 19.6) emerges from the historical record (see Introduction and Appendix 2).

17. The question presupposes an answer that is found in Virgil (Publius Vergilius Maro) *Eclogues* 10.69: "Omnia vincit Amor, et nos cedamus Amori" (Love conquers all; let us, too, yield to love).

18. Fourteenth-century itineraries to the Holy Land often included descriptions of places between the point of departure and the place of embarkation. See, for example, the "Pilgrimage of Lionardo di Niccolo Frescobaldi to the Holy Land" and the "Pilgrimage of Giorgio Gucci to the Holy Places," which include brief sections on the journey from Florence to Venice (*Visit to the Holy Places of Egypt, Sinai, Palestine, and Syria in 1384 by Frescobaldi, Gucci, and Sigoli,* trans. T. Bellorini and E. Hoade [Jerusalem: Franciscan Press, 1948], pp. 32–33 and 93).

19. Petrarch's first encounter with Genoa was as a boy during his family's transfer from Pisa to Carpentras in 1311 (see *Sen.* 10.2, to Guido Sette). He returned to Genoa at the end of November 1347 on the way to Rome to support Cola di Rienzo and wrote from there *Fam.* 7.13 informing Cola that he would not be continuing to Rome (for this trip, see also *Fam.* 7.5 and 7.10.4).

    Genoa and its coast are included among the tourist sites that Petrarch suggested he and his friends might enjoy together if they were to come to live with him in northern Italy (*Fam.* 8.5, to Olimpio [Luca Cristani]). In *Fam.* 14.5, written 1 November 1352 from Vaucluse and following the Genoese defeat of the Venetians in the Bosphorus (13 February 1352), Petrarch appealed to "the Doge and Council of Genoa for peace with the Venetians and civil harmony." Besides its political import the letter stresses the poet's personal affection and admiration for the city in a passage parallel to his treatment of Genoa in the *Itinerarium*: "I was then an infant, and I can remember, as if in a dream, when that shoreline of your gulf that looks both eastward and westward used to appear a heavenly and not an earthly dwelling, such as poets describe in the Elysian fields with their hilltops full of delightful pathways, green valleys, and blessed souls in the valleys. Who would not marvel from on high at the towers and palaces, and at nature so artfully subdued, at the stern hills covered with cedars, vines and olive trees, and under the high cliffs marble villas equal to any royal palace and worthy of any city? Who could behold without astonishment those delightful recesses where amidst the cliffs stood courtyards with gilded roofs? Resounding with the heavy waves of the sea and wet from stormy rains, these would attract seafarers' attention because of their beauty and would cause the sailor struck by the view's novelty to abandon his oar. When one finally arrived in your city, truly a regal city as it was said of Rome, one would think it was like entering the temple of happiness and the doorway to joy" (*Letters on Familiar Matters*, vol. 2, p. 241).

The departure point of Genoa for the pilgrimage projected by the *Itinerarium* is unusual. Venice was the normal point of embarkation for pilgrims to the Holy Land. Alfonso Paolella suggests that Petrarch's familiarity with Genoa and the Tyrrhenian coast may have motivated the selection of this route ("Petrarca e la letteratura odeporica del medioevo," *Studi e Problemi di Critica Testuale* 44 [1992], pp. 61–85).

20. For the epithet *superbam* ("proud" Genoa), cf. *Fam.* 14.5.6 and 17.3.22. For the civil strife of the Ligurians, cf. *Fam.* 15.7.6: "The seagoing Ligurians who dwell, as Florus attests between the Var and the Magra, whose capital was once Albenga and today is Genoa, are so managing their affairs and their time that, in accordance with their ancient custom, the end of a foreign war means the beginning of a civil one" (*Letters on Familiar Matters*, vol. 2, p. 268).

21. The two traditions explaining the name of Genoa that Petrarch appears to reject here are not unrelated, as Janus was the ancient Italic god of doors to houses and cities. For the name of Genoa "in ancient times," see Pliny *Naturalis historia* 3.48 and Pomponius Mela *De situ orbis* 2.72. Petrarch probably refers to the *Annali* of Caffarus (1080?-1163), begun in 1100 and continued after Caffarus's death by several other chroniclers. The *Annali* were eventually completed by Jacopo Doria in 1293. See *Annali genovesi di Caffaro e de' suoi continuatori dal MXCIX al MCCXCII*, 5 vols. (Genova: Fonti per la Storia d'Italia, 1890–1929).

22. For the form of the name Albenga, see Pomponius Mela *De situ orbis* 2.72, while Pliny *Naturalis historia* 3.48 has Album Ingaunum. The origins of Albenga (44 km from Savona on the Riviera del Ponente) go back to mythological times when, according to legend, it was founded by Alebion, Poseidon's son, who was Hercules' famous enemy. From the sixth century B.C., Albenga was the capital of the Ingauni Ligurian people, a fierce tribe of navigators who were subdued by the Roman Consul L. Emilius Paulus in 181 B.C. after a long and bloody war. After the Romans came the Byzantines, followed by the barbarians who destroyed the town, and then the Longobards who rebuilt it and made it one of their most highly fortified strongholds. In the twelfth century it became an independent sea town and enjoyed flourishing trade with the East until Genoa became

jealous of its powerful neighbor and allied with Pisa to send an army to destroy the town by fire and sword in 1165. The year 1179 marked the beginning of a slow process of submission to Genoa, and after being compelled to sign a series of increasingly humiliating concessions, Albenga was finally forced to capitulate completely.

23. The city was destroyed by Mago, the youngest brother of Hannibal, featured in a celebrated episode of Petrarch's *Africa*. Mago served his brother in Italy (218–216 B.C.), fighting at Trebia and Cannae. He fought in Spain from 215 until his defeat by P. Cornelius Scipio Africanus at Ilipa north of Seville (in 206). After failing to seize Carthago Nova and to reenter Gades, Mago attacked the Balearic isles and, in 205, crossed over to Genoa and destroyed the city. After lengthy recruiting he advanced to the Po valley, where he was defeated by the Romans and severely wounded (in 203). Soon afterwards he, with Hannibal, was ordered to return to Africa to face Scipio but died on the voyage. Cf. Livy 28.46.7, but the episode is known to Petrarch via Florus *Epitome* (an abridged history of Rome based on Livy's history) 1.21.5. Spurius Lucretius was given the task of rebuilding the city in 203 (Livy 30.1.9–10).

24. Tyre: a major city in southern Phoenicia with a large territory, built on an island but extending ashore and equipped with two harbors. Tyre is famed as the main founder of Phoenician colonies in the west, and its international trade from Spain to the Persian gulf is evoked in Ezechiel's prophecies (Ezekiel 26–28). Prof. Simone Marchesi informs me that the expression "cunctis terribilem tremendamque litoribus" is from Valerius Maximus *Facta et dicta memorabilia* 5.6ext.4: "Ubi sunt Karthaginis alta moenia? Ubi maritima gloria inclyti portus? Ubi cunctis litoribus terribilis classis?"

25. Petrarch cites Livy for the difficulties of the war against the Ligurians, but the basis for the passage is Florus *Epitome* 1.19.

26. The "sacro catino" (Holy Grail), a late-antique artifact, is still kept in the museum of the Cathedral of St. Lorenzo in Genoa (see Illustration 3). This cup or dish, made of green glass, though long supposed to have been carved from one huge emerald, is 14.5 inches in diameter and was supposedly given as a gift by the queen of Sheba to Solomon. Jesus is supposed to have drunk from it during the Last Supper. The "sacro catino," found in Caesarea in Palestine during the Crusades, is mentioned for the first time by William of Tyre, *Historia rerum in partibus transmarinis gestarum* (Recueil des historiens des Croisades, Historiens occidentaux 1 / 1 [Paris, 1844], p. 423). See also Jacobus de Voragine, *Cronaca* 2:309–15.

 Petrarch takes the term *parapside* from the Vulgate, Matthew 26.23: "at ipse respondens ait qui intinguit mecum manum in parapside hic me tradet" (And he answered and said, "He that dippeth [his] hand with me in the dish, the same shall betray me").

27. For the literary anthropologist Piero Camporesi, "Petrarch was the first of the moderns to describe the Ligurian and Tyrrhenian coasts observing them from the sea, from a point of view that was for the time unusual" ("Il mare e il littorale," *Le belle contrade: Nascita del paesaggio italiano* [Milano: Garzanti, 1992], p. 110). The description of the Tyrrhenian coast finds many points of contact with the description of the same coast in the first part of the famous episode of Mago's final journey in Petrarch's *Africa*, 6.839–84 (ed. Nicola Festa [Firenze: Sansoni, 1984, pp. 166–67]): "Now Mago, sailing / ill-omened

from the port of Genoa, / trusted his wounded body to the vast expanse of ocean, yet within him planned, / should Fortune so much grant, a swift return. / Up from the sea the hills of cedars rise— / in green luxuriant growth this coastline yields / to none—and on the beach the scattered groves / of palms grow verdant. On one side Delphinus / lies hidden in a sunlit grove that, walled / by mountains, ever turns aside the fierce / blasts from the south; its unvexed harbor lies / in dreaming peace. And on the other side / Siestrum with its winding slope extends. / 'Tis here they look upon the vineyards bathed / in warm sunbeams, by Bacchus held most dear. / Beyond arise steep Monte Rosso's crest / and the Cornelian peaks, famed far and wide/ for honeyed wines; to these might well defer— / and without shame—the storied Meroe / and the Falernian hills. Whether through dearth/ of talent or because as yet it lay / unknown to poets, that fair land had owned / no sacred song. To me therefore it falls / to hymn its beauty. As they plough the deep, / shoreward appear the island and the port / once dear to Venus, and behind is seen / sturdy Ausonian Eryx, with its name / borrowed from Sicily. Pallas, men say, / would linger in those lofty olive groves, / forgetful of the Athens of her heart. / Then rises the Corvinian cape; the sea / swells round about it, flashing white with foam, / and combers break upon the shallow shoals. / Amid them, as experienced mariners know, / a perilous reef protrudes its blackened crest, / but all around the cliffs are white with gleam, / seen from afar when Phoebus sheds his rays. / The coastline curves and Macra's mouth appears / and towering Luni's battlements. Beyond, / mark where the Arno flows serenely down/ to mingle with the deep. Upon that bank / fair Pisa can be seen. They point it out / and watch it pass and eye the Etrurian plain, / tiny Gorgona, Elba, looming large, / and stony beached Capraia; to port / Igilium, rich in gleaming marble, fades / behind; ahead to starboard comes in view/ the peak that takes two names from its twin mines of ore: one summit is called Plumbium, / the other Argentaro. Not far off, / under the sloping mountain lies the port / of Hercules, the Talamonian mass. / There Umbro, yet more baneful than the sea / to sailors, puts its slender current forth / in churling swirls. Right of their wind-swept course / tree mantled Corsica is left behind; / on one side in the distance they discern / the wasted hills of gaunt Sardinia / and on the other golden Rome herself / and Tiber's channel to the storm-racked coast" (*Petrarch's Africa*, trans. Thomas G. Bergin and Alice S. Wilson [New Haven: Yale University Press, 1977], vv. 1090–1150, pp. 138–40). The link with this passage of the *Africa* is made explicitly below, at *Itin.* 5.1.

28. In the nautical charts of the time, "Caput Montis" is indicated by various forms, including "co de monte." It corresponds to the mountain of today's Portofino. The places along the Tyrrhenian coast mentioned by Petrarch correspond in large measure to those given by the portolan maps of the period (also known as *compass charts,* or *rhumb charts*) that served Mediterranean pilots and travelers between 1300 and 1600. The portolan charts were characterized by rhumb lines, lines that radiate from the center in the direction of wind or compass points and that were used by pilots to lay courses from one harbor to another. The charts were usually drawn on vellum and embellished with a frame and other decorations. See Illustration 3. The earliest surviving dated chart was produced at Genoa by Petrus Vesconte in 1311. F. Friedersdorff, in noting Petrarch's geographical interests, advanced the hypothesis of contact between the poet and the Venetian Pizzigani

brothers in Parma, who were authors of portolan charts and an atlas (*Franz Petrarcas poetischen Briefen* [Halle, 1903], p. 140). For the history of the portolan chart, see Tony Campbell, "Portolan Charts from the Late Thirteenth Century to 1500," in *The History of Cartography*, ed. J. B. Harley and David Woodward (Chicago: University of Chicago Press, 1987–), vol. 1, pp. 371–463.

Petrarch's place names reveal a pattern of correspondences with the place names collated by Adolf Erik Nordenskiöld from major portolan charts of the fourteenth, fifteenth, and sixteenth centuries (in *Periplus:An Essay on the Early History of Charts and Sailing-Directions*, trans. Francis A. Bather [New York: B. Franklin, 1967; originally Stockholm, 1897])—including an anonymous chart of the fourteenth century, the Catalan atlas (also fourteenth century), the Giraldis chart of 1426, and the Voltius map of 1593. It is almost as if Petrarch had such a chart before him as he wrote, allowing for some departures from the portolan model for sites of personal interest, including those he had personally visited.

For example, for the first part of the coast, from Caput Montis (*Itin.* 4.0) to the mouth of the Magra river (*Itin.* 6.0), the places mentioned by Petrarch—Caput Montis, Port of Delfino (Portofino), Rapallo, Sestri, Portovenere, La Spezia (described but not named by Petrarch)—correspond to those presented by the portolans; all of the places mentioned by Petrarch, with the exception of Lerici, appear on the portolans collated by Nordenskiöld (Levanto, however, which is present in all the portolans is ignored by Petrarch, as is Nervi, which appears on the Catalan atlas). The addition of Lerici derives from the poet's firsthand reconnaissance of these places. Lerici is also mentioned in *Fam.* 3.22.11, where it is described as the home of the inventor of the olive (see below).

Petrarch's eye for the attractive tourist spot is noteworthy. Lerici, on the Gulf of La Spezia (or as it is more romantically called today, the Bay of Poets, because Byron, Shelley, and Keats visited it), is now a picturesque resort and considered an ideal location for exploring the pleasures of the Italian Riviera (which runs from the French border to the mouth of the Magra River). From Lerici, you can take boats across the gulf to the Cinque Terre, five villages strung along the coast north of Portovenere. Lerici is also mentioned by Petrarch in less idyllic circumstances in *Fam.* 5.3.4, where it is described as a point of embarkation during Petrarch's troubled journey to Naples of 1343.

Luni, Sarzana, Lavenza, Rio Freddo, Massa, and Pietrasanta, which follow in Petrarch's *Itinerary* but do not appear in the portolans, similarly derive from Petrarch's firsthand experience of these places during his journeys. From Mutrone, the correspondence with contemporary portolans resumes more or less as far as Salerno, at which point only major spots along the coasts of Italy are highlighted by Petrarch. See Illustrations 5, 6, and 9.

29. But see also *Fam.* 3.22.11, to Lelius (Lello di Pietro Stefano dei Tosetti), 1347: "Here [at the source of the Sorgue] I would say that the inventor of the olive, Minerva, dwells after having deserted Athens, except that sometime ago in my *Africa* I had already placed her on the shore of Genoa in Porto Venere and in Lerici" (*Letters on Familiar Matters*, vol. 1, 171).

30. Cf. *Afr.* 6.848 and 856–59; *Fam.* 3.22.11.

31. Cf. *Afr.* 6.858.

32. Erice, in northwestern Sicily (cf. Virgil *Aeneid* 5.759–61).

33. The Gulf of Spezia.

34. Cf. *Afr.* 6.842–44. "Minerva": cf. *Afr.* 6.849–50 and *Fam.* 3.22.11.

35. For Petrarch and his contemporaries, Meroe was a legendary Ethiopian island in the Nile. According to the *Oxford Classical Dictionary*, 3d ed., Meroe was a capital of Kush on the east bank of the Nile, between the Fifth and Sixth Cataracts. First referred to by Herodotus (2.29), it figures more prominently in Hellenistic and Roman literature. In later literature, it was a romanticized, exotic place.

36. Cf. *Afr.* 6.851–53; *Fam.* 5.4.5 and 12.15.5.

37. The episode of Hannibals's brother Mago, wounded in battle by the Romans in Liguria and called home by the Carthaginian senate, had been briefly mentioned by Livy 30.19.5. Petrarch developed the theme in one of the most famous passages of the *Africa*. The section dedicated to Mago's lament (*Africa* 6.885–916) was published by the author in Naples in 1341 and met with criticism that Petrarch had occasion to complain about in a letter to Boccaccio (*Sen.* 2.1). The unfinished *Africa*, in nine books, was dedicated to Robert of Anjou in 1341. The work was begun in Vaucluse in 1338–39, and a part was presented in Naples to King Robert on the occasion of Petrarch's examination for the laurel crown. That same year Petrarch took the work up again, initially at Selvapiana and then at Parma. Petrarch worked on the poem only intermittently after the death of King Robert in 1343, and the work was never completed. In this passage Petrarch appears to suggest that it might yet be completed and published. Even many years after his coronation as poet laureate, Petrarch evidently remained invested in the unfinished *Africa*. It continued to represent an important dimension of his literary reputation and foundation for his fame and is featured prominently in both the *Secretum* (ed. Enrico Fenzi [Milano: Mursia, 1992]; *Petrarch's Secret, or the Soul's Conflict with Passion,* trans. William H. Draper [London: Chatto and Windus, 1951]) and the *Posteritati* ("Letter to Posterity," *Sen.* 18.1).

38. Cf. *Afr.* 6.862–66 and *Fam.* 5.3.4.

39. Cf. Pliny *Naturalis historia* 3.48; Dante *Paradiso* 9.90. The *volgarizzamento meridionale*, as well as the Tuscan Trecento version, translates: "lo quale devide le confine marine de Lombardia da quilli de Toscana" (which divides the shores of Lombardy from those of Tuscany), thus collapsing Liguria into Lombardy (Paolella, *Volgarizzamento meridionale anonimo,* p. 69). Giovanni Villani, *Cronica* (ed. I. Moutier, 7 vols. [Firenze: Magheri, 1823]): "And to the south Tuscany has the sea called Tyrrhenian which bathes the shores of the Maremma, Piombino and Pisa, and the districts of Lucca and of Luni as far as the mouth of the river Magra that enters the sea at the cape of Mt. Corvo beyond Luni and to the west of Sarzana. And said river descends from the Apennines above Pontremoli, between the Genoese riviera and the country of Piacenza in Lombardy, in the territory of the marquesses of Malaspini" (book 1, chapter 43).

40. Cf. *Afr.* 6.867–68 and *Fam.* 5.3.4. Luni (originally Luna) was an Etruscan city but was seized by the Ligurians. At an uncertain date it was taken by the Romans under Domitius Calvinus. In 177 B.C., and under the Second Triumvirate, Roman colonies were established there. The port, though far from the city (the modern port of Spezia), was very important even in antiquity, and the marble of Luna, known today as Carrara marble, was very renowned. In the fifth century A.D. Luna was sacked by the Vandals, and in 650 by the Lombards. From the ninth century onwards it suffered the depredations of the

Saracens, the last time in 1016 at the hands of Mogehit, who was defeated the same year (8 June) by the Genoese and Pisan fleets. The city never recovered, however, and in 1058 the inhabitants emigrated to the modern Sarzana. Ruins are still visible of an amphitheater, a semicircular theater, a circus, and an aquarium.

41. This phrase picks up a signature theme of Petrarch, that of "flight" from love, beginning with his travels to flee from Laura. Cf. *Epyst.* 1.6.

42. "Della città di Luni" (concerning the city of Luni): see Villani, *Cronica:* "The city of Luni which is today in ruins was very ancient, and as we find in the stories of Troy, a fleet and troops from Luni went to help the Greeks against the Trojans. It was later destroyed by people from beyond the mountains because the wife of a lord who was on his way to Rome was corrupted and committed adultery there; for this reason said lord destroyed the city and today the area is deserted and unhealthy" (book 1, chapter 50). On the traditions surrounding the destruction of Luni, see G. Sforza, "La distruzione di Luni nella leggenda e nella storia," *Miscellanea di storia italiana* 3.19 (1922), pp. 1–138. For Troy as an example of lust punished, see *Sen.* 4.5.

43. None of the cities mentioned in this paragraph are present in the corresponding passage of the *Africa*. Sarzana in Lunigiana was a center on the Via Francigena of some importance since the eleventh century. Guido Cavalcanti was sent into exile there in 1300 during Dante's priorate and never recovered from the effects of the malarious climate of the place, dying in Florence in August of that same year.

44. Mention of Avenza connects this passage to Petrarch's account of his 1343 journey to Naples (*Fam.* 5.3), during which he was forced by storms to disembark along the coasts of Liguria during a war between Pisa and Milan: "So although I had started on a straight path, the fact that near Lavenza both armies had encamped, with the lord pressing forward seriously while on the other hand the Pisans defended their Mutrone with all their might—I was compelled at Lerici to entrust myself once again on a sea journey. Passing by Corvo, the huge cliff so called because of its color, and then the white cliffs and the entrance to Macra and then Luni, once famous and powerful but now carrying an empty and insignificant name" (*Letters on Familiar Matters*, vol. 1, pp. 232–30).

45. Villani reports from a Florentine perspective on the political context for the war-torn territory through which Petrarch traveled in 1343: "The Florentines, as we mentioned earlier, did the Pisans a disservice when they gave Pietrasanta to the bishop of Luni of the marquesses Malaspini for he was the brother-in-law by his sister of Messer Luchino Visconti lord of Milan, who was indignant with the Pisans because they held Sarzana and Avenza, and Massa of the marquesses of Malaspini and other Malaspini castles in Lunigiana, nor were they willing to give them up as he had requested, nor to him personally nor in lieu of the great debt of money owed him for the great service his troops had accomplished for them against our commune when he defeated us at Lucca" (*Cronica*, book 12, chapter 26).

46. The reference is to Guiscardo da Pietrasanta, a member of the Milanese family of the Pietrasanta, who served as podestà of Genoa, Bologna, Florence (1254), Modena, and Lucca. The *Cronichetta lucchese* (1164–1260), sec. 13/14 (in S. Bongi, *Antica cronichetta volgare lucchese*, in *Atti della Reale Accademia Lucchese di Scienze, Lettere ed Arti* 26 [1893], p. 254,

under the date: "1255. Fue podestade di Lucca d.no Guiscardo da Pietrasanta; edificossi Pietrasanta e lui impuose il nome" (1255. Lord Guiscardo da Pietrasanta was podestà of Lucca; Pietrasanta was built and he gave it its name).

47. Two strategically important medieval forts on the coast of Versilia: Motrone and Viareggio, in the pine forest between Migliarino and Motrone. Cf. *Afr.* 6.870–71 and *Fam.* 5.3.4.

48. The reference is to the Genoese victory over the Pisans in the battle of Meloria, 6 August 1284. The Genoese fleet of eighty-eight ships, commanded by Oberto Doria and Benedict Zaccaria, defeated the Pisan fleet of one hundred galleys under the command of the podestà Alberto Morosini and of the count Ugolino of the Gherardesca in the waters off Livorno. This battle marks the beginning of the decline of Pisa as a sea power. The battle is mentioned also in *Fam.* 14.5.26. Cf. Villani, *Cronica*, book 7, chapter 92.

49. The nautical charts show P(orto) Pis(s)ano. Livorno was a supporting port while Porto Pisano was active and important.

50. Two small off-shore islands. Cf. *Afr.* 6.871–74. The toponyms are in Pliny *Naturalis historia* 3.82 and Pomponius Mela *De situ orbis* 2.122. Cf. Dante *Inferno* 33.79–84: "Ahi Pisa, vituperio de le genti/ del bel paese là dove 'l sì suona, / poi che i vicini a te punir son lenti, / muovasi la Capraia e la Gorgona, e faccian siepe ad Arno in su la foce, / sì ch'elli annieghi in te ogne persona!" (*The Divine Comedy: Inferno,* trans. Charles S. Singleton [Princeton, N.J.: Princeton University Press, 1970], vol. 1, p. 355: Ah, Pisa! Shame of the peoples of the fair land where the sì is heard, since your neighbors are slow to punish you, let Capraia and Gorgona shift, and make a hedge for Arno at its mouth, so that it drown every soul in you!)

51. Corsica appears in fact directly in front of the Pisan coast in contemporary portolans when it is in reality situated farther south. Cf. *Fam.* 15.7.13, where Petrarch defines Corsica as "horrens et squalida." Cf. *Afr.* 6.881–82 and *Fam.* 15.7.13.

52. Cf. *Afr.* 6.875–77. Piombino is an important town on the Tuscan coast, situated on the southern side of the headland which bears the same name, below Mount Massoncello and opposite the island of Elba. It is situated 82 km south of Livorno and approximately 15 km south of Populonia. It is the ancient Roman Port Falesia. After the destruction of Populonia by the Longobards, Piombino became an important Pisan stronghold.

53. Cf. Virgil *Aeneid* 10.174. The Chalybes were a people of Pontus in Asia Minor, famous for their iron work. See also Herodotus 1.28; Xenophon *Anabasis* 4.4.8, 5.5.1, 7.8.25. Elba has an area of 86 square miles (223 square km) and is the largest island of the Tuscan archipelago. Cf. *Afr.* 6.873–874. Mention of Elba and Giglio (see below) also recalls the topography of a famous sonnet of Petrarch's, *RVF* 69, the last of a triptych of compositions commemorating Petrarch's first journey to Rome and his travel by sea along the same coast described here: "Ben sapeva io che natural consiglio, / Amor, contra di te già mai non valse, / tanti lacciuol', tante impromesse false, / tanto provato avea 'l tuo fiero artiglio. / Ma novamente, ond' io mi meraviglio / (diròl, come persona a cui ne calse, / et che 'l notai là sopra l' acque salse, / tra la riva toscana et l' Elba et Giglio), / i' fuggia le tue mani, et per camino, / agitandom' i vènti e 'l ciel et l' onde, / m' andava sconosciuto et pellegrino: / quando ecco i tuoi ministri, i' non so donde, / per darmi a diveder ch' al suo destino / mal chi contrasta, et mal chi si nasconde" (*Francesco Petrarca Canzoniere,* ed. Marco Santagata [Milano: Mondadori, 1996], p. 342); (*Petrarch: The Canzoniere, or Rerum*

Vulgarium Fragmenta, trans. Mark Musa [Bloomington: Indiana University Press, 1996], p. 108: "How well I knew that any human means / taken against you, Love, would never work; / so many snares and unkept promises / had made me feel the fierceness of your claw. / But recently, I am left surprised / (I'll tell it as a person who's concerned, / who took note of it while he sailed the seas / by Tuscan shores near Elba and near Giglio), / I fled your hands and went upon a journey, / that was unknown and quite unusual, / the winds and waves and heavens driving me; / when out of nowhere came your ministers / to make me see that from one's destiny / one cannot hide, one cannot fight it off").

54. Pisa lost Sardinia to the Aragonese in 1326 but had maintained control of Elba since 1309.

55. Populonia (Etruscan Pupluna) is actually north of Piombino. It is located on the promontory overlooking Porto Baratti and was the port of the metal-rich zone of northwest Tuscany and a smelting center for the iron of Elba. It flourished between the fourth and second centuries B.C. and was the only Etruscan city established directly on the sea. It was destroyed by the Longobards in 570 A.D. Charlemagne gave it to Pope Adrian I. The bishopric was transferred to Massa Marittima in 835 and in the eleventh century it appears to have been deserted. The surviving town dates to the fourteenth century and with its medieval castle, situated on a lofty and precipitous hill, is conspicuous from all sides. It is not mentioned in the *Africa* nor elsewhere in Petrarch's works as far as I know.

56. The Tuscan *volgarizzamento* calls it "Massa di Maremma." The earlier Massa Marittima is north of Lucca; this one is northwest of Grosseto. Massa Marittima is on the road from Siena to Follónica and approximately 30 km east of Populonia. Probably of Etruscan origin, Massa Marittima became an important center during the ninth century, when the bishopric was transferred there from Populonia. Massa Marittima took part in the struggles between the Tuscan cities as the sometime ally and sometime enemy of Pisa and as the sometime ally and sometime enemy of Siena until Siena established its dominion there after 1335.

57. Grosseto, a medieval town dating to the ninth century, and Massa Marittima are not mentioned in *Africa*. Grosseto is situated on a low-lying coastal plain, the Maremma, near the Ombrone River approximately 50 km southwest of Siena and 12 km from the sea. It originated as a castle along the road from Pisa to Rome and was a Ghibelline stronghold in the Maremma during the thirteenth and early fourteenth centuries until it came under Sienese dominion after 1336.

58. Cf. *Afr.* 6.874–75, where Talamone is considered the work of the hero Telamon, who was the father of Ajax "the greater." Modern Talamone, situated on a promontory in the southwestern extremity of the Sienese Maremma, about 6 km southeast of the mouth of the Ombrone, possesses a convenient anchorage, sheltered from the southwest gales by the island of Giglio and by Monte Argentario. In 1303 the harbor was purchased by the Sienese, who sought an outlet to the sea, but the enterprise was a failure due both to the constant dredging required to keep the entrance clear and to the malarious climate of the Maremma. Dante ridicules the project in *Purgatorio* 13.151–54. Modern Talamone emerged during the Middle Ages in connection with the port, while ancient Telamon, already inhabited during Etruscan times, was located on the Talamonaccio hill farther to the east.

In mythology, Telamon was the son of Aeacus and Endeis and brother of Peleus. He was one of the Argonauts and a participant in the Calydonian boar hunt. By his wife, Eriboae or Periboea, he fathered the great Aias—Ajax—Homer's "Bulwark of the Achaeans."

59. Cf. Pliny *Naturalis historia* 3.81 and Pomponius Mela *De situ orbis* 2.122. Giglio is the second largest island of the Tuscan archipelago and is located opposite from Mount Argentario. The island rises to 1,634 feet (498 m) and has an area of 8 square miles (21 square km). Between 1264 and 1406 it was under Pisan control.

60. Mt. Argentario is a conspicuous promontory having an elliptical form that rises 12 km from the coast to which it is connected by two sand and gravel bars (*tómboli*) 450 m wide, between which is enclosed the Orbetello lagoon. The promontory rises at its highest point (Mt. Telégrafo) to 635 m. Porto Santo Stefano is on the northeast coast of the Argentario while Port'Ercole is on the southeast coast.

61. Corneto, located on a high plateau about 90 km from Rome and 6 km inland, is the name of the castle town that rose in the ninth century near the ruins of ancient Tarquinia, the head of the twelve cities of Etruria. The walls of the city date to the ninth century, and it survived as a free commune until it was occupied by Egidio Albornoz and Giordano Orsini in 1355. The association between the Tarquini and Tarquinia derives from Roman historiography (Livy 1.34) and may explain Petrarch's interest in the place. Corneto does appear on the portolan charts right before Civitavecchia. Cf. Dante *Inferno* 13.9.

62. Civitavecchia, the principal port for Rome, situated on the Tyrrhenian Sea, was founded early in the second century by the emperor Trajan on a stretch of coast known as Centumcellae. The port was in reality constructed by Trajan in 106 A.D., and the Porto di Traiano ("Trajan's Port") is preserved in the central part of the modern port. For a vivid description, see Pliny *Epistulae* 6.31.

63. Cf. *Afr.* 6.882–84. Actually, Sardinia is lower in latitude.

64. Cf. Livy 1.33. 9; Florus *Epitome* 1.4.2 (1.3.4). Cf. Suetonius *De viris illustribus* Ancus 6.

65. Cf. Livy 2.65.11. Located on a peninsula jutting into the Tyrrhenian Sea, Anzio was founded, according to legend, by Anteias, son of Ulysses and the sorceress Circe. It was a stronghold of the Volsci, an ancient people prominent in the fifth century B.C., and was older than Rome, which conquered it in 338 B.C.

66. A small ancient island, today joined to the mainland, located at the mouth of the river of the same name. Cf. Pliny *Naturalis historia* 3.81. It appears on the portolans.

67. Circee (modern Circeo) is a prominent mountain on the coast south of Rome. It reaches a height of 541 m. Cf. the *Circaeae terrae* of Virgil *Aeneid* 7.10–20. The mountain also appears on the portolans.

68. The most important island of the Pontine archipelago. It was the place of exile for numerous members of the imperial families. The plural form is also in Pliny *Naturalis historia* 3.81 and Pomponius Mela *De situ orbis* 2.122.

69. Cf. Pliny *Naturalis historia* 3.59 and Livy 4.59. Originating as the Anxur of the Volsci tribe, it passed under Roman domination c. 400 B.C. and became known as Tarracina. An important city on the Appian Way, it assumed great importance as a resort, as witnessed still today by the remains of the forum, sumptuous temples, baths, theaters, and villas

of the emperors Tiberius, Galba, and Vitellius. Anxur is the name given for Terracina also in *Fam.* 5.7.4.

70. Cf. Virgil *Aeneid* 7.1–2. A town and seaport located on the Gulf of Gaeta, northwest of Naples. Gaeta first came under the influence of the Romans in the fourth century B.C.; a road was built c. 184 B.C. connecting the town with the port, and it became a favored Roman resort. Petrarch includes it in a list of Roman "winter delights" together with Anzio, Terracina, Formia, Naples, and Baiae in *Fam.* 5.4.7. Gaeta is recalled in *Fam.* 8.5.12 as the place where Scipio and Lelius enjoyed "ever-desirable leisure . . . after their military labors" (*Letters on Familiar Matters*, vol. 1, p. 411).

71. St. Erasmus was also known as St. Elmo. He was the bishop of Formia and suffered martyrdom during Diocletian's persecution of the Christians. Legend records that when a blue light appeared on the masts or riggings of ships before or after a storm, the seamen took it as a sign of Erasmus's protection. This blue electrical discharge was known as "St. Elmo's fire." According to Lo Monaco, *Itinerario in Terra Santa 1358*, p. 100, the tomb of St. Erasmus is found in the cathedral of Gaeta while another church in Formia dedicated to St. Erasmus also claims to hold his remains.

72. Formia is a town located on the Gulf of Gaeta between the mouth of the Garigliano and the Gaeta peninsula, northwest of Naples. A town of the ancient Volsci people, it was later taken by the Romans and became a popular Roman summer residence noted for the Caecuban and Falernian wines. There are ruins of prehistoric megalithic walls, and Roman remains include the villa of the statesman and orator Cicero and his restored mausoleum; Cicero was murdered nearby in 43 B.C. Petrarch describes the murder in *Rerum Memorandarum Libri* 2.17.8. The town was razed by the Saracens in the ninth century and during the fourteenth century constituted by two small centers, Castelnuovo and Moleta di Gaeta. Cicero informs us several times he had a villa at Formia, calling it Formianum (Cicero *Ad Atticum* 4.2.6 and 6.7).

73. Scipio the African spent his voluntary exile at Literno from 187 until his death. Cf. *Triumphus Pudicitie*, 168–71: "lassando, se n'andar dritto a Linterno. / In così angusta e solitaria villa / era il grand'uom che d'Affrica s'appella, / perché prima col ferro al vivo aprilla" (*Trionfi*, ed. Pacca and Paolino, pp. 259–60); (*The Triumphs of Petrarch*, trans. Ernest Hatch Wilkins [Chicago: University of Chicago Press, 1962], p. 46: "Straight to Linterno was its onward course. / There in his simple home, living in peace / Was the great Africanus, titled thus / Since 'twas his sword that opened Africa"). Seneca described firsthand the villa of Scipio as well as the moral stature of the hero in Epistle 86 to Lucilius and Petrarch recalls this example in *Fam.* 2.9.25: "Seneca seems to me to be rejoicing as he writes to Lucilius from the very villa of Scipio Africanus, nor did he take it lightly to have seen the place where such a great man was in exile and where the bones lay which he denied to his homeland" (*Letters on Familiar Matters*, vol. 1, p. 103). Aware of the pilgrimage to the site made by Livy (cf. Livy 38.56.3), Petrarch expressed his disappointed desire also to visit the site in *Fam.* 5.4.9: "I know that his small villa is not far from here, and there is nothing that I would look upon more eagerly if I could visit with some guide places renowned because of so great an occupant" (*Letters on Familiar Matters*, vol. 1, p. 240). Feo reports ("Inquietudini," pp. 116–17) that in the definitive redaction of Petrarch's life

of Scipio (*De Viris Illustribus,* Scipio 12.29), the poet attempted to liken himself to the example of his masters Seneca and Livy who had visited the site "as best he could" by adding the passage, "haud procul Campanie Cumis; quam ipse olim, dum loca illa peregrinus inviserem, ab amicis ostensam non sine quadam animi voluptate prospexi" (Francis Petrarch, *De Viris Illustribus,* ed. Martellotti [Firenze, 1964], vol. 1, p. 307). P. De Nolhac, *Pétrarque et l'humanisme* (Paris: Champion, 1907), vol. 1, p. 155, and vol. 2, p. 33, n. 2, took this to mean that Petrarch had indeed visited Literno, but Feo points out that *prospexi* does not mean "I visited" but "I saw from afar," and suggests that this passage from the *Itinerary* ("you will visit these places more in thought than with the eyes") alludes to an unsatisfied desire of Petrarch's to visit the place. Petrarch typically contrasts Literno with Baiae, as in *Fam.* 15.9.3: "Scipio in his exile preferred the roughness of Literno to the pleasures of Baiae" (*Letters on Familiar Matters,* vol. 2, p. 275).

74. Cf. Virgil *Aeneid* 9.715–16. Cf. *Triumphus Pudicitie,* vv. 112–14: "Non freme così 'l mar, quando s'adira, / non Inarime, allor che Tipheo piagne, / né Mongibel, s'Enchelado sospira" (*Trionfi,* ed. Pacca and Paolino, p. 246); (*The Triumphs of Petrarch,* p. 43: "Greater his (Love's) rage than that of the angry sea, / Or that of Ischia when Typhoeus weeps, / Or Aetna's when Enceladus laments). Petrarch follows the tradition that has Typhoeus buried beneath Ischia. Petrarch annotated this point in his copy of Pomponius Mela *De situ orbis* 1.13.76, "Nota contra Dantem," in contrast to Dante *Paradiso* 8.67–70, which has Typhoeus buried beneath Sicily, following Ovid *Metamorphoses* 5.346–58. See Giuseppe Billanovich, "Tra Dante e Petrarca," *Italia medioevale e umanistica* (1965), pp. 39–40; and Billanovich, "Uno Svetonio della biblioteca di Petrarca (Berlinese lat. Fol. 337)," *Studi petrarcheschi* 6 (1956), p. 30, n. 4.

75. Giovanni da Procida, who according to the tradition of Trecento chroniclers is credited with inspiring the Sicilian Vespers (cf. Villani, *Cronica,* book 7, chapter 61; and Giovanni Boccaccio *De Casibus Virorum Illustrium* 9.19). He was born in Salerno in 1210 and was Lord of Procida and associated with the Hohenstaufen imperial party in Italy. When Charles I (Charles of Anjou), 1227–85, count of Anjou and Provence, youngest brother of King Louis IX of France, defeated the emperor Frederick II's illegitimate son Manfredi at Benevento in 1266, Giovanni conspired against Charles I. When discovered, he was exiled and was welcomed at the court of James I in Aragon. He later supported the territorial expansion of the Aragonese in Sicily during and after the Sicilian Vespers.

The *Sicilian Vespers* is the name given to the massacre, signaled to begin by the first stroke of the vesper bell, of the French in Sicily on Easter Monday, 30 March 1282. Charles I had aroused the hatred of the Sicilians by imposing heavy taxes and especially by putting the island under the control of French officials and soldiers. On that Monday evening the inhabitants of Palermo rose against their oppressors. Their example was followed in other towns, until almost all the French in Sicily had been massacred. Charles made a determined attempt to reconquer the island, but the Sicilians summoned to their aid Pedro III, king of Aragon (1239–85), who was elected king of Sicily that same year. A twenty-year war followed between the Aragonese and the Angevin kings of Naples for control of Sicily, with the Aragonese ultimately prevailing.

76. The acropolis of Cuma is described at the beginning of book 6 of Virgil's *Aeneid.* Petrarch might have learned about the refuge of Superbus at Cuma from Livy 2.21.2; Aurelius

Victor (known as Pliny) *De viris illustribus* 8.6; or Cicero *Tusculanae disputationes* 3.12.27.

77. The mistake *Cuma* for *Comum* was common in the medieval tradition of Como from the thirteenth century. For an analogous passage on this point, see *Fam.* 17.6.1, to Bernardo Anguissola.

78. Cf. Virgil *Aeneid* 6.212–35 and Pomponius Mela *De situ orbis* 2.70. See also *Epyst.* 2.7.49–50 and 2.17.8.

79. The words, "is maintained by some (in any case the matter is very uncertain)," are added to the text after 1365. Feo, "Inquietudini," p. 151–54, shows how, after reading *Odyssey* 10–12 in the Latin translation of Leontius Pilatus in 1365, Petrarch revised a network of passages throughout his writings, including this one, to conform to his new knowledge of Homer's works (including *Fam.* 5.4.5, *De Vita Solitaria* 2.12, and perhaps *Epyst.* 2.15, vv. 77–81). In fact, Petrarch read in Leontius Pilatus's translation about the meeting between Ulysses with the ghost of Elpenor, who revealed that the youth's death was by chance and occurred before the departure from Circe and not near the Avernus. Therefore Petrarch distances himself from the opinion of Servius, who was likely Petrarch's original source for the idea that Aeneas had sacrificed Misenus in the same place as Ulysses had Elpenor.

80. Cf. Virgil *Aeneid* 6.124–29: "Talibus orabat dictis arasque tenebat, / cum sic orsa loqui vates: 'sate sanguine divum, / Tros Anchisiade, facilis descensus Averno: noctes atque dies patet atri ianua Ditis; / sed revocare gradum superasque evadere ad auras, / hoc opus, hic labor est'" (In such times he prayed and clasped the altar, when thus the prophetess began to speak: "Sprung from blood of gods, son of Trojan Anchises, easy is the descent to Avernus: night and day the door of gloomy Dis stands open; but to recall thy steps and pass out to the upper air, this is the task, this the toil!")

81. The toponyms given here also appear in *Epyst.* 2.7.43–45, *Epyst.* 2.16.39–43, and *Fam.* 5.4.5.

82. Cf. *Epyst.* 2.16.30 and *Fam.* 5.4.5–6.

83. An early trace of the reception of the *Itinerarium* is in Benvenuto da Imola's commentary on *Inferno* 3, referring to "il lago d'Averno." See Introduction, note 48.

84. For the notion that the Adriatic is "above" while the Tyrrhenian is located "below" Italy, cf. the *Peutinger Table*, where the Adriatic is styled "Mare Superum" and the Tyrrhenian "Mare Inferum." See also Virgil *Georgics* 2.158: "an mare, quod supra, memorem, quodque adluit infra?" (Shall I tell of the seas washing the land above and below?).

85. The source for this information is Suetonius *De vita caesarum* Augustus 49.1, a passage that Petrarch annotated in his personal copy (Oxford, Exeter College, manuscript 186, f. 16v) with a reference to a passage of Vegetius, also annotated by Petrarch in his personal copy (Vatican City, Vatican Library, manuscript Vat. Lat. 2193, f. 117r). See Giuseppe Billanovich, "Nella biblioteca del Petrarca II: Un altro Svetonio del Petrarca (Oxford, Exeter College, 186)," *Italia medioevale e umanistica* 3 (1960), p. 53.

86. For the toponym, see Servius *Aeneid* 3.441 and 6.107.

87. Baiae flourished as a fashionable spa and resort, thanks to volcanic hot springs. By the mid-first century B.C. many of the Roman aristocracy owned houses there. Several imperial palaces were built and it remained fashionable until the third century A.D., when

earthquakes and malaria sent it into decline. For classical references to Baiae with which Petrarch would have been familiar, see *Francesco Petrarca Triumphi*, ed. Marco Ariani (Milano: Mursia, 1988), p. 220.

But this section of the *Itinerary* also reflects Petrarch's firsthand knowledge of these places and corresponds to a passage in one of Petrarch's travel letters from his second visit to Naples in 1343, *Fam.* 5.4: "I saw Baiae along with the very famous Giovanni Barrili and my Barbato. I do not recall a happier day in my life, not only because of my friends' company and the variety of notable sights but because of the experience of many sad days. . . . I saw the places described by Virgil; I saw the lake Avernus and Lucrinus as well as the stagnant waters of Acheron; the laguna of Augusta rendered unhappy by the fierceness of her son; the once-proud road of Gaius Caligula now buried under the waves; and the obstacle against the sea built by Julius Caesar. I saw the native land and the home of the Sibyl and that dreadful cave from which fools do not return and which learned men do not enter. I saw Mt. Falernus distinguished from its famous vineyards and the parched soil exhaling continuously the vapors that are good for diseases. . . . I saw not only what is called the Neapolitan grotto which Annaeus Seneca recalls in his letter to Lucilius, but everywhere mountains full of perforations and suspended on marble vaults gleaming with brilliant whiteness, and sculpted figures indicating with pointing hands what water is most appropriate for each part of the body" (*Letters on Familiar Matters*, vol. 1, pp. 238–39).

88. This same monument is referred to in *Fam.* 5.4.7–8—"The laguna of Augusta rendered unhappy by the fierceness of her son" (*Letters on Familiar Matters*, vol. 1, p. 239)—and probably corresponds to what is today termed the "piscina mirabile" (marvelous pool) on Cape Miseno south of Bacoli, an enormous rectangular cistern 70 m long 26 m wide and 15 m high, which the contemporary travel writer Guido Piovene describes as "the most impressive monument between Miseno and Baiae. . . . Naples never erected a more august cathedral than that cistern" (*Viaggio in Italia* [Milano: Baldini e Castoldi, 1993; originally, 1956], p. 469).

89. The works of Nero mentioned here are those in Suetonius *De vita caesarum* Nero 31.7.

90. Cf. Virgil *Georgics* 2.161–64: "an memorem portus Lucrinoque addita claustra / atque indignatum magnis stridoribus aequor, / Iulia qua ponto longe sonat unda refuso / Tyrrhenusue fretis immittitur aestus Avernis?" (*Virgil*, trans H. Rushton Fairclough, Loeb Classical Library [Cambridge: Harvard University Press, 1967], vol. 1, p. 515–16: "Shall I tell of our havens, and the barrier thrown across the Lucrine, and how Ocean roars aloud in wrath, where the Julian waters echo afar as the sea is flung back and the Tyrrhenian tide pours into the channels of Avernus?").

91. Cf. *Fam.* 4.5.5: "the obstacle against the sea built by Julius Caesar." The detail is from Suetonius *De vita caesarum* Augustus 16.1, a passage annotated by Petrarch in the Oxford Suetonius and in his Virgil (Milano, Biblioteca Ambrosiana, manuscript S.P. Arm. 10, f. 28v a Serv. *Georg.* 2, 164). According to H. Rushton Fairclough's translation of Virgil *Georgics* 2.161–64 (*Virgil*, pp. 515–16), Agrippa provided the Lucrine lake with a ship channel from the sea and a breakwater, and united it with an inland lake, that of Avernus. Thus he secured for the Roman fleet a protected harbor that he called Julian in honor of Augustus.

92. Cf. *Fam.* 5.4.5: "the once-proud road of Gaius Caligula now buried under the waves" (*Letters on Familiar Matters*, vol. 1, p. 239).

93. The question of whether the "mons Falernus" should be taken to refer to the hill of St. Elmo (as in the *Cronaca di Partenope*) west of Naples, or the cape / hill of Posillipo (according to Boccaccio), or some other locale is discussed in M. Porena, "Il *Mons Falernus* secondo F. P.," *Rendiconti dell' Accademia di Archeologia, Lettere e Belle Arti di Napoli* 27 (1952), pp. 75–79. Porena argues against E. Cocchia, who had held for St. Elmo on the basis of Trecento sources including Petrarch, Benvenuto da Imola, the *Cronaca di Partenope*, and the Neapolitan poem "The Baths of Pozzuoli" (*Rendiconti dell'Accademia di Archeologia, Lettere e Belle Arti di Napoli*, new series 4 [1915]). Petrarch had already spoken of Mt. Falernus in *Fam.* 5.4. But Porena takes this passage from the *Itinerarium* as decisive for showing that Mt. Falernus for Petrarch was neither Posillipo nor the Vomero nor St. Elmo but rather an area between Pozzuoli and Fuorigrotta. The description of *Fam.* 5.4 also corresponds to a description of the volcanic manifestations that characterize the area of the Campi Flegrei. In fact, Petrarch explicitly says that the high ground or "hill of Falernus rises not far from Pozzuoli," which would seem to rule out the hill of St. Elmo just to the west of Naples and closer to Naples than to Pozzuoli (the option favored by Lo Monaco, *Itinerario in Terra Santa*, p. 105). The "crypta neapolitana" or "grotto of Posillipo" is between Falernus and the sea, which would rule out the hill / cape of Posillipo as Petrarch's Mt. Falernus. Porena concludes that there were two traditions on the location of Mt. Falernus, the first, which he calls the Boccaccian, identified Falernus as the hill / cape of Posillipo (which comprehends the option of St. Elmo insofar as they are part of the same chain), and the second, which located Mt. Falernus between Pozzuoli and Fuorigrotta, and which is followed here by Petrarch, possibly informed by his local guides Giovanni Barrili and Barbato da Sulmona, who had accompanied him on his visit to these sites in 1343. Petrarch had spoken of the classical Falernus earlier in the *Itinerarium* at 5.1. For classical sources regarding Falernus, see Horace *Epodes* 1.20 and Pliny *Naturalis historia* 14.62.

94. Regarding this legend, see Domenico Comparetti, *Virgil in the Middle Ages* (Hamden, Conn.: Archon Books, 1966), pp. 342–43.

95. The exchange probably took place in 1341 during Petrarch's first visit to Naples. Robert of Anjou, king of Naples (1309–43), was titular king of Sicily, and leader of the Italian Guelphs. He was Petrarch's sponsor at his coronation as poet laureate in Rome, 8 April 1341. See *Petrarch's Remedies for Fortune Fair and Foul*, vol. 4, p. 238, for Petrarchan references to King Robert; see also Ernest Hatch Wilkins, *The Making of the* Canzoniere *and Other Petrarchan Studies* (Rome: Edizioni di Storia e Letteratura, 1951), chapter 2, pp. 28 and 46–53, where references to King Robert are listed. Cf.: *Fam.* 4.2: "it is my considered opinion that nothing contributes more than familiarity with noble talents, and conversation with outstanding men. . . . 'Who is more outstanding than Themistocles in Greece' said Tullius; and I faithfully repeat: 'Who in Italy and indeed throughout Europe is more outstanding than Robert?'" (*Letters on familiar letters*, vol. 1, p. 182). See Fabio Stok, "Il Virgilio del Petrarca," *Preveggenze umanistiche di Petrarca: Atti delle giornate petrarchesche di Tor Vergata (Roma/Cortona 1–2 giugno 1992)* (Pisa: ETS, 1993), pp. 171–212.

96. Cf. Seneca *Epistulae* 57.1–2; cf. *Fam.* 5.4.6. The Neapolitian crypt, better known as the Grotta di Pozzuoli, begins nearby Virgil's tomb. It connected directly the Flegrean area with Naples through the hill of Pozzuoli from the first century down to the beginning of this century. The entrance is approximately 20 m high and the length of the tunnel is approximately 700 m (see Illustrations 7a, 7b, and 8).

97. The reputed tomb of Virgil on the Via Puteolana is a mausoleum set on the hillside above the Grotto of Posillipo. Cf. *Epyst.* 2.7.38–41. An accurate and recent bibliography on the question of the identification of the tomb as Virgil's is found in M. Capasso, *Il sepolcro di Virgilio* (Napoli: Giannini, 1983). See also J. B. Trapp, "The Grave of Virgil," *Journal of the Warburg and Courtauld Institute* 47 (1984), pp. 7–10. The reputed tomb of Virgil eventually became a required stopping place in Naples for Grand Tour travelers and was a popular and lucrative subject for artists. See Illustration 8.

98. The church is Santa Maria di Piedigrotta, built in 1352 and, already during the Angevin period, the site of an important popular festival still celebrated on 8 September. See Giuseppe Porcaro, *Piedigrotta: Leggenda, storia, folklore* (Napoli: F. Fiorentino, 1958).

99. The chapel of Robert of Anjou is in Castel Nuovo. It contained frescoes, now lost, painted by Giotto between 1329 and 1333. For celebrations of Giotto, see *Fam.* 5.17: "I know two outstanding painters who were not handsome: Giotto, a Florentine citizen whose reputation is very great among the moderns, and Simone di Siena" (*Letters on Familiar Matters*, vol. 1, p. 273). See also Dante *Purgatorio* 11.94–96; Boccaccio *Decameron* 6.5, *Amorosa Visione* 4.16–18, *Genealogia Deorum Gentilium* 14.6; Sacchetti, *Trecentonovelle* 63, 75, and 136. The castle was built between 1279 and 1282 by order of Charles I of Anjou, from whom it gets its original name, the Maschio Angioino (the Angevin Keep). It was called the "new" castle after extensive renovations commissioned by Alfonso of Aragon following his victory over the French.

100. The Certosa of San Martino on the hill of the same name. Petrarch visited there in 1341 with King Robert (cf. *Epyst.* 2.6.8). To anyone arriving at Naples by sea, and from the point of view of the historical center as well, the city is dominated by the imposing fortress of Castel Sant'Elmo and by the white walls of the Certosa di San Martino beneath it. The Certosa was founded in 1325 by Charles the Illustrious, son of King Robert. Following Charles's death in 1328, King Robert continued the work. Following Robert's death in 1343, his granddaughter Joanna I completed the work in 1363.

101. The church and cloister of St. Clare. Cf. *Fam.* 5.3.20 and 5.4.2. Petrarch calls the widow of King Robert, Sancha di Maiorca, "the elder queen" (regine senioris) to distinguish her from Joanna I of Anjou (1326–82), queen of Naples (1343–81) granddaughter of King Robert of Naples, who succeeded Robert with her husband, Andrew of Hungary. Cf. *Fam.* 5.3.20—"The elder queen, formerly the royal spouse, now the most wretched of widows" (*Letters on Familiar Matters*, vol. 1, p. 237)—and *Fam.* 5.4.2. The monumental complex of S. Chiara (St. Clare) is still considered the most important religious structure ever to be built at Naples. The queen entrusted the construction of the monastery to the architect Gagliardo Primario in 1310. The work was finished in 1328 and the church consecrated in 1340.

102. The Black Death, beginning in 1348, marks a watershed in medieval and Renaissance European history. In just two years perhaps one-third to one-half of Europe's popula-

tion died. In many of the major European cities stricken by the plague in the first two years, up to two-thirds of the population succumbed, including Petrarch's Laura, whose death the poet recorded 19 May 1348 on the first flyleaf of his codex of Virgil (Milano, Biblioteca Ambrosiana, Sala Prefetto, manuscript Arm. 10). See the introduction to Boccaccio's *Decameron* and the dedicatory letter to Petrarch's epistolary, which also begins under the sign of the plague of 1348, *Fam.* 1.1: "The year of 1348 left us alone and helpless; it did not deprive us of things that can be restored by the Indian or Caspian or Carpathian Sea. It subjected us to irreparable losses. Whatever death wrought is now an incurable wound. There is only one consolation in all this: we too shall follow those who preceded us" (*Letters on Familiar Matters*, vol. 1, p. 3).

Feo has clarified the meaning of this passage of the *Itinerarium:* "I have exhorted you to visit the neighborhoods of Nido and Capuana famous for the soldiers they provide, but I do not exhort you to go to Castel dell'Ovo, the seat of fables and legends: you are a 'miles' therefore I send you 'ad militie pelagus,' to the sea of the militia (an extravagant but rational image); you are a seeker of truth and I do not send you 'ad fabulas'" ("Inquietudini," p. 182).

According to Comparetti, *Virgil in the Middle Ages,* p. 257, there existed an earlier legend of a palladium of Naples, originally a model of the city in a glass bottle that Konrad von Querfurt, chancellor of Emperor Henry VI, described seeing and himself handling in a letter written from Sicily in 1194 describing impressions of his journey through Italy (published by Leibnitz in the *Scriptores rerum brunsvicensium,* vol. 2, pp. 695–98): "The model . . . perhaps came to grief in the hands of the imperialists; anyhow later legends substituted for it an egg, preserved in a glass bottle, which was itself enclosed in an iron vessel. This form of the legend, which is a much later one, supplanted the former one at the time when the castle, built in 1154 by William I and enlarged by Frederick II, changed its name from 'Castello marino' or 'di mare' to 'Castel dell'uovo' (Castle of the Egg). The latter name does not occur, as far as I know, in any document earlier than the fourteenth century."

103. Virgil *Georgics* 4.563–66: "illo Vergilium me tempore dulcis alebat / Parthenope, studiis florentem ignobilis oti, / carmina qui lusi pastorum audaxque iuventa, / Tityre, te patulae cecini sub tegmine fagi" (In those days I, Virgil, was nursed of sweet Parthenope, and rejoiced in the arts of inglorious ease—I who dallied with shepherds' songs, and, in youth's boldness, sang, Tityrus, of thee under thy spreading beech's covert). Stok, "Il Virgilio del Petrarca," p. 192, notes that Petrarch's information about Virgil's studies in Naples derives from Servius's life of Virgil: "diversis in loci operam dedit nam et Cremonae et Mediolani et Neapoli studuit."

104. The mythical tomb of the siren Parthenope was supposedly at the site where Naples grew up. As a result, the city has become known as Parthenopaea. "Dulcis Parthenope" is a Virgilian stileme. Cf. Virgil *Georgics* 4.563–64.

105. A Petrarchan interpretation of the famous funerary monument epitaph on Virgil's tomb, attributed to the poet and reported by St. Jerome in his *Chronicon* and by Donatus and Servius to have been dictated by the poet while dying: "Mantua me genuit, Calabri rapuere, tenet nunc / Parthenope, cecini pascua, rura, duces" (Mantua bore me, Calabria snatched me away, now Naples holds me: I sang of pastures, fields, and kings).

106. The two peaks are the crater of Vesuvius and the so-called Mt. Soma, that is, a second crater that emerged during the eruption of 79 A.D. The expression "biceps Vesevus" occurs also in *Epyst.* 2.7.31 and "bifidumque Vesevum" in *Epyst.* 2.17.9.

107. A parallel passage on the death of Pliny the Elder is found in *Fam.* 13.4.19: "Pliny could have died in Verona and Virgil in Mantua, except that the former's desire for experience crushed him under the cinders of Vesuvius, while the latter's drive for fame caused his great talent to be felled by a painful death" (*Letters on Familiar Matters*, vol. 2, p. 184). Pliny's noble death is also recalled in *Fam.* 17.8.5 and *Epyst.* 2.7.29–34. Also *Triumphus Fame* 3.43–45 (*Trionfi*, ed. Pacca and Paolino, p. 46): "Mentr'io mirava, subito ebbi scorto / quel Plinio veronese, suo vicino, / a scriver molto, a morir poco accorto" (*The Triumphs of Petrarch*, p. 87: "While I was watching him [Livy] I chanced to see / Pliny, his neighbor of Verona, who, / Wise in his writings, was unwise in death").

108. The fact that Virgil is buried in Naples is recalled also in *Epyst.* 2.7.31–34 and 2.15.125–28; *Rer. Mem.* 2.125.110, p. 245; *Fam.* 13.4.19 and 17.8.5. Pliny was actually from Como and not Verona. Petrarch's error probably derives from the preface of Pliny's *Natural History*, where Catullus (who was known to be Veronese) is referred to in a broad sense as "conterraneum meum," and / or from the manuscript tradition of Pliny's works, which were often attributed to Plinius Secundus Veronensis. See Raffaele Sabbadini, *Le scoperte dei codici greci e latini ne' secoli XIV XV: Nuove ricerche* (Firenze: Sansoni, 1967), p. 90.

109. The abundance of grapes on the slopes of Vesuvius is also mentioned in *Epyst.* 2.7.29–31.

110. Cf. *Fam.* 7.1.4: "But a portion of Italy keeps me concerned, namely, the part formerly known as Magna Graecia, including Abruzzi, Calabria, Puglia, and the Terra di Lavoro now truly so called, and Capua once a powerful city, and Naples now the queen of cities" (*Letters on Familiar Matters*, vol. 1, p. 331).

111. Cf. Suetonius *De vita caesarum* Tiberius 40.

112. Lo Monaco, *Itinerario in Terra Santa 1358*, notes that Herculaneum actually precedes Pompei proceeding south from Naples but the succession Pompei–Herculaneum follows textual rather than topographical reality; this is according to the vivid description of the earthquake of 63 A.D. that destroyed the better part of the two centers as given in Seneca *Naturales quaestiones* 6.1.1, to which Petrarch refers.

113. Cf. Pliny *Naturalis historia* 3.62 and Pomponius Mela *De situ orbis* 2.70.

114. Ceres was an ancient Roman goddess of growth commonly identified in antiquity with Demeter. Ceres is also known as goddess of grain, while Liber was an Italian god of fertility and especially wine, later commonly identified with Dionysius. Petrarch's reference to the fertility of the territory "Leboria," part of Campania, is modeled after Pliny *Naturalis historia* 18.111, and the struggle between Ceres and Bacchus follows Pliny *Naturalis historia* 3.60. See also *Fam.* 11.5: "From my most productive and pleasing country place, I scornfully observe the battle in Campania between Bacchus and Ceres, feeling in my heart wealthier than any King" (*Letters on Familiar Matters*, vol. 2, p. 95). For part of Campania as "Terra laboris" (land of labor), cf. *Fam.* 15.7.9. The name of the region termed by Petrarch "land of labor" corresponds to what the ancients called the "Leboriae terrae" named for the ancient people called Leborini who inhabited this part

of Campania, roughly between Mount Màssico and the peninsula of Sorrento. The name was corrupted from "terra Leboriae" to "Terra laboris" (land of labor) quite naturally by association with the agricultural fertility of the area. On the appellation "Terra laboris," see P. Gribaudi, "Sul nome di 'Terra di Lavoro'," in *Rivista geografica italiana* 14 (1907), pp. 193–210.

115. After doubling the cape at St. Campanella, one enters the Gulf of Salerno and then the delta plain of the mouth of the Sele (cf. Pomponius Mela *De situ orbis* 2.69). The river Sileris is also mentioned by Petrarch in *Epyst.* 2.17.9 as defining the borders of Campania.

116. Salerno was the site of one of the earliest and greatest medical schools of the Middle Ages. It was noted for its physicians as early as the tenth century, and by the eleventh century it was attracting students from all over Europe, as well as Asia and Africa. In 1221 the Holy Roman emperor Frederick II decreed that no doctor in the kingdom could legally practice medicine until he had been examined and publicly approved by the school at Salerno. For a panoramic treatment of medicine at Salerno between the thirteenth and fourteenth centuries, see Paul Oskar Kristeller, "La scuola di Salerno," in *Studi sulla scuola medica salernitana* (Napoli: Istituto Italiano per gli Studi Filosofici, 1986), pp. 58–77. See also Patricia Skinner, *Health and Medicine in Early Medieval Southern Italy* (Leiden: Brill, 1997). Petrarch's dismissal of contemporary medicine at Salerno is probably an extension of his general disdain for the profession as expressed in his *Invective contra medicum.* See B. Martinelli, "Petrarca e la medicina," in *Invective contra medicum,* ed. P. G. Ricci, Storia e letteratura: Raccolta di studi e testi (Roma: Edizioni di Storia e Letteratura, 1978), pp. 204–49.

117. Cf. Virgil *Aeneid* 1.50–54 on the kingdom of Aeolus, the ruler of the winds, as well as 8.416–22 on Lipari and Vulcano. Cf. Pliny *Naturalis historia* 3.92 and Pomponius Mela *De situ orbis* 2.69.

118. Probably based on Virgil *Aeneid* 8.416–22. Other sources on the these islands include Pliny *Naturalis historia* 3.92; Pomponius Mela *De situ orbis* 2.69; Solinus 6. Vulcan and Lipari are paired also in *Africa* 8.312–14, to indicate the Aeolian group during Hannibal's flight to Ephesus (see below, note 129): "they glide between / Vulcan and Lipari and look with awe / at the black plumes of smoke, the fearsome flames / that rise from the twin peaks" (*Petrarch's Africa,* p. 193).

119. Scalea, located on the northern coast of Calabria, takes its name from its terraced layout on the hillside (*scale,* "stairs"), at the bottom of the promontory of Cape Scalea. It is believed that the town of Lao, of pre-Indo-European origin and colonized by the Sybarites in the sixth to fifth century B.C., once stood on the plain South of Scalea, near the mouth of the river Lao.

There does not seem to be any source for Petrarch's erroneous assertion that Scalea is the place where Italy grows most narrow; it may derive from his consultation of portolan charts where Scalea, sometimes in red letters, can occur close to a point where the peninsula does appear most narrow (see Illustration 9: Scalia (Scalea) is at the base of the bootleg of Italy at a point where the peninsula might appear to be narrowest). Lo Monaco, *Itinerario in Terra Santa,* p. 109, notes that the town apparently developed in the late medieval period, given the modernity of the name, which is not mentioned in any of the classical sources.

120. Petrarch discusses this lighthouse in his gloss on Virgil *Aeneid* 3.411 (f. 95r of the poet's Ambrosian codex of Virgil), where he also cites Pomponius Mela on the "tower of Reggio": "Columpnam Massanam dicunt moderni, sed de hac apud autenticos nichil quod meminerunt legi. Est et Columpna Regia in adverso litore Ytalie, non procul a Regio, cuius et Pomponius in Cosmographia (2.68) et carte vetustissime meminerunt. De hac intelligitur hic. Ait enim a continenti usque ad Pharon, quem constat esse in insula Trinacrie, ubi est Pelorus" (cf. Pierre de Nolhac, *Pétrarque et l'humanism*, 2 vols. [Paris: Champion, 1907], vol. 1, p. 150).

121. In the straits of Messina, between Sicily and the Italian mainland, were located famed Scylla and Charybdis. According to the *Oxford Classical Dictionary*, 3d ed., Scylla was "a fantastic monster with twelve feet and six heads who lurked in a cave situated high up on the cliff opposite Charybdis, darting her necks out like a kind of multiple moray eel to seize dolphins, sharks or passing sailors. Charybdis is a sort of whirlpool or maelstrom in a narrow channel of the sea (later identified with the Straits of Messina, where there is nothing of the kind), opposite Scylla; it sucks in and casts out water three times a day and no ship can possibly live in it."

   Cf. *RVF* 189: "Passa la nave mia colma d'oblio / per aspro mare, a mezza notte il verno, / enfra Scilla et Caribdi; et al governo / siede 'l signore, anzi 'l nimico mio" (*Petrarch: The Canzoniere, or Rerum Vulgarium Fragmenta*, p. 281: "My ship full of forgetful cargo sails / through rough seas at midnight of a winter / between Charybdis and the Scylla reef"). For the significance of Scylla and Charybdis in this key poem of the *Canzoniere* in connection with the *navigatio vitae* theme of that work and the theme of Ulysses in Petrarch's ouevre, see Michelangelo Picone, "Il sonetto CLXXXIX," *Atti e memorie dell'Academia Patavina di Scienze, Lettere ed Arti* 1–2 (1989–90), part 2: Classe di Scienze Morali, Lettere ed Arti, pp. 151–67. Petrarch speaks of "the fury of Scylla and the blows of Charybdis" in *Fam.* 7.12.18. He recalls Ulysses' struggles in *Fam.* 9.13.25: "Rather than grow old at home, he preferred to age between Scylla and Charybdis, among the black whirlpools of Avernus, and in the midst of such difficult circumstances and locations as to weary even the reader's mind" (*Letters on Familiar Matters*, vol. 2, p. 40); see also *Fam.* 1.7.5, 2.9.13, 15.3.8, 18.2.6, 23.4.3; *Sen.* 10.1. Petrarch sometimes speaks of Charybdis singly, as at *Fam.* 5.8.4: "I tremble at this harborless Charybdis, notorious for the shipwreck of so many, in which he is now navigating" (*Letters on Familiar Matters*, vol. 1, p. 257); see also *Fam.* 10.3.21 and 23.18; *Sen.* 2.1. *Sen.* 12.1 refers to "ill-famed Charybdis bobbing in the thunderous eddies" (*Letters of Old Age*, vol. 1, pp. 441–42).

   For his classical sources, Petrarch explicitly cites here "the third book of the divine poem." See Virgil *Aeneid* 3.420–21, "Dextrum Scylla latus, laevum implacata Charybdis/obsidet"(Scylla guards the right side; Charybdis, insatiate, the left), and 3.684. See *Petrarch's Remedies*, vol. 4, p. 334, for a listing of other classical and medieval sources, including Ovid *Amores* 2.11.18, Ovid *Metamorphoses* 7.62–65 and 13.730 ff.; Lucan *Pharsalia* 4.459–61; Isidore *Etymologiae* 2.12.6, 12.3.32, 13.18.4–5, 14.6.32.

122. See the journey towards Italy from Africa prophesized by Helenus to Aeneas (Virgil *Aeneid* 3.410–28).

123. The pause for this explanation is suggested and informed by the same passage from Virgil *Aeneid* 3.414–19: "These lands they say, of old broke asunder, torn by force of mighty upheaval—such vast change can length of time effect—when the two countries were one unbroken whole. The sea came in might between, cut off with its waters the Hesperian from the Sicilian coast, and with narrow tideway laves fields and cities on severed shores" (*Virgil*, trans. Faircloth, vol. 2, p. 377). It is interesting and significant that Petrarch differs from Virgil in attributing separation to the powers of the waves over time rather than to a telluric event. In this he sides with the historical source, Pliny *Naturalis historia* 3.86: "In former times it was attached to the southern part of Italy, but later it was separated from it by an overflow of the sea" (Pliny, *Natural History*, trans. H. Rackham, 10 vols. [Cambridge: Harvard University Press, 1989], p. 65). Other sources include Ovid *Metamorphoses* 15.290–92; Lucan *Pharsalia* 2.435–38; Claudian *De raptu Proserpinae* 1.242–43; Seneca *Dialogi* 6.17.2 and *Naturales quaestiones* 6.30; Justin *Historia* 4.1; Servius *Aeneid* 3.414; and Isidore *Etymologiae* 14.6.34.

    Petrarch alludes to the same separation of lands in the context of remarks on the passing of time in *Sen.* 12.1: "Cliffs yield and mountain ranges change their appearance and nature; for example, Vesuvius has grown cold, Etna cooled, in many places the Alps have sunk, the Sicilian Peloro and the Italian Apennines, split by waves where once they stood with wooded hills, now look down upon ill-famed Charybdis bobbing in the thunderous eddies. Finally, though great men may deny this one thing—great I mean in other matters but small in this—the world, as we believe, will yield to age" (*Letters of Old Age*, vol. 2, p. 442).

124. For the three summits of Sicily, see Pliny *Naturalis historia* 3.87 and Pomponius Mela *De situ orbis* 2.116. Due to its triangular shape, Sicily was once called Trinacria, meaning "Three Capes," after Peloro, Passero, and Lilibeo, which were its three corners. For Pliny, "Sicily itself is triangular in shape, its points being the promontory mentioned before named Pelorum, pointing towards Italy, opposite Scylla, Pachynum towards Greece, the Morea being 440 miles away and Lilybaeum towards Africa, at a distance of 180 miles from the promontory of Mercury and 190 from Cape Carbonara in Sardinia" (*Natural History*, p. 65).

125. Cf. *Fam.* 9.5: "Because of slight suspicion, Hannibal slew his loyal helmsman; a famous Sicilian mountain named after the buried helmsman bears witness to the crime" (*Letters on Familiar Matters*, vol. 2, p. 22). The murder of the pilot Pelorus, suspected of treachery, is recounted by Strabo (1.1.17), but Strabo's Pelorus is the Greek pilot of the Persian fleet, killed by his suspicious commander after the battle of Salamis. The association of the tale of Pelorus with Hannibal (historically without basis) is found in Valerius Maximus and Pomponius Mela. Cf. the journey in which Hannibal flees from Carthage toward Ephesus in *Africa* 8.315–29: "Between Trinacria's fields and Italy / a bay extends, / so placed that mariners / who visit it from afar are oft deceived / until experience has rectified / their first opinion: one would deem the shores / are not divided but compose the coast / of one land only and two peaks stand / close joined together, as indeed men

say / they stood of old. And thither by design / or chance the helmsman of the Punic ship, / Pelorus steered his bark. The wily chief / fearful of treachery, trusting no man / had the unhappy pilot put to death, / though guiltless and desiring no such end. / The leader when he learned of his mistake regretted bitterly his savage act / and there on that Sicilian hillside gave him honored burial and raised / a tomb above it, with a monument / and altar. Now the mountain keeps and will forever keep the memory of his name" (*Petrarch's Africa*, 8.452–72).

Petrarch takes the opportunity in the *Itinerary* to express his preference for the version of the killing of the pilot Pelorus given by Pomponius Mela, who had described it as having taken place during a journey from Carthage to Ephesus, while the version given by Valerius Maximus had it taking place during a journey from Crotone to Africa (an account confirmed by Servius *Aeneid* 3.411: "on a return trip to his homeland with only one ship fleeing from the Romans").

While two journeys are documented by the historical sources (including Livy), none gives any information about the routes followed by Hannibal. Vincenzo Fera has documented traces of Petrarch's study of the problem in connection with the passage above from the *Africa* as it can be traced in numerous passages and annotations scattered through Petrarch's works (*La revisione petrarchesca dell'*Africa [Messina: Centro di Studi Umanistici, 1984], pp. 371–76).

126.   Cf. Virgil *Aeneid* 3.551–53: "hinc sinus Herculei, si vera est fama, Tarenti / cernitur; attollit se diva Lacinia contra / Caulonisque arces et navifragum Scylaceum" (*Virgil*, trans. Faircloth, vol. 1, pp. 384–85: "Next is described the bay of Tarentum, a town of Hercules if the tale be true; while over against it rise the Lacinian goddess [Juno], the towers of Caulon and shipwrecking Scyaceum").

127.   The importance of Crotone is described in Livy 24.3.1–15; Petrarch had annotated the passage carefully in his copy (British Library, manuscript Harleian 2493, f. 134r). The emphasis on the decadence of Crotone together with its importance as the site of Juno's temple is also in *Africa* 6.452–58: "In Italy's remotest part the town / of Croton lies, once far renowned and now / a wretched port bearing a noble name. Here, sited to salute the morning light / of Phoebus, stood a temple consecrate / to Juno, rich in the embellishment / of precious pictures that with Grecian art / great Zeuxis had created to endure, / by all men cherished and revered" (*Petrarch's Africa*, p. 125). Cf. also *Rer. Mem.* 3.70.

128.   St. Jerome had identified Taranto as the birthplace of Ennius in *Chronicon, Olymp.* 135 (see also *Bucolicum Carmen* 10.181). The passage had been marked with an asterisk by Petrarch in his copy (see Giuseppe Billanovich, "Un nuovo esempio delle scoperte e delle letture del Petrarca: L'Eusebio—Girolamo—Pseudo Prospero," *Schriften und Vorträge des Petrarcas Instituts Köln* 3 (1954), p. 39 no. 157). Virgil's place of death was a subject of controversy. Fabio Stok notes that the news of Virgil's death at Taranto derives from the *Vita serviana*, Servius's life of Virgil. It is noteworthy that Petrarch gives greater credit to Servius than to Jerome and others, including Dante *Purgatorio* 3.27—"da Brandizio è tolto" (see G. C. Alessio and C. Villa, "Per *Inferno* I 67–87," in *Vestigia: Studi in onore di G. Billanovich* [Roma: Edizioni di Storia e Letteratura, 1984], p. 6, n. 22)—and perhaps

Donatus. On the debate about whether or not Petrarch knew the *Vita vergilii* of Suetonius-Donatus, see Stok, "Il Virgilio del Petrarca," pp. 186–212.

129. The first island encountered, Corcyra or Corfu, is the northernmost of the western Greek islands. It was in Angevin hands at the time. In the parallel passage from *Africa* 8.331–34, the first island encountered by Hannibal on his trip to Ephesus is instead Cephalonia: "and first ahead / is Cephalonia sighted, then the isle / Zacynthus, moderate in acreage. / To port a narrow passage could be won / if the Corinthian isthmus, a high sill / between two seas, would give way to the waves" (*Petrarch's Africa*, p. 194). According to Lo Monaco, *Itinerario in Terra Santa*, p. 111, Petrarch may have been uncertain about the relative positions of these islands, because during the phases of elaboration of the *Africa* he made a note to remind himself to do some further checking (cf. Fera, *La revisione*, 374–75). However, the variation between *Africa* and *Itinerarium* on this point probably results from the fact that Hannibal passed directly from Sicily toward the Greek isles without further skirting the Ionian coasts of Italy, as Petrarch does in the imaginary journey of the *Itinerarium*, which passes from Otranto directly east across the Adriatic to Corfu.

      The toponym "Achaea" appears to indicate the entire peninsula here, but, as Lo Monaco notes, *Itinerario in Terra Santa*, p. 111, Petrarch gave a much more detailed breakdown of the peninsula in a gloss to his Pliny (Paris, Bibliothèque Nationale, manuscript Par. lat. 6802, f. 31r): "Attendendum in cartis cosmographis quod in illa quam peninsula, isthmos facit et quam multi Achaiam solam putant, est primum Peloponesus ad dexteram contra Italiam et super Corinthium sinum, ubi est Patras. Secundo est Achaia in medio ubi est Moton et Coron, contra meridiem. Tertio Messenia simulque Laconica, contra orientem Cretamque insulam, ubi mons Maleus. Quarto sinus Argolicus ad Scilleum reflexus ad Arthon ipsumque ad isthmum, quo in tractu Argos ipsa est, quamvis in mensura ultima videatur Peloponesus hec universa comprehendere, quasi nomen."

130. Petrarch refers to the desirability of the creation of such a passage also in the *Africa* 8.333–34. The isthmus of Corinth was cut by the canal of Corinth only in the last century (1882–93), but the idea was already proposed in antiquity (cf. Pliny *Naturalis historia* 4.10). The idea was also Nero's, according to Suetonius *De vita caesarum* Nero, 19.

131. Petrarch's principal sources for this war would be Florus *Epitome* 2.16 and Justin *Historia* 34.2.6. The reference to Cicero is to *De officiis* 1.35: "nollem Corinthum, sed credo aliquid secutos, opportunitatem loci maxime, ne posset aliquando ad bellum faciendum locus ipse adhortari" (*Cicero De officiis*, trans. Walter Miller [London: William Heinemann Ltd; New York: G. P. Putnam's Sons, 1928], pp. 36–37: "I wish they had not destroyed Corinth; but I believe they had some special reason for what they did—its convenient situation, probably—and feared that its very location might some day furnish a temptation to renew the war").

132. The navigation along this coast is also described in *Africa* 8.337–39. Modon and Coron were Venetian maritime stations from the beginning of the thirteenth century.

133. The richest mythographic source concerning Crete is Pomponius Mela *De situ orbis* 2.122, but see also Virgil *Aeneid* 3.103–13. The Venetians occupied Crete after the fourth

Crusade (1204), making it an important commercial center. It is described as the place of origin of religious beliefs in *Fam.* 15.7.14—"Crete, that ancient center of superstitions, is living with new ones" (*Letters on Familiar Matters*, vol. 2, p. 269)—and as sacred to Jupiter in *Fam.* 15.8.19. See also the description of the island in *Sen.* 4.1, to the *condottiere* Luchino dal Verme, who was departing on an expedition to suppress the rebellious island on behalf of the Venetians and whom Petrarch informs in a context not unlike that of his letter to Mandelli: "It is a large island, indeed, the largest island in our sea after Trinacria, a famous and powerful island with a hundred cities at one time, where there was Jupiter's palace and tomb, and the horrible Minotaur, and the pathless Labyrinth. None of our islands, unless I am mistaken, lie so far from the continent; it is surrounded on all sides by a vast sea, and its shores are harborless. On land, the inhabitants are turncoats, cunning, false, and were always considered not only by ancient Greek and Latin poets, but even by the Apostle Paul, as liars, evil beasts, lazy bellies" (*Letters of Old Age*, vol. 1, p. 116).

134.   Achilles, whom his mother Thetis had disguised as a woman in order to avoid the war against Troy, seduced Deidamia, daughter of Nicomede king of Skyros, but later abandoned her. See Ovid *Ars amatoria* 1.679–702; Statius *Achilleid* 1.285–960; Dante *Inferno* 26.61–62; Boccaccio *Amorosa Visione* 23.31–24. 6.

See *Sen.* 13.3 for the figure of Pythagoras: "It is well known that, by being born, Pythagoras raised Samos to prominence and Theophrastus Lesbos" (*Letters of Old Age*, vol. 2, p. 484). Cf. *Rer. Mem.* 1.24 and *Triumphus fame* 3.7–9: "Aristotele poi, pien d'alto ingegno; / Pythagora, che primo umilemente / philosophia chiamò per nome degno." According to the tradition and to Petrarch (*Sen.* 12.2), Pythagoras refused to take the name of one who knows (*sophos*), preferring the more modest title of one who loves knowledge (*philosophus*). On Pythagoras's travel to Italy, "more inflamed with the love of truth than of country," see *Fam.* 9.13. See also Ovid *Metamorphoses* 15.60–64.

135.   The reference is to Hero and Leander, also mentioned in Pomponius Mela *De situ orbis* 1.97 and 2.26. Leander was called the "youth of Abydos" from the name of the place in Asia Minor where he lived. In order to be with Hero, Leander swam across the Hellespont, guided by a flame that Hero put on the window; one night the flame was blown out, Leander drowned, and Hero, seeing his body wash up, threw herself out of the window. Cf. *Triumphus Cupidinis* 3.20; Ovid *Epistulae* 18 and 19; Ovid *Ars amatoria* 2.249–50; Virgil *Georgics* 3.258–63.

136.   Although Lo Monaco, *Itinerario in Terra Santa*, p. 69, translates "emulatione" with "imitation," here the Trecento *volgarizzamenti* translate "famoso per l'odio del romano impero" (famous for its hate of the Roman empire). For Byzantium's emulation of Rome, there is a parallel passage in *Sen.* 3.6: "for the Greeks call Constantinople another Rome. They have dared to call it not only equal to the ancient city, but greater in monuments and graced with riches. But if this were true on both counts as it is false (I would say it to Sozomen who wrote this), surely no Greek, however impudent, would dare to call them equal in men, arms, virtues, and glory" (*Letters of Old Age*, vol. 1, p. 101).

137.   Petrarch's sources for the existence of a flourishing cult of Helios include Horace *Carmen saeculare* 1.7.1; Horace *Epistulae* 1.11.17 and 21; and Pliny *Naturalis historia* 34.41, which tells

of an enormous statue in Rhodes dedicated to the sun. The Knights of the Order of St. John captured Rhodes in 1308 and remained there until 1522 when they were driven out, eventually settling in Malta. Cf. *Fam.* 15.7: "Rhodes, protector of the faith, lies inglorious without wounds" (*Letters on Familiar Matters*, vol. 2, p. 269).

138. Cf. *Sen.* 7.1, to Urban V: "You know the plight of your Christians throughout the East. Indeed the evil is close. Have you not heard how the unsoldierly peoples of Asia, whom our slackness makes valiant—especially the former Phrygians, now Turks—endlessly plunder wretched Greece and ravage the Cyclades that are scattered throughout the Aegean" (*Letters of Old Age*, vol. 1, pp. 254–55). Osman I (1258–c. 1326), founder of the Ottoman Empire, undertook the conquest and unification of Asia Minor, and the expansion of Turkish control continued throughout the fourteenth century.

139. The principal source for this passage is Florus *Epitome* 3.6. Pompey conducted the war against the pirates in 67 B.C. having arrived in Syria in 64 B.C. (Lucan 1.122). Cf. *Fam.* 23.1: "O great Pompey, who quickly subdued the shameful bands of plunderers threatening Roman ships and Italian shores and raging over all the seas, and then put them in chains, would that you were alive—I would speak to you, and I would beg you to cleanse now, just as you once cleansed all the infected seas, if not all lands, at least your Italy so pitifully stained with a new band of plunderers" (*Letters on Familiar Matters*, vol. 2, p. 254).

140. The story of a forced migration of pirates to Lodi by Pompey the Great derives from the local historiographical traditions of Lodi. Pliny *Naturalis historia* 3.124 speaks of "Laus Pompei" which Pompey Strabo established as a Roman colony in 89 and which received Roman citizenship in 49 from Julius Caesar. The city was destroyed in 1111 by the Milanese and was rebuilt on the bank of the Adda after a privilege was granted by Federico Barbarossa in 1158.

141. For the position of Cyprus, see Pliny *Naturalis historia* 5.129 and Pomponius Mela *De situ orbis* 2.102. A Petrarchan parallel on the luxury of Cyprus is *Tr. Cup.* 4.100–102: "Giace oltra ove l'Egeo sospira e piagne / un'isoletta dilicata e molle / più d'altra che'l sol scalde, o che 'l mar bagne." Cf. *Fam.* 15.7.14: "Cyprus is an unfit abode for a strong man; lesser Armenia fluctuates between the danger of temporal and eternal death, besieged on all sides by enemies of the cross" (*Letters on Familiar Matters*, vol. 2, p. 269). The itinerary of Petrarch's guide to the eastern Mediterranean (from Crete to Rhodes to Cyprus to Lesser Armenia) follows to some extent the progress of this passage of *Fam.* 15.7, addressed to Stefano Colonna, "concerning the unsettled condition of nearly the entire world," which also presents Petrarch's mental map of the area (from Rhodes to Crete to Cyprus to Lesser Armenia). Not being delimited by permanent natural boundaries, the territory covered by Armenia has varied at different epochs of the world's history. At the time of the ancient Romans there was recognized a Lesser as well as a Greater Armenia, the former embracing a portion of Asia Minor. Lesser Armenia is a region in southern Turkey corresponding to ancient Cilicia. Cf. *Sen.* 3.9: "In recent days, the Venetian fleet set forth for Cyprus to Alexandria. . . . When it was driven from the shores of Crete, until lately loyal and subject but now hostile, to a city named Sittia on the island's furthest side where it looks toward Asia, toward Lesser Armenia" (*Letters of Old Age*, vol. 1, p. 112).

142. St. Hilarion was founder of anchoritic life in Palestine. He was born at Tabatha, south
      of Gaza, Palestine, about 291 and died on the island of Cyprus about 371. The chief
      source of information regarding him is the biography written by St. Jerome (ed. A.
      Hamman, Supplement vol. 23 of Patrologia Latina, ed. J. P. Migne, 221 vols. plus sup-
      plements [Paris, 1844–55; 1958–74], pp. 29–54). Hilarion is discussed at length in *De
      Vita Solitaria* 2.1: "Ciprum insulam suis [of S. Ilarione] moribus longe dissimilem")
      where Petrarch's source is St. Jerome's *Vita Hilarionis*. But St. Jerome says that Hilarion's
      friend Hesychius brought the body from Cyprus to Majuma, and that the location of
      his burial is an open question (*Vita Hilarionis*, in *Vita Dei Santi*, vol. 4, ed. A.A.R.
      Bastiaensen and J. Smit, trans. L. Canalie and C. Moreschini, introduction by C.
      Mohrmann [Milano: Fondazioni Lorenzo Valla; Mondadori, 1975], 9:33.3–4): "Cernas
      usque hodie miram inter Palestinos et Cyprios contentionem, his corpus Hilarionis,
      illis spiritum se habere certantibus. Et tamen in utrisque locis magna quotidie signa
      fiunt, sed magis in hortulo Cypri, forsitan quia plus illum locum dilexerit" (Even at
      the present day one may see a great dispute between the people of Palestine and the
      Cypriotes, the one contending that they have the body, the other the spirit of Hilarion.
      And yet in both places great miracles are wrought daily, but to a greater extent in the
      garden of Cyprus, perhaps because that spot was dearest to him).

143. For the border of Lesser Armenia, see Pliny *Naturalis historia* 6.25.

144. Cf. Cicero *De officiis* 2.33; W. Walther, *Proverbia Sententiaeque Latinitatis Medii ac Recentioris
      Aevi*, new series, ed. P. G. Schmidt (Göttingen, 1982), n. 660a.

145. Petrarch's Latin text reads "Sur" for the city of Tyre, which is called in Hebrew, *Zor*, and
      in Arabic, *Sour*, from two words meaning rock. For Petrarch's "Sur" for Tyre, cf. Virgil
      Aeneid 1.350; Vulgate Ezekiel 26 and 27; Vulgate Matthew 11.21.

146. All of these places were in Arab hands at the time of Petrarch's writing and basically
      impracticable. Acre is a Syrian seaport on the Mediterranean, in a plain with Mount
      Carmel on the south and the mountains of Galilee on the east. One of the best har-
      bors on the Syrian coast, the city was taken by the Moslems in 638, by the Crusaders
      in 1104, again by the Moslems in 1187, by the Crusaders again in 1191, and finally by
      the Moslems in 1291. For all of these ports, see H. L. Savage, "Pilgrimages and Pilgrim
      Shrines in Palestine and Syria after 1095," in *A History of the Crusades*, ed. K. M. Setton
      and H. M. Hazard (Madison: University of Wisconsin Press, 1977), vol. 4, pp. 36–68.

147. Damascus is a very ancient city and is almost the chief among the cities of the east for
      size and population. It was the capital city of Lesser Syria, called Lebanon of Phoenicia
      (cf. Isaiah 7.8: "The head of Syria is Damascus"). The Pilgrims' Society editor notes
      that "no pilgrim seems able to refrain from making the quotation" (Jacques de Vitry,
      The History of Jerusalem A.D. 1180, trans. Aubrey Stewart [London: Palestine Pilgrims'
      Text Society, 1896], p.23). "Damascus was formerly the capital of Syria, but the hon-
      our was transferred by Antiochus to Antioch" (*Feltellus* [c. 1130], trans. James Rose
      Macpherson [London: Palestine Pilgrims' Text Society 1892], vol. 5, p. 3).

148. A fourth-century translator of the *Jewish War* of Flavius Josephus. The name is based
      on an error. In the manuscripts of the work "Iosippus" appears quite regularly for
      "Josephus." From *Iosippus* a copyist derived *Hegesippus*, which name, therefore, is merely

that of the original author, erroneously transcribed. In the best manuscripts, the translator is said to be St. Ambrose. Although formerly much contested, this claim is today acknowledged by the greater number of philologists. The work began to circulate about the time of the death of the bishop of Milan (398), or shortly after a letter of St. Jerome (*Epistula* 71), written between 386 and 400, bears witness to this. But there is nothing to prove that St. Ambrose wrote this translation at the end of his life. The reference is therefore to Hegesippus *Hist.* 1.13, which derives in turn from Flavius Josephus's *Antiquities of the Jews* (3.29): "And now Vespasian took along with him his army from Antioch, which is the metropolis of Syria, and without dispute deserves the place of the third city in the habitable earth, that was under the Roman empire, both in magnitude, and other marks of prosperity" (*The Complete Works of Flavius Josephus,* trans. William Whiston [Chicago: Thompson and Thomas, 1902], p. 587). Petrarch is unpersuaded by Josephus's claim for the importance of Antioch during Roman times and grants the palm to Damascus by virtue of the greater antiquity and the sacred sanction of its claim.

149. Cf. Aristotle *Nicomachean Ethics* 3.3.1112b.23–24. On "intention," see *Fam.* 20.4.28–31. The idea of mental pilgrimage through reading sacred texts returns explicitly later in the *Itinerarium* (16.5). On the importance for the traveler of having a goal or destination, see *Fam.* 20.4.28–31: "Nothing is worse for a wayfarer than not knowing where he is going, nothing more shameful for a man than not knowing what he knows. . . . From the beginning we must have fixed in our minds where we wish to go, lest with continual changing we think, as happens at night when the path is lost, that we are going forward when we are going backward" (*Letters on Familiar Matters,* vol. 3, p. 132).

150. Petrarch's guide becomes increasingly a mental and meditational support as it undertakes to treat the Holy Land itself. He makes little or no attempt to provide practical or detailed information about the Holy Land sites, as was typical in the *descriptiones* and *itineraria* of the late medieval period. Rather, he appears to revert to an earlier medieval pilgrimage mode more akin to that of Paula or Egeria (both to compensate for his lack of direct knowledge and, perhaps, as a literary homage to the classical literature of pilgrimage: see the echoes of the so-called *Epitaphium Paulae* noted below), as described by Mary B. Campbell: "we tend not to *see* place description in the tissue of anecdote and scriptural quotation that constitutes these pilgrimage accounts" ("'The Object of One's Gaze': Landscape, Writing, and Early Medieval Pilgrimage," in *Discovering New Worlds: Essays on Medieval Exploration and Imagination,* ed. Scott D. Westrem [New York: Garland Publishing, 1991], p. 6). The part of the text dedicated to the Holy Land has less of a guidebook character than the Italian portion and appears designed to assist the pilgrim in his meditations.

The Jordan River is the river where Jesus was baptized (Matthew 3.1–17); the Temple is described as "in ruins" since the building was destroyed by Titus (son of the emperor Vespasian and later himself emperor, 79–81 A.D.), who conquered and destroyed Jerusalem in April of the year 70, after a siege of five months. Mount Calvary is the place of the execution of Jesus Christ. Since the sixth century the usage has been to designate Calvary as a mountain, but the Gospel styles it merely a "place" (Matthew 27.33; Mark 15.22; Luke 23.33; John 19.17). The Evangelists tell us that Jesus' tomb was

Joseph of Arimathea's own new monument, which he had hewn out of a rock, and that it was closed by a great stone rolled to the door (Matthew 27.60; Mark 15.46; Luke 23.53). Knowledge of the place was handed down by oral tradition, and the correctness of this knowledge was proved by the investigations caused to be made in 326 by the emperor Constantine, who then marked the site for future ages by erecting over the tomb of Jesus a basilica, in the place of which, according to an unbroken written tradition, now stands the Church of the Holy Sepulcher.

Lo Monaco notes (*Itinerario in Terra Santa,* p. 115) that the only Gospel authority for the detail of the sleeping guards, mentioned by Petrarch, is Matthew 28.1–15. But the detail had been strikingly developed by Dante in his encounter, in *Inferno* 10.9, with the Epicureans, who are represented in open tombs that recall the iconography of Christ's resurrection, "and no one is standing guard" (see the note to this passage in *The Divine Comedy of Dante Alighieri,* trans. Robert Durling [Oxford: Oxford University Press, 1996], vol. 1, p. 162).

The contiguous evocation of Christ's descent to the underworld adds to the Dantesque flavor of this meditation (for the theme in Dante, see Amilcare A. Iannucci, *Forma ed evento nella* Divina commedia [Roma: Bulzoni, 1984]). In fact, more than the Gospel sources for Christ's descent (Romans 10.6–10; 1 Corinthians 15.20–23), Petrarch may be influenced here by the literature and iconography associated with the medieval representations of Christ's "harrowing of hell," which, while ultimately based upon the New Testament and the Fathers, have been found to largely derive from the apocryphal Gospel of Nicodemus, the literary form of a part of which is said to date back to the second or third century. In any event, Petrarch's interest in Christ's conquest of the underworld is consistent with his own personal passion for military travel and conquest that is evident throughout his writings and that characterizes (also in the allusion to the destruction of the Temple) this first frame of the pilgrim's pious meditation (coloring even the high point of this opening meditation below at *Itin.* 16.3).

151.   Sion is the name of the ancient stronghold of Jerusalem, which through its association with the Last Supper (based upon Luke 22.12 and Acts 14.15) was a pilgrimage site already in the sixth century when Jerome's friend Paula visited there: "Leaving that place she ascended Sion, which signifies 'citadel,' or 'watch-tower'" (*The Pilgrimage of the Holy Paula by St. Jerome,* trans. Aubrey Stewart [London: Adelphi, 1887], p. 6). For an extensive treatment of the topography of Mount Sion, upon which part of the city of Jerusalem is situated, see *Burchard of Mount Sion, A.D. 1280,* trans. Aubrey Stewart [London: Palestine Pilgrims' Text Society, 1896], vol. 12, pp. 65–71.

To Christians, Mt. Olivet (not so much a hill as a range of hills separated by low depressions to the east of Jerusalem) is a holy place because it was much frequented by Jesus during the last days of his public life. Petrarch singles out several in the Gospels: Bethany, the home of Lazarus and of Simon the Leper (Mark 14.3; Matthew 26.6); Bethphage, from which began the triumphal procession to Jerusalem (Matthew 21.1); the place where the fig tree cursed by Jesus stood (Matthew 21.18–22; Mark 11.12–14, 20–21); the spot where Jesus wept over Jerusalem (Luke 19:41); the site where he prophesied the destruction of the Temple, the ruin of the city, and the end of the world (Matthew 24.1); the Garden of Gethsemani; lastly the place where Jesus imparted his farewell blessing to the apostles and ascended into heaven (Luke 24.50–51). All these spots the piety of Christian ages has, with more or less success, sought to locate and to consecrate by erecting sanctuaries.

Petrarch begins with the mention of two specific places, Sion and Mt. Olivet, but the series of sites becomes increasingly difficult to localize topographically as it develops ("where he gave sight to the blind"), culminating in the "place" where Christ "restored to liberty the soul." Petrarch collapses the topography of the Holy Land in spite of the fact that literature on these sites was copious. For example, he does not specifically name the Valley of Jehoshaphat, which lies between Mount Sion and Mount Olivet and is the place where "it is believed that the Lord will come to judge the World" (cf. Jacques de Vitry, *The History of Jerusalem A.D. 1180*, trans. Aubrey Stewart [London: Palestine Pilgrim's Text Society, 1896], vol. 11, p. 46).

152. A version of the same anecdote is given in *Rer. Mem.* 3.37.

153. Petrarch focuses on the indifference of the Jews to the mission of Jesus. The entire passage revisits a theme treated in the *De otio* (1) of 1347 (*Opere latine di Francesco Petrarca*, ed. Antonietta Bufano [Torino: UTET, 1975], pp. 620–21). Cf. also *Fam.* 23.1.7: "O noble couple, Vespasian and Titus, worthy of one another, the son of the father and the father of the son, who in a single chariot, a sight never seen before, achieved a glorious vengeance for Christ at the acclaimed triumph over Jerusalem," (*Letters on Familiar Matters*, vol. 3, p. 255). That the Roman destruction of Jerusalem was visited upon the city for the killing of Christ is a concept expressed by Dante, who emphasized the avenging role of the Roman Empire in *Purgatorio* 21.83–84 and in *Paradiso* 6.88–93. In both passages reference is made to the destruction of Jerusalem by Titus, which Dante says was the vengeance upon the Jews for the crucifixion of Christ, whereby in its turn the sin of Adam was avenged. According to Charles S. Singleton, the "theory that Titus, as the destroyer of Jerusalem, was the avenger of the death of Christ, was borrowed by Dante from Orosius [*Historia* 7.3.8 and 9.9]" (Dante Alighieri, *The Divine Comedy*, trans. Charles S. Singleton, *Purgatorio*, Bollingen Series 80 [Princeton: Princeton University Press], vol. 2, pp. 512–13).

154. Vulgate Psalm 40 [Ps. 41], v. 11.

155. Cf. *Triumphus Fame* 1.103–5: "e in ciò sembiate il veritero ebreo / Iosefo ed Egisippo, in cinque libri / che poi l'istoria sua più breve feo." Flavius Josephus (37/38 B.C.–100 A.D.) is called "veritiero" (a truthful witness) because he was an eyewitness of the fall of Jerusalem in 70. See Vincenzo Ussani, "Il Petrarca e Flavio Giuseppe," *Atti della Pontificia Accademia Romana di Archeologia Rendiconti* 3, 20 (1943–44), pp. 447–67.

156. See Feo, "Un Ulisse in Terrasanta," pp. 383–87. The appearance of Ulysses in the context of sacred pilgrimage may well appear incongruous, but the travels of the Greek hero and their significance are often revisited by Petrarch throughout his writings, and Ulysses comes to represent a signature theme. *Fam.* 1.1.21–22: "Compare my wanderings to those of Ulysses. If the reputation of our name and of our achievements were the same, he indeed traveled neither more nor farther than I. He went beyond the borders of his fatherland when already old. Though it may be true that nothing at any age is long lasting, all things are very brief in old age" (*Letters on Familiar Matters*, vol. 1, p. 8). See also: *Fam.*

9.13.24–25: "Ulysses too went to Troy, and even further, crossing lands and seas; nor did he stop before he had founded a city bearing his name on a most distant western shore. At home he had an aged father, a young son, a youthful wife beset by suitors, while he fought with Circe's poisonous cups, the sirens' songs, the violent Cyclops, sea monsters and tempests. This man, famous for his wanderings, put aside his affections, neglected his throne, and scorned his responsibilities. Rather than grow old at home, he preferred to age between Scylla and Charybdis, among the black whirlpools of Avernus, and in the midst of such difficult circumstances and locations as to weary even the reader's mind. He did all this for no other reason than return one day to his country more learned in his old age" (*Letters on Familiar Matters*, vol. 2, p. 40). *Fam.* 13.4.10–11: "Ulysses could have lived in peace had his implacable desire for knowledge not driven him to many lands and shores" (*Letters on Familiar Matters*, vol. 2, p. 182). *Fam.* 23.2.32: "Tender feelings and inconsequential advice by wives, children and ordinary friends have always been in conflict with lofty designs; one must block his ears like Ulysses in order to sail into the port of glory, avoiding the reeflike sirens" (*Letters on Familiar Matters*, vol. 3, p. 263). But see particularly, for its intersection with this passage, Petrarch's praise of Dante in a letter to Boccaccio, *Fam.* 21.5: "In this (neglecting all else and desiring only glory) I can scarcely admire and praise him too highly when nothing—not the injustice suffered at the hands of his fellow citizens, not exile, poverty, or the stings of envy, not his wife's love or his devotion to his children—diverted him from his course once he had embarked upon it. When many other great talents, being weak of purpose, would be distracted by the least disturbance" (*Letters on Familiar Matters*, vol. 3, p. 203). See also Introduction, note 95.

157. Cf. *Fam.* 7.2.4 and 15: "For who, even of mediocre ability, having read both sacred and secular writings, does not realize how much Christ, our master of humility, always loved humble things?... He could have been born not in that narrow district of Bethlehem but in Rome to which Judea was subject among the others, and in a golden bed rather than in a stable" (*Letters on Familiar Matters*, vol.1, pp. 334 and 336–37). See also *RVF* 4.9–11.

158. Lo Monaco, *Itinerario in Terra Santa*, p. 116, suggests that this paragraph and the next, integrated with material from the Gospels, are modeled on a passage from St. Jerome's letter on the pilgrimage of his friend Paula: "she could see the Infant Lord, wrapped in swaddling clothes, wailing in the manger, the Magi adoring, the star shining above, the Virgin mother, the careful nursing, the shepherds coming by night that they might see the Word which had been made flesh. . . . the little children massacred, Herod raging, Joseph and Mary fleeing into Egypt" (*The Pilgrimage of the Holy Paula by St. Jerome*, p. 7).

159. Cf. *Fam.* 10.4.29: "The Jor and the Dan are names of streams from which derive the river and its name; it descends into the Sea of the Sodomites where it is said fields are ashen because of the burning of the city" (*Letters on Familiar Matters*, vol. 2, p. 74). The Old Testament makes frequent reference to the Dead Sea under a variety of titles; once only, however, by its present one.

160. The Sinai desert.

161. Virgil *Aeneid* 6.688; this hemistich recurs often in Petrarch as a supporting citation in similar contexts, for example in Petrarch's most famous travel narrative, the "Ascent of Mt. Ventoux" (Fam. 4.1): "It is a steep mountain with rocky and almost inaccessible cliffs. It was well said by the poet, however: 'Persistent toil overcomes all things'" (*Letters on Familiar Matters*, vol. 1, p. 173). Cf. also *Fam.* 4.6.3: "As you saw, I finally came to you despite the rigors of winter, of the sea, and of war. Love does indeed overcome all difficulties, and as Maro says, 'devotion conquered the difficult journey'" (*Letters on Familiar Matters*, vol. 1, p. 191). Cf. also *Fam.* 4.6.3, 11.10.1, 16.6.10, 22.4.8.

162. A statement of Cato's, before beginning the march in the desert (Lucan 9.385). The preceding evocation of Ulysses in the context of pilgrimage to the Holy Land is just one example of Petrarch's classicizing approach to the theme. This paragraph recalls the crossing of the northern Sahara in Libya by Cato the Younger and his army during the war of the Roman Senate, supporting Pompey the Great against Julius Caesar. The primary literary source for this episode (also recalled by Dante in *Inferno* 14.13) is Lucan's *Pharsalia* (in particular, book 9). Cato's march in the desert is another heroic exemplary theme that Petrarch has occasion to revisit elsewhere, although never as here in conjunction with the Israelites' crossing of the desert to escape from Egypt (Exodus 15.22–18.27). Cf. *Fam.* 10.3.46: "When, however, you will have communication with God through prayer, joy will contend with reverence so that you can prove yourself sleepless and diligent in the eyes of such an observer. In histories you have read that the soldiers of Marcus Cato endured in his presence thirst, dust, heat, serpent bites, and died in his presence without a groan or lament" (*Letters on Familiar Matters*, vol. 2, p. 65). Cf. also *Fam.* 13.4: "What shall I say of Cato? Could he not have lived in his own home? He preferred instead to cross parched deserts, subjecting his life to Libyan serpents, so great was the virtue and the love of freedom which enkindled him" (*Letters on Familiar Matters*, vol. 2, p. 183).

163. Petrarch presents Julius Caesar in a positive light here ("the mild dominion of Caesar") and in the last paragraphs of this work (*Itin.* 20). In the *Africa* Petrarch had taken a strong stand against Caesar, but as the poet grew older he modified his view. According to Hans Baron, "by the time [Petrarch] grew old, he was to ask whether Cato's suicide was not due to envy of Caesar's glory, whether it was really necessary to fear Caesar so much, 'the most clement and benevolent, not only of all tyrants but of all princes.' In 1366 (in part somewhat later) he composed the *De Gestis Cesaris*, the first modern picture of Caesar as a great statesman and personality" (*Petrarch's Secretum: Its Making and Its Meaning* [Cambridge: Medieval Academy of America, 1985], pp. 163–64.) On Petrarch and Caesar, see Guido Martellotti, "Petrarca e Cesare" (1947); reprinted in Guido Martellotti, *Scritti petrarcheschi*, ed. Michele Feo and Silvia Rizzo (Padova: Antenore, 1983), pp. 77–89.

164. Cf. Lucan 9.379–406; "Syrtis Libyca" is in Lucan 8.444.

165. The poet is Virgil—"litore rubro"—but also Dante has "lito rubro" (*Parardiso* 6.79). Petrarch understands Virgil's "litore rubro" to refer to the Red Sea (Virgil *Aeneid* 8.685–88): "hinc ope barbarica variisque Antonius armis, / victor ab Aurorae populis et litore rubro, / Aegyptum viresque Orientis et ultima secum / Bactra vehit, sequiturque

(nefas) Aegyptia coiniunx" (*Virgil*, trans. Faircloth, vol. 2, p. 107: "Here Antonius with barbaric might and varied arms, victor from the nations of the dawn and from the ruddy sea, brings with him Egypt and the strength of the East and utmost Bactria; and there follows him [O shame!] his Egyptian wife"). But according to Faircloth, "This is the mare Erythraeum, or Indian Ocean, not the Red Sea as we know it" (*Virgil*, vol. 2, p. 107). In fact, the name Erythra Thalassa, "from a legendary eponymous king of the Persian Gulf was extended by the ancients to cover all eastern waters, including the Indian Ocean; it specifically referred to the modern Red Sea and the Persian Gulf" (*Oxford Classical Dictionary*, 3d ed., p. 1296). The remark on the color of the water of the Red Sea represents a commonplace of Holy Land descriptions that appears in the narratives of the more naturalistic and curious of pilgrims like Ludolph Von Suchem: "Its water is not red, but the earth and the bottom thereof is red; the water appears red to one looking down upon it because of the red bottom, but at a distance it is of the same colour as other water, and its water is exceedingly clear and pellucid, so that a penny can be clearly seen on its bottom and due to the clearness of its water it looks like the clearest red wine" (Ludolph Von Suchem, *Description of the Holy Land and of the Way Thither, Written in the Year A.D. 1350*, trans. Aubrey Stewart [London: Palestine Pilgrims' Text Society, 1895], vol. 12, p. 83).

166. Manlio Pastore Stocchi, *Tradizione medievale e gusto umanistico nel* Del Montibus *del Boccaccio* (Firenze: Olschki, 1963), p. 48, notes that Petrarch has in common here with Boccaccio's entry on "Sinai mons" in the *De montibus* the passage from the Breviary: "Deus qui dedisti legem Moysi in summitate montis Sinai, et in eodem loco per sanctos Angelos tuos corpus Beatae Catharinae virginis et martyris tuae collocasti" (*Breviario Romano*, 25 November). Giuseppe Billanovich, *Petrarca letterato*, vol. 1, *Lo scrittoio del Petrarca* (Roma: Edizioni di Storia e Letteratura, 1947), p. 225, mistakenly asserted Boccaccio's dependence upon Petrarch's *Itinerario*.

The monastery of St. Catherine is situated on Mount Sinai, at an altitude of 4854 feet (1479.5 m), in a picturesque gorge below the Jebel-Musa, the reputed Mountain of the Law. The earliest known historical fact about the site is the erection of a church by Emperor Justinian about A.D. 550. A Byzantine mosaic, which is still in existence, shows that this was formerly called the Church of the Transfiguration; here were gathered the hermits who had previously lived in separate cells and caves among the rocks of Mount Sinai. It is not known when or how the monastery obtained possession of the remains of St. Catherine of Alexandria and adopted her name. According to legend her body was transported there by the hands of angels. The name, however, does not appear in literature before the tenth century. While the itineraries of the ancient pilgrims who visited Sinai do not contain the slightest allusion to the miraculous translation of the saint's body to Mount Sinai, devotion to St. Catherine assumed vast proportions in Europe after the Crusades, and the monastery became an important pilgrimage site that is regularly mentioned in the literature. Cf. Ludolph Von Suchem: "It was to the top of another taller mountain beside a deep valley in the same place that the body of the glorious virgin Catherine was borne by angels from Alexandria, and miraculously discovered by the hermits who dwelt thereon" (*Description of the Holy Land*, vol. 12, p. 88). See G. H. Forsyth et al., *The Monastery of Saint Catherine at Mount Sinai: The Church and Fortress of Justinian* (Ann Arbor: University of Michigan Press, 1973–74).

167. Hostility of the Christian sources toward the Saracens who supervised the holy sites and exacted tribute from pilgrims in the Holy Land was typical. According to Giuliano Pinto: "the Christian travelers define with a nearly unanimous chorus of insults the people of the east and the Muslims in particular" ("I costi del pellegrinaggio in terrasanta," *Toscana e Terrasanta nel medioevo*, ed. Franco Cardini [Firenze: Alinea, 1982], with citations from Trecento pilgrims, including Niccolò Da Poggibonsi, Roberto Da Sanseverino, and Simone Sigoli, p. 272). But Petrarch's list here of obstacles to be confronted by the pilgrim is more conventional and metaphorical than specifically referential. That Petrarch describes as the greatest danger facing the pilgrim that he might "lose his way" seems to express a personal preoccupation of the poet with the theme of the wayfarer and the journey more than anything particular about the historical reality of Holy Land travel and topography. Cf. the typical passage from *Fam.* 20.4.28–31, quoted above in note 149.

168. The "New Babylon" or "Babylon of Egypt" is the common name for Cairo during the Middle Ages. Cf. Flavius Josephus *Jewish Antiquities* 2.10 and 15.1. Cf. *Sine Nom.* 10 for the association of Avignon with the other two Babylons of the east: "You are surprised by the addresses on my letters. As well you might be. Since you have read of only two Babylons, the Assyrian one of long ago enshrining the famous name of Semiramis, and the Egyptian one founded by Cambyses which still flourishes in our own day, you wonder about this unheard of Babylon with which you are now confronted" (*Petrarch's Book without a Name*, trans. Norman P. Zacour [Toronto: Pontifical Institute of Medieval Studies, 1973], p. 71). Cambyses, the eldest son of Cyrus, acceded on the death of his father (530 B.C.) and completed his father's grand plan by conquering Egypt. Petrarch annotated a passage in his copy of Flavius Josephus that attributed the founding of Cairo (Babylon) to Cambyses (Josephus *Antiquities of the Jews* 2.15, in *The Complete Works of Flavius Josephus*, trans. Whiston, p. 70: "where Babylon was built afterward, when Cambyses laid Egypt waste"); the gloss is in Nolhac, *Pétrarque*, vol. 2, p. 155). Petrarch speaks further of Cambyses in the *Sine Nomine* cited above: "Here is a Cambyses [the pope in Avignon] madder than the eastern one who first drove his chariot over the necks of kings but later, worn out from feasting and surfeited by the slaughter of his men, was reduced from haughty lordship to wretched poverty" (*Petrarch's Book without a Name*, p. 72). The story of the mad Cambyses who sought the mysterious source of the Nile is in Lucan 10.279–83.

In referring to both names together as Petrarch does here ("the new Babylon . . . and Cairo of Egypt"), a usage which is common in pilgrimage texts of the period, it is not clear whether Petrarch understood Babylon and Cairo to be one and the same city, as Lo Monaco seems to suggest (*Itinerario in Terra Santa*, p. 117). Ludolph Von Suchem describes them as two separate cities: "one goes along the highroad and comes to Carra (Cairo) and New Babylon, which are two exceeding great cities not far apart" (*Description of the Holy Land*, vol. 12, p. 66). And there are precedents for distinguishing between New Babylon and Cairo, for example in the "Stato (attuale) dell'Egitto e di Babilonia" of the chronicler Arnoldo, dated 1175, one reads that "New Babylon is situated in a plane near to the Nile, and in the past it was a great city and still today it is rather illustrious and well-populated. . . near to New Babylon, at a distance of a third of a mile, there is another magnificent city called Cairo where the king resides" (*Itinera Hierosolymitana crucesignatorum* (saec. 12–13), ed. Sabino de Sandoli [Jerusalem: Franciscan Printing Press, 1978], vol. 2, p. 400). Petrarch's "Carras Assyrias" (Assyrian Cairo) appears to correspond to Carrhae (modern Harran), a city of north Mesopotamia about 16 km southwest of Edessa, at the junction of important trade routes. It was an important provincial capital, trading city, and fortress in the Assyrian empire (cf. Lucan 1.105; Pliny *Naturalis historia* 5.85).

169. Tanaïs, the ancient name for the river Don, was conventionally taken to be the boundary between Europe and Asia (cf. Pliny *Naturalis historia* 3.3 and 4.78; Pomponius Mela *De situ orbis* 1.8), while the Nile marked the border between Asia and Africa (Pomponius Mela *De situ orbis* 1.8). The Don and the Nile together formed the two arms of the *T* in the medieval maps of the world of the type commonly termed *T-O* maps. According to this cartographic form of representation, the Tanaïs in the north divided Asia and Europe while the Nile (or sometimes the Red Sea) in the south divided Africa and Asia; the Mediterranean Sea, dividing Europe from Africa, formed the vertical stroke of the *T*. The circling ocean shaped the encompassing *O* of the T-O map, and Jerusalem was always situated roughly at the center. For medieval maps of the world (mappaemundi), including the T-O type, see David Woodward, "Medieval Mappaemundi," in *The History of Cartography*, vol. 1, pp. 286– 370, especially, pp. 301–3 and 343–58.

   As Leonardo Dati (1365–1424) wrote in his poetic cosmography, *La Sfera*, written around 1420: "A *T* in an *O* gives us the division of the world into three parts. / The upper part and the greatest empire take nearly the half of the world. / It is Asia; the vertical bar is the limit dividing the third from the second, Africa, / I say, from Europe; between them appears the Mediterranean Sea." From this perspective Petrarch describes the Nile as "adversum Tanai" (opposite the Tanaïs). See Illustrations 10 and 11.

   Christian scholars from Isidore to Petrarch adopted the T-O map for its simplicity, as had the classical writers who first employed it. Petrarch, however, appears to use this traditional schematic perspective only in the Holy Land portion of his *Itinerary*, after having adopted the more modern and empirical portolan cartographic perspective in the text from the embarkation in Genoa to the debarkation in the Holy Land (most striking in the voyage along the Italian coast).

   For the Tanaïs as an element in Petrarch's personal mental map of the world, cf. *Fam.* 6.3.62, which imagines a heroic Giovanni Colonna traveling the world were it not for his gout: "You would now be, as I surmise, in some other corner of the world: you would be swimming at times in the Nile, at times in the Indian Ocean or the Tanaïs, or you would be climbing the Rhiphaen mountains or the thickets of the Hercynian passes, an eternal wanderer and fugitive on land" (*Letters on Familiar Matters*, vol. 1, p. 311). See also *Fam.* 24.1.28 and 24.4.15; *De Vita Solitaria* 2 (*The Life of Solitude*, pp. 466–67).

170. The Nile River, which marked the border between Asia and Africa. Cf. Pomponius Mela *De situ orbis* 1.8.

171. Petrarch refers here to the *Liber de inundacione Nili*, "which seems to be a genuine work of Aristotle for which the Greek original does not survive, though it has not generally been included in collected works of Aristotle, nor taken account of in the interpretive studies" (Charles B. Schmitt and Dilwyn Know, *Pseudo-Aristoteles Latinus: A Guide to Latin Works Falsely Attributed to Aristotle before 1500* [London: Warburgh Institute, 1985], p. 45). The work survives in a Latin translation of the thirteenth century, possibly by Bartolomeo da Messina (fl. 1258–66) (see the entry on him in *Dizionario biografico degli italiani*, vol. 6 [1964], pp. 729–30). Over eighty-two surviving manuscripts testify to the work's wide diffusion. The text is available in Valentini Rose, *Aristoteles Pseudepigraphus* (Leipzig: B. G. Teubner, 1863), pp. 631–43; and in D. Bonneau, "Liber Aristotelis de inundatione Nili," *Études de papyrologie* 9 (1971), pp. 1–33.

172. Petrarch's unusual account of the sources of the Nile derives from an apochryphal tradition according to which, during the flight to Egypt, Jesus brought forth waters to refresh his mother. As the Gospel of pseudo-Matthew reports: "Then Christ said to it: 'Raise thyself, O palm tree, and be strong, and be the companion of my trees, which are in the paradise of my Father; and open from thy roots a vein of water which has been hid in the earth, and let the waters flow, so that we may be satisfied from thee.' And it rose up immediately, and at its root there began to come forth a spring of water exceedingly clear and cool and sparkling" (chapter 20). The same source appears to have inspired a similar traveler's tale concerning the fount of "Mathalia" by Niccolò da Poggibonsi, *Libro d'Oltramare: A Voyage beyond the Seas (1346–1350)*, trans. T. Bellorini and E. Hoade (Jerusalem: Franciscan Press, 1945), p. 93. Lo Monaco, *Itinerario in Terra Santa*, p. 118, notes, however, that Petrarch himself appears to credit an oral tradition in this passage when he speaks of having "learned it from illustrious persons."

    As Petrarch also informs us, the possible source of the Nile was one of the most debated questions by classical and medieval sources. For another signal evocation of the *topos* in an Italian literary context, see Dante's great song of exile "Tre donne intorno al cor mi son venute" (*Le rime*, ed. Piero Cudini [Milano: Garzanti, 1979], 47 [104], vv. 45–50, p. 237). Petrarch's inclusion of this miraculous, naive account of the source of the Nile corresponds to the fascination that he exhibits throughout his writings with fountains or springs. See, for example, the geographical *canzone*, *RVF* 135, "Qual più diversa e nova" (The strangest, rarest thing), which features a series of marvelous springs from all parts of the world, including Ethiopia, Epirus, the Fortunate Islands, and last, but most important, "a closed vale where Sorgue springs." This passage on the sources of the Nile thus appears to represent yet another signature theme, one in a series of characteristically Petrarchan *loci*, by means of which the pilgrimage guide serves as a self-portrait of its author.

173. Alexandria was founded by Alexander the Great in 331 B.C. when he took Egypt from the Persians. The city rapidly became one of the largest and grandest cities of the Mediterranean world, famed for the monumental magnificence of its two main intersecting streets, its palace quarter with the tomb of Alexander and the museum and library, its Serapeum, gymnasium, and Pharus, the lighthouse at the entrance to its two capacious artificial towers.

For another late medieval evocation of Alexander's tomb, cf. Walter of Châtillon's *Alexandreis* 10.448–50: "A five foot house constructed of hewn marble inside a deeply-dug grave sufficed for the man who had previously found the whole world insufficient. Here his noble body rested, covered by but a little earth, until Ptolemy, who, one reads, gained Egypt as his share, tranferred the world-wide respected ward of revered fate to the city named after his sovereign" (Walter of Châtillon, *The Alexandreis,* trans. R. Telfryn Pritchard [Toronto: Pontifical Institute of Mediaeval Studies, 1986], p. 231). For Petrarch's generally negative view of Alexander, see George Cary, "Petrarch and Alexander the Great," *Italian Studies* 5 (1950), pp. 43–55.

174. The source for Caesar's entering the city "almost as if rendering religious devotion" is Lucan 10.14–24. Caesar's defeat of Pompey took place at Pharsalus in Thessaly, 9 August 48, for which Petrarch's primary poetic source is Lucan, also for the cremation and burial of Pompey in Alexandria. In addition, the events surrounding Julius Caesar's conquest of Alexandria were described in an anonymous *De bello Alex.* (*The Alexandrian War*), which Petrarch read in a personal corpus of Ceasarean texts upon which he based his own *De Gestis Cesaris* (see G. Martellotti, "Il *De Gestis Cesaris* ed il cod. Neapolitanus dei *Commentarii,*" in *Scritti petrarcheschi,* Studi sul Petrarca [Padova: Ente Nazionale Francesco Petrarca, 1983], vol. 16, p. 525).

Caesar's conquest of Alexandria, following which he established Cleopatra VII on the throne, is also recalled by Petrarch in *De Vita Solitaria* 2:"I don't ask by what right he did so: I admire that force of will and that energy, which would be needed in our own times" (*The Life of Solitude,* pp. 470–71).

175. Octavian defeated Marcus Antonius at Actium 2 September 31 B.C. Antony and Cleopatra managed to break the blockade at Actium and escape southwards, but their supporters defected to Octavian in the following months. Antony committed suicide as Octavian entered Alexandria (30 August). The anecdote about Augustus Caesar asking to see the tomb of Alexander is from Suetonius *De vita caesarum* Augustus 2.18. Petrarch recalled the same anecdote in the introduction to the *De Viris* (see *Francesco Petrarca, Prose,* ed. G. Martellotti et al. [Milan: Ricciardi, 1955], p. 222), where, according to Thomas Greene, it is used "to vindicate his right to select his own material as biographer. . . . Augustus refuses the conventional guided tour and refuses the conventional title of king to the late Ptolemy. The true sovereign chooses to divert his attention to another true sovereign; his diversion or deviation demonstrates his distinction just as Petrarch's unconventional selection of materials in this book [the *De Viris*] will demonstrate his own" ("Petrarch *Viator:* The Displacements of Heroism," *Yearbook of English Studies* 12 [1982], pp. 43–44).

The notion that the authority of a king derives from his virtue and the virtue of his deeds is also expressed, with regard to King Robert, in *Fam.* 4.2.11–12: "When thinking about him I find I admire his character more than his kingdom. Him do I indeed call king who rules and controls not only his subjects but himself, who takes command of the passions which rebel against the mind and would crush him if he yielded" (*Letters on Familiar Matters,* vol. 1, p. 182). See also *Fam.* 12.2.10–11 and 30.

176. Cf. Lucan 8.712–822.

177. Cf. *Fam*. 1.4.6: "They recount that King Charles, whom they dare equate to Pompey and Alexander by giving him the surname of 'the Great'" (*Letters on Familiar Matters*, vol. 1, p. 26).

178. Pella was founded c. 400 B.C. as the new capital of Macedonia by King Archelaus. The city was the birthplace of Philip II and Alexander the Great and it grew in size and prestige at a pace with the Hellenistic empire. The city reached its peak in political and artistic influence c. 274–239 B.C. With the defeat of the last king of Macedonia in 168 B.C. Pella lost importance and was overshadowed by the growing city of Thessalonica on the coast. Cf. *Triumphus Fame* 2.11 (*Trionfi*, ed. Pacca and Paolino, p. 396): "Philippo e 'l figlio, che, da Pella a gl'Indi / correndo, vinse paesi diversi" (Philip and his son, who, racing from Pella to the Indies conquered various countries). Note that Epirus is given as being in the north also in *RVF* 135, "Qual più diversa e nova," vv. 61–64.

179. Pharus island at Alexandria, upon which the famous 100 m (328-foot) lighthouse was built, gave its name to the architectural genre (built c. 300–280 B.C. by Sostratus of Cnidus). Together with the colossus Helios at Rhodes, the lighthouse at Pharus was among the Seven Wonders of the Ancient World. The etymology of the word for lighthouse from the name of the island is given in Solinus 32.

180. According to the account in Lucan, the soldiers saw the body of Pompey without its head while Caesar saw only the head that was brought to him by an emissary of Ptolemy (Lucan 8.700 ff. and 9.1000–1060).

    The death of Pompey and Caesar's reaction to it is another Petrarchan theme that derived largely from Lucan. Cf. *Petrarca Canzoniere*, ed. Santagata, 44.1–4: "Que' ch 'n Tesaglia ebbe le man' sì pronte / a farla del civil sangue vermiglia, / pianse morto il marito di sua figlia, / raffigurato a le fatezze conte" (*Petrarch: The Canzoniere, or Rerum vulgarium fragmenta*, pp. 72–73: "That man in Thessaly with hands so anxious / to turn it crimson bathed in civil blood, / wept for the death of his own daughter's husband / recognized by his features known to all"). See also *Petrarca Canzoniere*, ed. Santagata, 102.1–4: "Cesare, poi che 'l traditor d'Egitto / li fece il don de l'onorata testa, / celando l'allegrezza manifesta, / pianse per gli occhi fuor sì come è scritto" (*Petrarch: The Canzoniere or Rerum vulgarium fragmenta*, pp. 156–57: "Caesar, the time that the Egyptian traitor / gave him the gift of that great, honored head, / hiding the joy he clearly felt inside, / wept outwardly with tears, as it is written"). This second passage, from an early composition of the *Rerum Vulgarium Fragmenta*, dated before 1336, follows Lucan's version, which presented Caesar's tears as insincere and apparently reflects Petrarch's anti-Caesarean sentiment in the early part of his career (see note 163 above). *RVF* 44 on the other hand is also dated around 1336 and is apparently a more sympathetic treatment of Caesar. The contrast represents a critical problem (see *Petrarca Canzoniere*, ed. Santagata, pp. 232–33 and 477–78). Pompey had married Caesar's daughter Giulia ("his daughter's husband" in *RVF* 44, while here "his son-in-law"). Both victor and vanquished, however, are ultimately presented as equals within the ironic perspective of their dividing in death the world between them, north and west, Pompey buried along the Nile and Caesar by the Tiber.

    This concluding image of Caesar and Pompey, victor and vanquished, both ultimately overcome by inevitable death, expresses the deeper inspiration of Petrarch's mature humanism, which was rooted in the common struggle against time and death that united winners and losers, Caesar and Pompey here, no less than *Africa's* Scipio and Hannibal, another pair of heroic Petrarchan adversaries who are no less indispensible to one another. On Petrarch's humanism in this aspect, see Enrico Fenzi, "Dall'*Africa* al *Secretum:* Nuove ipotesi sul 'Sogno di Scipione' e sulla composizione del poema," *Il Petrarca ad Arquà,* ed. Giuseppe Billanovich and Giuseppe Frasso (Padova: Antenore, 1975), pp. 61–115, especially pp. 110–13 .

181.   Petrarch addresses Giovanni Mandelli directly and evokes the "quick and ready intelligence" of his epistolary interlocutor before closing. The author has made good on his promise to include, besides religious and antiquarian material, "memorable examples that are capable of inspiring courage"—but not before writing-in his signature ambivalence through the final example's counterpoint of majesty, treachery, and death.

BIBLIOGRAPHY

Petrarch's Works

Latin Works

Opere latine di Francesco Petrarca. Edited by Antonietta Bufano. Torino: UTET, 1975.
  De Otio Religioso, vol. 3, pp. 567–809.
  De Sui Ipsius et Multorum Ignorantia, vol. 4, pp. 1026–1150.
  De Vita Solitaria, vol. 3, pp. 262–564.
  Invective Contra Medicum, vol. 4, pp. 818–980.

Prose. Edited by G. Martellotti. Milano: R. Ricciardi, 1955.

Afr. Africa

Africa. Edited by N. Festa. Firenze: Sansoni, 1926.

Petrarch's Africa. Translated by Thomas G. Bergin and Alice S. Wilson. New Haven: Yale University Press, 1977.

Buc. Carm. Bucolicum Carmen

Il Bucolicum Carmen e i suoi commenti inediti. Edited by A. Avena. Padova: Società Cooperativa Tipografica, 1906.

Canzoniere see *RVF*

De Remediis De Remediis Utriusque Fortune

Petrarch's Remedies for Fortune Fair and Foul. Translated, with a commentary, by Conrad H. Rawski. 5 vols. Bloomington: Indiana University Press, 1991.

De Viris Ill.   De Viris Illustribus

De Viris Illustribus. Edited by G. Martellotti. Firenze: Sansoni, 1962.

Disp.   Lettere Disperse

Lettere Disperse. Edited by Alessandro Pancheri. Parma: Ugo Guanda, 1994.

Epyst.   Epystole

Epystole. In *Francisci Petrarchae poëmata minora,* edited by D. Rossetti, vols. 2–3. Milano: Società Tipografica de' Classici Italiani, 1831 and 1834.

Fam.   Rerum Familiarium Libri

Le familiari. Edited by Vittorio Rossi and U. Bosco. 4 vols. Firenze: Sansoni, 1933–42.

Letters on Familiar Matters, Rerum Familiarium Libri. 3 vols. Translated by Aldo S. Bernardo.
   Vol. 1, *Fam.* 1–8. Albany: State University of New York Press, 1975.
   Vol. 2, *Fam.* 9–16. Baltimore: Johns Hopkins University Press, 1982.
   Vol. 3, *Fam.* 17–24. Baltimore: Johns Hopkins University Press, 1985.

In difesa dell'Italia

In difesa dell'Italia (Contra Eum Qui Maledixit Italie). Edited by Giuliana Crevatin. Padova: Marsilio, 1995.

Itin.   Itinerarium

Itinerario in Terra Santa 1358. Edited by Francesco Lo Monaco. Bergamo: Lubrina, 1990.

Viaggio in Terrasanta, volgarizzamento inedito del Quatrocento. Edited by A. Altamura. Napoli, 1979.

Volgarizzamento meridionale anonimo di Francesco Petrarca Itinerarium breve de Ianua usque ad Ierusalem et Terram Sanctam. Edited by Alfonso Paolella. Bologna: Commissione per i Testi di Lingua, 1993.

Rer. Mem.   Rerum Memorandarum Libri

Rerum Memorandarum Libri. Edited by Giuseppe Billanovich. Firenze: Sansoni, 1943–45.

RVF   Rerum Vulgarium Fragmenta (Canzoniere)

Francesco Petrarca Canzoniere. Edited by Marco Santagata. Milano: Mondadori, 1996.

Canzoniere. Edited by Gianfranco Contini. Torino: Einaudi, 1964.

Petrarch: The Canzoniere, or Rerum vulgarium fragmenta. Translated, with notes and commentary, by Mark Musa. Bloomington: Indiana University Press, 1996.

Secr. *Secretum*

Secretum. Edited by Enrico Fenzi. Milano: Mursia, 1992.

Petrarch's Secret, or the Soul's Conflict with Passion. Translated by William H. Draper. London: Chatto and Windus, 1951.

Sen. *Rerum Senilium Libri*

Letters of Old Age, Rerum Senilium Libri. Translated by Aldo S. Bernardo, Saul Levin, and Reta A. Bernardo. Baltimore: Johns Hopkins University Press, 1992.

Sine Nomine *Liber sine Nomine*

Petrarch's Book without a Name. Translated by Norman P. Zacour. Toronto: Pontifical Institute of Medieval Studies, 1973.

Sol. *De Vita Solitaria*

De Vita Solitaria. In *Opere latine.*

The Life of Solitude. Translated by Jacob Zeitlin. Urbana: University of Illinois Press, 1924.

Test. *Testamentum*

Petrarch's Testament. Edited and translated by Theodor E. Mommsen. Ithaca: Cornell University Press, 1957.

Tr. *Trionfi*

Francesco Petrarca Triumphi. Edited by Marco Ariani. Milano: Mursia, 1988.

Trionfi, rime estravaganti, codice degli abbozzi. Edited by Vinicio Pacca and Laura Paolino, introduction by Marco Santagata. Milano: Mondadori, 1996.

The Triumphs of Petrarch. Translated by Ernest Hatch Wilkins. Chicago: University of Chicago Press, 1962.

Other Works Cited

Alessio, G. C., and C. Villa. "Per *Inferno* I, 67–87." In *Vestigia: Studi in onore di G. Billanovich.* Roma: Edizioni di Storia e Letteratura, 1984.

Almagià, R. "Intorno a quattro codici fiorentini e ad uno ferrarese dell'erudito veneziano Alessandro Zorzi." *La bibliofilia* 38 (1936), pp. 313–47.

Anderson, Benedict. *Imagined Communities: Reflections on the Origin and Spread of Nationalism.* London: Verso, 1983.

Annali genovesi di Caffaro e de' suoi continuatori dal MXCIX al MCCXCII. 5 vols. Genova: Fonti per la Storia d'Italia, 1890–1929.

Antica Cronichetta volgare lucchese. Edited by S. Bongi. In *Atti della Reale Accademia Lucchese di Scienze, Lettere ed Arti* 26 (1893).

Ariani, Marco. "Petrarca." In *Storia della letteratura italiana,* edited by Enrico Malato, vol. 2, pp. 632–33. Roma: Salerno Editrice, 1995.

Ariosto, Ludovico. *Satire e lettere.* Edited by C. Segre. Torino: Einaudi, 1976.

———. *The Satires of Ludovico Ariosto: A Renaissance Autobiography.* Translated by Peter DeSa Wiggins. Athens: Ohio University Press, 1976.

Asher, Lyell. "Petrarch at the Peak of Fame." *Publications of the Modern Language Association of America* 108/5 (Oct. 1993), pp. 1050–63.

Azarii, Petri. *Liber gestorum in Lombardia.* Edited by F. Cognasso. In *Rer. Ital. Script.* 16, P. 4. Bologna: Zanichelli, 1926–39.

Barolini, Teodolinda. "Ulysses, Geryon, and the Aeronautics of Narrative Transition." In *The Undivine Comedy: Detheologizing Dante,* pp. 48–73. Princeton: Princeton University Press, 1992.

Baron, Hans. *Petrarch's Secretum: Its Making and Its Meaning.* Cambridge: Medieval Academy of America, 1985.

Bartolini, Gabriella. *Nel nome di Dio facemmo vela: Viaggio in Oriente di un pellegrino medievale.* Roma: Laterza, 1991.

Benso S., L. Formisano, J. Guérin Dalle Mese, M. Guglielminetti, M. Masoero, M. Pregliasco, and A. Rossebastiano. *La letteratura di viaggio dal medioevo al rinascimento: Generi e problemi.* Alessandria: Edizioni dell'Orso, 1989.

Benvenuto da Imola. *Comentum super Dantis Aldigherij Comoediam.* Edited by J. P. Lacaita. 5 vols. Florence: Barbèra, 1887.

Bertone, Giorgio. "Il monte: gli occhi di Laura, i passi di Francesco." In *Lo sguardo escluso: L'idea di paesaggio nella letteratura occidentale,* pp. 95–147. Novara: Interlinea, 1999.

Bettarini, Rosanna. *Lacrime e inchiostro nel Canzoniere di Petrarca.* Bologna: CLUEB, 1998.

Billanovich, Giuseppe. "Dall' antica Ravenna alle biblioteche umanistiche." *Annuario dell' Università Cattolica del Sacro Cuore* (1955–56/1956–57), pp. 91–106.

———. "Nella biblioteca del Petrarca II: Un altro Svetonio del Petrarca (Oxford, Exeter College, 186)." *Italia medioevale e umanistica* 3 (1960), pp. 28–58.

———. *Petrarca letterato.* Vol. 1: *Lo scrittoio del Petrarca.* Roma: Edizioni di Storia e Letteratura, 1947.

———. "Tra Dante e Petrarca." *Italia medioevale e umanistica* (1965), pp. 1–44.

———. "Uno Svetonio della biblioteca di Petrarca (Berlinese lat. Fol. 337)." *Studi petrarcheschi* 6 (1956), pp. 23–33.

————. *Un nuovo esempio delle scoperte e delle letture del Petrarca: L'Eusebio—Girolamo—Pseudo Prospero*. Schriften und Vortrage des Petrarcas Instituts 3. Köln: Petrarca Institut, 1954.

Biondo, Flavio. *Roma ristaurata et Italia illustrata di Biondo da Forli*. Vernacular translation by Lucio Fauno. Venezia: Tramezzino, 1542.

Blumemberg, Hans. *Shipwreck with Spectator: Paradigm of a Metaphor for Existence*. Translated by Steven Rendall. Cambridge: MIT Press, 1997.

Boitani, Piero. *The Shadow of Ulysses: Figures of a Myth*. Oxford: Oxford University Press, 1994.

Bonneau, D. "Liber Aristotelis de inundatione Nili." *Etudes de papyrologie* 9 (1971), pp. 1–33.

Braudel, Fernand. *The Mediterranean and the Mediterranean World in the Age of Philip II.* 2 vols. Berkeley: University of California Press, 1995.

Burchard of Mount Sion, A.D. 1280. Translated by Aubrey Stewart. London: Palestine Pilgrims' Text Society, 1896.

Cachey, Theodore J., Jr. "'Peregrinus (quasi) ubique': Petrarca e la storia del viaggio." *Intersezioni: Rivista di storia delle idee* 27 (December 1997), pp. 369–84.

————. "Petrarch, Boccaccio and the New World Encounter." *Stanford Italian Review: Perspectives on the Italian Renaissance* 10 (1991), pp. 45–59.

Campbell, Mary. "'The Object of One's Gaze': Landscape, Writing, and Early Medieval Pilgrimage." In *Discovering New Worlds: Essays on Medieval Exploration and Imagination*, edited by Scott D. Westrem, pp. 3–15. New York: Garland Publishing, 1991.

————. *The Witness and the Other World: Exotic European Travel Writing, 400–1600*. Ithaca: Cornell University Press, 1988.

Campbell, Tony. "Portolan Charts from the Late Thirteenth Century to 1500." In *The History of Cartography*, edited by J.B. Harley and David Woodward, vol. 1, pp. 371–463. Chicago: University of Chicago Press, 1987.

Camporesi, Piero. *Le belle contrade: nascita del paesaggio italiano*. Milano: Garzanti, 1992.

Capasso, M. *Il sepolcro di Virgilio*. Napoli: Giannini, 1983.

Cardini, Franco. *La peregrinación: Una dimensión de la vida medieval* [= *Il pellegrinaggio: Una dimensione della vita medievale*]. Manziana [Roma]: Vecchiarelli, 1999.

————. "I viaggi di religione, d'ambasceria e di mercatura." In *Storia della società italiana*. Vol. 7, *La crisi del sistema comunale*. Torino: Einaudi, 1982.

————. "Viaggiatori medioevali in Terrasanta: A proposito di alcune recenti pubblicazioni italiane." *Rivista storica italiana* 80/2, pp. 332–39. Napoli: Edizioni Scientifiche Italiane, 1968.

Cardini, Franco, ed. *Toscana e Terrasanta nel medioevo*. Firenze: Alinea, 1982.

Cardona, G. R. "I viaggi e le scoperte." In *Letteratura italiana: Le questioni*, edited by A. Asor Rosa, vol. 5, pp. 687–716. Torino: Einaudi, 1986.

Cary, George. "Petrarch and Alexander the Great." *Italian Studies* 5 (1950), pp. 43–55.

Cesareo, G. A. "La 'Carta d'Italia' del Petrarca." In *Dai tempi antichi ai tempi moderni*, pp. 221–25. Milano: Hoepli, 1904.

Cherchi, Paolo. "Il sonetto LXVII." *Lectura Petrarce* 11 (1991), pp. 237–58.

Cherubini, Giovanni, ed. *Santiago di Compostella: Il pellegrinaggio medievale*. Siena: Protagon, 1998.

Clifford, James. *Routes: Travel and Translation in the Late Twentieth Century*. Cambridge: Harvard University Press, 1997.

Cochin, Henry. *Un ami de Pétrarque: Lettres de Francesco Nelli à Pétrarque*. Paris: Champion, 1892.

Cohen, Erik. "Pilgrimage and Tourism: Convergence and Divergence." In *Sacred Journeys: The Anthropology of Pilgrimage*, edited by Alan Morinis, foreword by Victor Turner, pp. 47–61. Westport: Greenwood Press, 1992.

Comparetti, Domenico. *Virgil in the Middle Ages*. Hamden, Conn.: Archon Books, 1966.

Conley, Tom. *The Self-Made Map: Cartographic Writing in Early Modern France*. Minneapolis: University of Minnesota Press, 1996.

Constable, Giles. "Opposition to Pilgrimage in the Middle Ages." In *Melanges G. Fransen*, edited by Stephan Kuttner, Alfons M. Stickler, E. Van Balberghe, D. Van den Auweele. Studia Gratiana 19–20. Roma: Libreria Ateneo Salesiano, 1976.

Contini, Gianfranco. "Preliminari sulla lingua di Petrarca." In *Francesco Petrarca Canzoniere*, edited by Gianfranco Contini, pp. vi–xxxviii. Torino: Einaudi, 1964.

D'Agostini, Maria Enrica. *La Letteratura di viaggio: Storia e prospettive di un genere letterario*. Milano: Guerini, 1987.

Dante Alighieri. *The Divine Comedy*. Translated by Charles S. Singleton. 3 vol. in 6. Bollingen Series 80. Princeton: Princeton University Press, 1970.

———. *The Divine Comedy of Dante Alighieri*. Translated by Robert Durling. Introduction and notes by Ronald L. Martinez and Robert M. Durling. Oxford: Oxford University Press, 1996.

———. *Le rime*. Edited by Piero Cudini. Milano: Garzanti, 1979.

———. *Tutte le opere*. Edited by Luigi Blasucci. Firenze: Sansoni, 1981.

Dionisotti, Carlo. *Geografia e storia della letteratura italiana*. Torino: Einaudi, 1971.

D'Onofrio, Mario. *Romei e Giubilei: Il pellegrinaggio medievale a San Pietro (350–1350)*. Roma: Electa, 1999.

Doroszlai, A.; J. Guidi, M. F. Piéjus, and A. Rochon, eds. *Espaces réals et espaces imaginaires dans Le Roland furieux*. Paris: Université de la Sorbonne Nouvelle, 1991.

Dotti, Ugo. "L'ottavo libro delle *Familiari*: Contributo per una storia dell'umanesimo petrarchesco." *Belfagor* 28 (1973), pp. 273–74.

———. *Vita di Petrarca*. Roma and Bari: Laterza, 1987.

Feltellus (c. 1130 A.D.). Translated by James Rose Macpherson. London: Palestine Pilgrims' Text Society, 1892.

Fenzi, Enrico. "Dall'*Africa* al *Secretum:* Nuove ipotesi sul 'Sogno di Scipione' e sulla composizione del poema." In *Il Petrarca ad Arquà*, edited by Giuseppe Billanovich and Giuseppe Frasso, pp. 61–115. Padova: Antenore, 1975.

Feo, Michele. "Di alcuni rusticani cestelli di pomi." *Quaderni Petrarcheschi* 1 (1983), pp. 23–75.

———. "Inquietudini filologiche del Petrarca: Il luogo della discesa agli inferi (storia di una citazione)." *Italia medioevale e umanistica* 27 (1974), pp. 115–83.

———. "Un Ulisse in Terrasanta." *Rivista di cultura classica e medievale* 19 (1977), pp. 383–87.

Feo, Michele, ed. *Codici latini del Petrarca nelle biblioteche fiorentine*. Firenze: Le Lettere, 1991.

Fera, Vincenzo. *La revisione petrarchesca dell'Africa*. Messina: Centro di Studi Umanistici, 1984.

Flavius Josephus. *The Complete Works of Flavius Josephus*. Translated by William Whiston. Chicago: Thompson and Thomas, 1902.

Foresti, Arnaldo. *Aneddoti della vita di Francesco Petrarca*. Edited by Antonia Tissoni Benvenuti. Padova: Antenore, 1977.

Forsyth, G. H., et al. *The Monastery of Saint Catherine at Mount Sinai: The Church and Fortress of Justinian*. Ann Arbor: University of Michigan Press, 1973–74.

Foscolo, Ugo. *Saggi e discorsi critici, Saggi sul Petrarca, Discorso sul testo del Decameron, Scritti minori su poeti italiani e stranieri (1821–26)*. Edited by Cesare Foligno. Firenze: F. Le Monnier, 1953.

Frasso, G. *Itinerari con Francesco Petrarca*. Preface by Giuseppe Billanovich. Padova: Antenore, 1974.

Friedersdorff, Franz. *Franz Petrarcas poetischen Briefen*. Halle: M. Niemayer, 1903.

Gaeta, Franco. "Dal comune alla corte rinascimentale." In *Letteratura italiana*, vol. 1: *Il letterato e le istituzioni*, pp. 149–255. Milano: Einaudi, 1982.

Giannetto, N. *Bernardo Bembo umanista e politico veneziano*. Firenze: Olschki, 1985.

Greenblatt, Stephen. *Marvelous Possessions: The Wonder of the New World*. Chicago: University of Chicago Press, 1991.

———. *Renaissance Self-Fashioning: From More to Shakespeare*. Chicago: University of Chicago Press, 1980.

Greene, Thomas M. "Petrarch's *Viator*: The Displacements of Heroism." *Yearbook of English Studies* 12 (1982), pp. 25–57.

Greppi, Claudio. "Una carta per la corte: il viaggiatore immobile." In *The Renaissance in Ferrara and Its European Horizons*, edited by J. Salmons and W. Moretti, pp. 199–222. Cardiff: University of Wales Press; Ravenna: Edited by Del Girasole, 1984.

Gribaudi, P. "Sul nome di 'Terra di Lavoro.'" *Rivista geografica italiana* 14 (1907), pp. 193–210.

Harvey, David. *The Condition of Postmodernity.* Oxford: Basil Blackwell, 1989.

Heitmann, K. *Fortuna und Virtus: Eine Studie zu Petrarcas Lebensweisheit.* Köln and Graz: Bohlau, 1958.

———. "La genesi del *De Remediis Utriusque Fortune* del Petrarca." *Convivium* 25 (1957), pp. 9–30.

Helms, M. W. *Ulysses' Sail: An Ethnographic Odyssey of Power, Knowledge, and Geographical Distance.* Princeton: Princeton University Press, 1988.

Hortis, Attilio. *Scritti inediti di Francesco Petrarca.* Trieste, Tipografia del Lloyd Austro-Ungarico, 1874.

Iannucci, Amilcare A. *Forma ed evento nella* Divina commedia. Roma: Bulzoni, 1984.

Itinera Hierosolymitana crucesignatorum (saec. xii–xiii). Edited by Sabino de Sandoli. Jerusalem: Franciscan Printing Press, 1978.

Jacques de Vitry. *The History of Jerusalem A.D. 1180.* Translated by Aubrey Stewart. London: Palestine Pilgrim's Text Society, 1896.

Jerome, Saint. *The Pilgrimage of the Holy Paula by St. Jerome.* Translated by Aubrey Stewart. London: Adelphi, 1887.

Jones, Philip. *The Italian City-State: From Commune to Signoria.* Oxford: Claredon Press, 1977.

Kristeller, Paul Oskar. "La scuola di Salerno." In *Studi sulla scuola medica salernitana,* pp. 58–77. Napoli: Istituto Italiano per gli Studi Filosofici, 1986.

Leach, Eleanor Winsor. *The Rhetoric of Space: Literary and Artistic Representations of Landscape in Republican and Augustan Rome.* Princeton: Princeton University Press, 1988.

Leed, Eric J. *The Mind of the Traveler: From Gilgamesh to Global Tourism.* New York: Basic Books, 1988.

Lefebvre, Henri. *The Production of Space.* Translated by Donald Nicholson-Smith. Oxford: Basil Blackwell, 1991.

Levati A. *Viaggi di Francesco Petrarca in Francia, in Germania ed in Italia.* Milano: Società Tipografica de' Classici Italiani, 1820.

Lo Parco, F. "Il Petrarca e gli antipodi etnografici in rapporto con la concezione patristica e dantesca." *Romania* 37 (1908), pp. 337–57.

———. "L'ultima Thule nell'intuizione e nella divinizzazione di F. Petrarca." *Rivista geografica italiana* 17 (1911), pp. 459–74.

———. "Il viaggio di Francesco Petrarca 'ad extrema terrarum'." In *Studii dedicati a Francesco Torraca,* pp. 87–100. Napoli: F. Perrella, 1912.

Ludolph von Suchem. *Description of the Holy Land and of the Way Thither, Written in the Year A.D. 1350.* Translated by Aubrey Stewart. London: Palestine Pilgrims' Text Society, 1895.

MacCannell, Dean. *The Tourist: A New Theory of the Leisure Class.* New York: Schocken Books, 1976.

Maragno, Mary, ed. *Il Pellegrinaggio nella formazione dell'Europa: Aspetti culturali e religiosi.* Padova: Centro Studi Antoniani, 1990.

Martellotti, G. "Il *De Gestis Cesaris* ed il cod. Neapolitanus dei *Commentarii.*" In *Scritti petrarcheschi. Studi sul Petrarca.* Padova: Ente Nazionale Francesco Petrarca, 1983.

Martinelli, B. "Petrarca e la medicina." In *Invective contra medicum,* edited by P. G. Ricci, pp. 204–49. Storia e letteratura: Raccolta di studi e testi. Roma: Edizioni di Storia e Letteratura, 1978.

Mattesini, Enzo, ed. *Vie di pellegrinaggio medievale attraverso l'Alta Valle del Tevere, Atti del Convegno: Sansepolcro, 27–28 settembre 1996.* Città di Castello [Perugia]: Petruzzi; Sansepolcro: Comune di Sansepolcro, 1998.

Mazzotta, Giuseppe. *The Worlds of Petrarch.* Durham: Duke University Press, 1993.

Mézières, Alfred Jean François. *Pétrarque: Etude d'après de nouveaux documents.* Paris: Didier, 1868.

Monga, Luigi, ed. *L'Odeporica/Hodoeporics: On Travel Literature.* Special issue, *Annali d'italianistica* 14 (1996).

Monti, Carla Maria. "Mirabilia e geografia nel *Canzoniere:* Pomponio Mela e Vibio Sequestre (*RVF* CXXXV and CXLVIII)." *Studi petrarcheschi* 6 (1989), pp. 91–123.

Niccolò da Poggibonsi. *Libro d'Oltramare: A Voyage beyond the Seas (1346–1350).* Translated by T. Bellorini and E. Hoade. Jerusalem: Franciscan Press, 1945.

Nolhac, Pierre de. *Pétrarque et l'humanisme.* 2 vols. Paris: Champion, 1907.

Nordenskiöld, Adolf Erik. *Periplus: An Essay on the Early History of Charts and Sailing-Directions.* Translated by Francis A. Bather. New York: B. Franklin, 1967; originally Stockholm, 1897.

Nori, G. "La corte itinerante: Il pellegrinaggio di Nicolò III in Terrasanta." In *La Corte e lo spazio, Ferrara estense,* edited by Giuseppe Papagno and Amedeo Quondam, pp. 233–46. Roma: Bulzoni, 1982.

Novati, F. "Il Petrarca e i Visconti." In *Francesco Petrarca e la Lombardia,* pp. 42–45. Milano: Hoepli, 1904.

Paolella, Alfonso. "Petrarca e la letteratura odeporica del medioevo." *Studi e problemi di critica testuale* 44 (1992), pp. 61–85.

Pastore Stocchi, Manlio. "Itinerari in Terrasanta nei secoli XIV–XV." In *Dizionario critico della letteratura italiana,* vol. 2, pp. 520–23. Torino: UTET, 1986.

———. *Tradizione medievale e gusto umanistico nel* De Montibus *del Boccaccio.* Firenze: Olschki, 1963.

Perocco, Daria. *Viaggiare e raccontare: Narrazione di viaggio ed esperienze di racconto tra Cinque e Seicento.* Alessandria: Edizioni dell'Orso, 1997.

Petrucci, Armando. *La Scrittura di Petrarca.* Città del Vaticano: Biblioteca Apostolica Vaticana, 1967.

Picone, Michelangelo. "Il sonetto CLXXXIX." *Atti e memorie dell'Accademia Patavina di Scienze, Lettere ed Arti* 102 (1989–90), part 2: Classe di Scienze Morali, Lettere ed Arti, pp. 151–67.

Piovene, Guido. *Viaggio in Italia.* Milano: Baldini e Castoldi, 1993; originally published, 1956.

Porcaro, Giuseppe. *Piedigrotta: Leggenda, storia, folklore.* Napoli: F. Fiorentino, 1958.

Porena, M. "Il *Mons Falernus* secondo F. P." *Rendiconti dell'Accademia di Archeologia, Lettere e Belle Arti di Napoli* 27 (1952), pp. 75–79.

Pozzi, Mario. *Ai confini della letteratura: Aspetti e momenti di storia della letteratura italiana.* Alessandria: Edizioni dell'Orso, 1998.

Rahner, H. "Odysseus at the Mast." *Greek Myths and Christian Mystery,* pp. 328–86. London: Burns and Oates, 1963.

Ricci, Giulivo, ed. *Il pellegrinaggio medievale per Roma e Santiago de Compostela: Itinerari di Val di Magra.* Aulla: Assessorato all'Istruzione e Cultura del Comune di Aulla, Centro Aullese di Ricerche e di Studi Lunigianesi, 1992.

Romm, James. *The Edges of the Earth in Ancient Thought.* Princeton: Princeton University Press, 1992.

Rose, Valentini. *Aristoteles pseudepigraphus,* pp. 631–43. Lipzig: B. G. Teubner, 1863.

Sabbadini, Raffaele. *Le scoperte dei codici greci e latini ne' secoli XIV–XV: Nuove ricerche.* Firenze: Sansoni, 1967.

Sacchetto, A. *Il pellegrino viandante.* Firenze: Le Monnier, 1955.

Santagata, Marco. *Per moderne carte: La biblioteca volgare di Petrarca.* Bologna: Il Mulino, 1990.

Savage, H. L. "Pilgrimages and Pilgrim Shrines in Palestine and Syria after 1095." In *A History of the Crusades,* edited by K. M. Setton and H. M. Hazard, vol. 4, pp. 36–68. Madison: University of Wisconsin Press, 1977.

Schiaffini, A. "Il lavorio della forma in F. P." In *Momenti di storia della lingua.* Roma: Editrice Studium, 1953.

Schmitt, Charles B., and Dilwyn Know. *Pseudo-Aristoteles Latinus: A Guide to Latin Works Falsely Attributed to Aristotle before 1500.* London: Warburgh Institute, 1985.

Sforza, G. "La distruzione di Luni nella leggenda e nella storia." *Miscellanea di Storia italiana* 3/19 (1922), pp. 1–138.

Skinner, Patricia. *Health and Medicine in Early Medieval Southern Italy.* Leiden: Brill, 1997.

Stierle, Karlheinz. *Petrarcas Landschaften: Zur Geschichte ästhetischer Landschaftserfahrung.* Krefeld: Scherpe Verlag, 1979.

Stok, Fabio. "Il Virgilio del Petrarca." In *Preveggenze umanistiche di Petrarca:Atti delle giornate petrarchesche di Tor Vergata, Roma/Cortona 1–2 giugno 1992*, pp. 171–212. Pisa: ETS, 1993.

Struever, Nancy. "Petrarchan Ethics: Inventing a Practice." In *Theory as Practice: Ethical Inquiry in the Renaissance*. Chicago: University of Chicago Press, 1992.

Tiraboschi, Girolamo. *Storia della letteratura italiana*. 9 vols. Modena: Presso la Società Tipografica, 1787–94; first published in Modena, 1771–82.

Trapp, J. B. "The Grave of Virgil." *Journal of the Warburg and Courtauld Institute* 47 (1984), pp. 7–10.

Tuan, Yi-fu. *Cosmos and Hearth: A Cosmopolite's Viewpoint*. Minneapolis: University of Minnesota Press, 1996.

Turner, Victor. *Dramas, Fields, and Metaphors: Symbolic Action in Human Society*. Ithaca: Cornell University Press, 1974.

Ullman, B. L. "Petrarch's Acquaintance with Catullus, Tibullus, Propertius." In *Studies in the Italian Renaissance*, pp. 181– 200. Roma: Edizioni di Storia e Letteratura, 1955.

Ussani, Vincenzo. "Il Petrarca e Flavio Giuseppe." Atti della Pontificia Accademia Romana di Archeologia. *Rendiconti s* 3/20 (1943–44), pp. 447–67.

Van Den Abbeele, Georges. *Travel as Metaphor from Montaigne to Rousseau*. Minneapolis: University of Minnesota Press, 1992.

Villani, Giovanni. *Cronica*. Edited by I. Moutier. 7 vols. Firenze: Magheri, 1823.

Visit to the Holy Places of Egypt, Sinai, Palestine and Syria in 1384 by Frescobaldi, Gucci, and Sigoli. Translated by T. Bellorini and E. Hoade. Jerusalem: Franciscan Press, 1948.

Walter of Châtillon. *The Alexandreis*. Translated with an introduction and notes by R. Telfryn Pritchard. Toronto: Pontifical Institute of Mediaeval Studies, 1986.

Wilkins, Ernest Hatch. *The Making of the* Canzoniere *and Other Petrarchan Studies*. Roma: Edizioni di Storia e Letteratura, 1951.

———. *Petrarch's Eight Years in Milan*. Cambridge: Medieval Academy of America, 1958.

William of Tyre. *Historia rerum in partibus transmarinis gestarum*. Recueil des historiens des Croisades, historiens occidentaux 1/1. Paris, 1844.

Woodward, David. "Medieval Mappaemundi." In *The History of Cartography*, edited by J. B. Harley and David Woodward, vol. 1, pp. 286–370. Chicago: University of Chicago Press, 1987.

Yates, Frances. *The Art of Memory*. Chicago: University of Chicago Press, 1966.

ACKNOWLEDGMENTS

The idea for this volume came during a fellowship year at Villa I Tatti, the Harvard University Center for Italian Renaissance Studies, supported in part by the Institute for Scholarship in the Liberal Arts, University of Notre Dame. I would like to thank Walter Kaiser, then director of I Tatti, for creating such a congenial community that year; I shall always be grateful for having had the privilege to be part of it.

I have also to thank for valuable corrections and suggestions many colleagues, friends, students, and teachers who read and criticized the manuscript or parts of it: Zygmunt G. Barański, Piero Boitani, Salvatore Camporeale, Paolo Cherchi, Paul Collili, Dennis Dutschke, Steve Fallon, Paul Gehl, Louis Jordan, John Kerr, Elizabeth Krager, Valerio Manfredi, Ilaria Marchesi, Simone Marchesi, Alfonso Paolella, Francesco Sberlati, Marcello Simonetta, and Justin Steinberg.

I am especially grateful to my friend Jeannette Morgenroth, who dedicated so much energy, time, and skill to editing the book; and to Barbara Hanrahan, director of the University of Notre Dame Press, who welcomed the proposal of a facsimile edition of Petrarch's *Guide*.

Finally, I would also like to thank Robert E. Bjork, director of the Arizona Center for Medieval and Renaissance Studies and director and general editor of Medieval and Renaissance Texts Society for his support of the project, as well as the readers of an early version of the manuscript, whose criticisms and suggestions much improved the work.

INDEX OF PETRARCH'S WORKS

References immediately following the title of one of Petrarch's works refer to where the work is discussed in general. References to specific passages are listed in two columns: the left column gives the passage of the work; the right column, where the passage is discussed or quoted. References to notes appear in *italics*.

GENERAL INDEX